# Social and Organizational Psychology

# SOCIAL AND ORGANIZATIONAL PSYCHOLOGY

K.N. Pillai

CENTRUM PRESS
NEW DELHI-110002 (INDIA)

**CENTRUM PRESS**
**H.O.:** 4360/4, Ansari Road, Daryaganj,
New Delhi-110002 (India)
Tel: 23278000, 23261597, 23255577, 23286875

**B.O.:** No. 1015, Ist Main Road, BSK IIIrd Stage,
IIIrd Phase, IIIrd Block, Bengaluru-560085 (INDIA)
Tel: 080-41723429

*Email:* centrumpress@gmail.com
*Visit us at:* www.centrumpress.com

*Social and Organizational Psychology*



First Edition, 2011

ISBN 978-93-81293-52-2

PRINTED IN INDIA

---

*Printed at* Suman Printers, Jagatpuri Extn., Delhi

# Contents

# Preface

Social work has no explicitly formulated knowledge base, indeed it has no knowledge base of its own at all, drawing widely in its professional training from social 'administration, sociology, and a variety of fields which might very loosely be regarded as 'psychological'. The central contradiction of social work is that it has been 'singular among the disciplines, claiming a professional status in the absence of a knowledge-base'. It is a calling without a communicable core of knowledge. Psychoanalytic theories, often in vitiated form, are still a component of many social work training courses, where they occupy an important place in understanding child development. Theories are taught without the concept of experimental test, and the student is left with the impossible task of forming his or her own personal synthesis according to personal preferences or pressures within the given course. Without the concept of experiment there can be no objective test of rival theories, and no evaluation of the resultant practices, The social worker's 'psychology' is rich in ideas, and very thin indeed on demonstrable techniques.

Organizational Behaviour scientists have conducted extensive studies on job definitions and the tasks a job comprises. They have looked at how each job fit into different groups within the organization, a process called departmentalization. The researchers have studied managerial spans of control, i.e., the number of people an individual manager can manage most effectively. The process required that researchers reduce to its most basic level each task performed and then find ways to perform jobs more efficiently and effectively. Many researchers have suggested viable ways that organizations could restructure jobs and relationships to stimulate job satisfaction and productivity simultaneously. They have devised better communications programs, identified the elements that create stress, and explained how it could be better managed. Organizational Behaviour scientists performed extensive studies on company cultures and climates with an eye to upgrading employees' quality of life in the workplace. They have sought ways to include more people in the managerial and decision-making processes. Their suggestions have included such techniques as quality circles and participative management programs.

Social psychology is an interdisciplinary domain that bridges the gap between psychology and sociology. During the years immediately following World War II, there was frequent collaboration between psychologists and sociologists. However, the two disciplines have become increasingly specialized and isolated from each other in recent years, with sociologists focusing on "macro variables" (e.g. social structure) to a much greater extent. Nevertheless, sociological approaches to social psychology remain an important counterpart to psychological research in this area.

The book will prove to be an essential text for students, researchers, academicians and planners.

*—Editor*

# 1

# Introduction

Humans are social animals. We spend much of our time interacting with other people. It is therefore not surprising that human thought, emotion, and Behaviour is strongly affected and shaped by social interactions. We truly have a social brain. The Department of Social and Organizational Psychology focuses on social interaction, cooperation, and leadership, as they occur in the context of dyads, groups, and organizations.

Traditional Industrial-Organizational Psychology focuses more on the "I" than on the "O", that is, it focuses on assessing individual differences and developing a deeper understanding of the person, as opposed to the context within which an individual is operating.

Various topics that are examined in I/O Psychology are the individual skills required for a particular job and how individual differences influence an individual's work performance. A goal of I/O Psychology is to improve organizational performance by placing the right people in the right jobs, thus enhancing the fit between the individual and the organization. I/O Psychologists work in such areas as selection, training, performance measurement, and evaluation.

A central component of a program in Social-Organizational Psychology is the belief that Behaviour must be understood from the point of view of the individual and the context within which the individual is behaving. Kurt Lewin's famous statement that Behaviour is a function of the person and the environment is the foundation on which a program in Social-

Organizational Psychology rests. Such programs examine the psychology of organizations and apply theories of both Social Psychology and Organizational Psychology to different organizational contexts. Instead of focusing solely on the individual, Social-Organizational Psychology emphasizes the impact that social forces have on performance and the factors that result in similar individual Behaviour across situations. A goal of Social-Organizational Psychology is to ultimately improve organizational performance through the creation of a suitable social environment. Social-Organizational Psychologists focus on such topics as motivation, rewards and recognition, leadership, group processes, conflict resolution, organizational culture, organizational change, and organizational performance.

## What makes our Program Unique

In addition to analysing Behaviour from the point of view of both the individual and the environment, we believe that it is important to utilize more than one perspective when examining an organization. Hence, our program examines organizational issues at the individual, the group, and the organizational levels. The individual level is focused on topics such as individual differences, motivation, and diversity. The group level emphasizes groups and teams and the dynamics involved therein. The organizational level deals with topics such as leadership, organizational culture, organizational change, and organizational effectiveness. Each of these three levels is taken into consideration when examining an organizational problem or issue so that one can determine which level(s) is/are the most relevant to consider in a particular situation.

In addition, our program is guided by a scientist-practitioner model that emphasizes both the systematic study of primary, foundational areas of theory and research in a particular discipline and the application of such theory and research to organizational settings. The curriculum is a reflection of this in that our theory courses expose our students to the core concepts of Social-Organizational Psychology and our applied courses and practica help guide them in the application of such principles. Our faculty reflects the scientist-practitioner model since they focus on both theory and research and publish in the top journals in the field. In addition, many of them are also practitioners and take on such roles as that of the consultant, the executive coach, or the head of an executive education program.

## WHAT IS SOCIAL PSYCHOLOGY?

### Social Psychology of Human Interaction

What is it that makes people trust one another? What is it that makes people to get along, or not? What is that makes so sensitive to justice? What is that helps people control their feelings, and resist unhealthy temptations? Social psychology addresses such intriguing question. The field is defined in terms of the influences between people and their social environment. Themes such as interpersonal trust, human cooperation, social justice, forgiveness versus retaliation, self-regulation, and culture, are among the more important themes studied in the department.

### Social Influences

One basic assumption underlying social psychology is that people are sensitive and responsive to other people's feelings, thoughts, and behaviour. One example is the study of empathy. We tend to be highly responsive to other's pain, and before we realize, we express emotions and other bodily states that prepare us for action-often to help. Another example is the study of social interactions between strangers. Often, before we realize, we formed an impression of another person, often based on superficial qualities. For example, men with 'baby-faces' are trusted more than people with pointier faces. The social context is important not only to individuals but also to groups. For example, relatively subtle cues that we as individuals are dealing with another group might sometimes activate competitive motives, distrust, and sometimes even hostility, with members of another group. Social influences can also sometimes take the form of cultural influences. In individualistic cultures, such as most of the western world, people tend to reason from their individual perspective, but in collectivistic cultures, people tend to emphasize the role of the family and communities. For example, individual shame is more deeply felt among family members in collectivistic than in individualistic cultures.

## Research

Social psychology asks intriguing questions, and seeks to answer those questions with various new research techniques. In addition to questionnaires and surveys, the field has creatively designed new measures of behaviour. For example, the size of our signatures appears to be an indicator of our self-esteem; how often people refer to 'we' rather than 'I' in describing their relationship is related to one's commitment to that relationship. We also see that social psychology increasingly uses biological and neuroscientific measures, to understand the social functions of hormones and the workings of the brain in dealing with social experiences. For example, does oxytocin increase interpersonal trust? How do experiences such as feelings of acceptance and love versus social exclusion affect neurological processes: Is social pain similar to other forms of physical pain?

## Everyday Life

All of these questions are exceptionally important to understanding everyday life. How can we promote trust and cooperation is of course essential to healthy functioning in relationships and organizations. How do we, in times of economic crises, make consumer decisions? How should management communicate particular decisions to people in the work place? How can one optimize performance in top sport. Can a bad apple spoil the barrel? How can we motivate people to take account of the long-term consequences of their actions? These topics are important to promoting healthy behaviours, such as effective dieting, and promoting the types of social behaviour that are desired by others, such as forgiveness or apology, rather than retaliation or apathy. Indeed, social psychology is at the heart of phenomena we witness in everyday life. Other people matter to us-which is why social psychology matters.

## WHAT IS WORK AND ORGANIZATIONAL PSYCHOLOGY?

The psychology of human behaviour in groups, work and organizational settings. Why do some people lead, and why do others follow? How do we ensure that we recruit ambitious, competent and honest staff members into our organization? How do groups and organizations manage diversity and what role do leaders have? Does personality affect the way people communicate? Can we develop skills tests for employees that are culturally unbiased?

Work and Organizational Psychology focuses on understanding human behaviour in social, work, and organizational settings. The program is part of the newly established Department of Social and Organizational Psychology at the VU University, which offers a scientific, practical and multidisciplinary 1 year Masters degree in Work and Organizational Psychology. The scientific knowledge of Work and Organizational Psychology is very relevant for any job in the field involving the selection, recruitment and management of staff.

## Multidisciplinary Approach

The field of Work and Organizational Psychology is an applied discipline which means that it borrows theories from a wide range of fields including social psychology, evolutionary psychology, cognitive psychology, biological psychology, developmental psychology, cognitive neuroscience, and behavioural economics and applies it to study and teach about group, work and organizational processes.

## Research Programme

Our research program titled, The Psychology of Leadership, Groups, and Organizations (LEGO, in short) identifies three specific areas of research expertise: (1) Leadership, (2) Personality at Work, (3) Group Dynamics and Organizational Performance. Ongoing research projects include the evolutionary psychology of organizational behaviour, leadership and followership, managing diversity in groups, emotions in the workplace, conflict management, personality and communication styles of leaders, organizational dilemmas, and organizational change and effectiveness. Descriptions of the LEGO-research projects can be found under the submenu 'Research'.

## WHAT IS A PERSONALITY/SOCIAL PSYCHOLOGIST?

A boy, barely a teenager, sprays his schoolyard with bullets. A black woman and white man become lifelong friends despite living in a town filled with racial conflict and strife. A group of top-level executives—the best and the brightest—blunder into an avoidable decision that bankrupts their company, all because they fail to share crucial information with one another.

What causes people to become murderously violent? Why do some people maintain their racial prejudices throughout their lives whereas others replace their hatreds with tolerance and respect? When do people work best as a group and when are they better off alone? If you find questions such as these intriguing, you should consider a career in personality and/or social psychology.

## Topics of Study

How do people come to be who they are? How do people think about, influence, and relate to one another? These are the broad questions that personality and social psychologists strive to answer. By exploring forces within the person (such as traits, attitudes, and goals) as well as forces within the situation (such as social norms and incentives), personality and social psychologists seek to unravel the mysteries of individual and social life in areas as wide-ranging as prejudice, romantic attraction, persuasion, friendship, helping, aggression, conformity, and group interaction. Although personality psychology has traditionally focused on aspects of the individual, and social psychology on aspects of the situation, the two perspectives are tightly interwoven in psychological explanations of human Behaviour.

## A Scientific Approach

At some level, we are all personality and social psychologists, observing our social worlds and trying to understand why people behave, think, and feel as they do. In the aftermath of schoolyard shootings we can hardly help but hypothesize answers to the many questions that come to mind. We do the same when we encounter less dramatic events in our everyday lives: Why is that person smiling at me? Will my professor be a hard grader? How might I persuade my neighbour to keep his cats off my car? But personality and social psychologists go beyond pondering such questions and their possible answers. If the lives of individuals and social groups are full of mystery, then personality and social psychologists are the detectives investigating these mysteries. Systematically observing and describing people's actions, measuring or manipulating aspects of social situations, these sleuths use the methods of science to reveal the answers to the kinds of puzzling questions we each encounter every day.

## Basic and Applied Research

Scientists in all fields distinguish between basic and applied research. Basic research in personality and social psychology tends to focus on fundamental questions about people and their thoughts, feelings, and Behaviours. Where does an individual's personality come from? What causes us to fall in love, hate our neighbour, or join with others to clean our neighbourhoods? How are the psychologies of being male and female similar, how are they different, and why? How does culture shape who we become and how we interact with one another? Questions such as these aim at the very heart of human nature.

Applied research in personality and social psychology focuses on more narrow arenas of human life, such as health, business, and law. By employing the lessons learned from basic research, and by searching for insights specific to particular domains, applied research often seeks to enhance the quality of our everyday lives. Personality and social psychologists contribute to areas as diverse as health, business, law, the environment, education, and politics. For example, personality and social psychologists have designed, implemented, and evaluated programs to help employers hire and train better workers; to make it easier for people with cancer to cope successfully with their challenge; to increase the likelihood that people will reduce pollution by relying on public transportation; to reduce prejudices and intergroup conflict in the classroom and in international negotiations; to make computers and other technologies more user-friendly; and to make many other societal contributions as well.

Of course, the distinction between basic and applied research is often a fuzzy one. One can certainly perform basic research in applied domains, and the findings from each type of research enrich the other. Indeed, it would be fair to say that most personality and social psychologists have both basic and applied interests.

## Career Options

Because personality and social psychologists combine an understanding of human Behaviour with training in sophisticated research methods, they have many opportunities for employment. Many psychologists teach and do research in universities and colleges, housed mostly in departments of psychology but also in departments of business, education, political science, justice studies, law, health sciences, and medicine. The research of such individuals may be based in the laboratory, in the field, in the clinic, or in historical archives. Many personality and social psychologists are employed in the private sector as consultants, researchers, marketing directors, managers, political strategists, technology designers, and so on. Personality and social psychologists also work in government and nonprofit organizations, designing and evaluating policy and programs in education, conflict resolution, environmental protection, and the like.

## Becoming a Social/Personality Psychologist

Although some personality and social psychologists go to graduate school to earn a terminal masters degree (M.S. or M.A.), most seek a doctoral degree (Ph.D.). For some careers, a masters degree may be sufficient. Generally, however, the doctorate is preferred by employers and is usually necessary for employment as a professor at a university or college.

Most Ph.D. programs in personality and social psychology require 4-5 years of training and study. The goal of most programs is similar: To prepare each student to become an independent, professional researcher. As a result, most programs teach the conceptual foundations and knowledge of the discipline, develop the student's ability to think theoretically, and train the student in research methodology, data analysis, and research writing and presentation. Programs differ, however, in the areas of research they focus on and in their emphasis on training students for academic versus nonacademic careers. Because graduate training revolves around research, it is important that students pay particular attention to the specific faculty members with whom they are likely to work. Prospective students should give full consideration not only to the perspectives and research activities of a potential graduate program on the whole, but also to those of their probable faculty mentors.

Admission to graduate programs in personality and social psychology is very competitive; there are far more applicants than openings (most programs enroll just a few new students each year). As a result, entry qualifications are rigorous: Most admitted students have earned high undergraduate grades and a bachelor's degree from an accredited university or college; many have been undergraduate psychology majors, although this isn't a requirement in many programs; most have had experience doing psychology research; most have demonstrated strong quantitative, verbal, and analytical abilities, as revealed in their scores on the Graduate Record Exam (GRE); and most have been evaluated by their undergraduate teachers in confidential letters of recommendation as being smart, talented, creative, hard-working, and conscientious. Of course, different programs have different standards and criteria for admission, and the prospective student should explore those articulated by programs of interest.

Most personality and social psychology programs provide financial assistance to their graduate students in the form of teaching or research assistantships, and many schools waive tuition and fees at the graduate level. This, too, varies from school to school.

## SOCIAL WORKERS' PSYCHOLOGY

'Despite widespread disillusion, however, the majority of social work institutions (both employing and 'professional') remain firmly committed to 'psychological' understandings of the problems facing them, and there are still very many individual 'believers', social workers who hold fast to the old beliefs. There are after all powerful structural encouragements for explanations of poverty that depend upon personal, rather than economic factors, and whilst moral turpitude has 'lost its credibility, the 'cycle of disadvantage' (Joseph, 1972) serves to focus attention upon individual rather than societal imperfections. Many of the new generation of social workers are too sophisticated to accept mentalistic explanations of the problems that face them in their daily work, yet the constraints of their jobs allow them little alternative in many instances: they must either act on that model, or get out.

## The Old School

Social work has no explicitly formulated knowledge base, indeed it has no knowledge base of its own at all, drawing widely in its professional training from social 'administration, sociology, and a variety of fields which might very loosely be regarded as 'psychological'. The central contradiction of social work is that it has been 'singular among the disciplines, claiming a professional status in the absence of a knowledge-base' (Bitensky, 1978). It is a calling without a communicable core of knowledge. Further, it should be noted, the fields that it draws from are largely American. The professional training for British *public service* social workers draws heavily from the literature of American social work, and also fairly widely from what in the United States are called psychotherapy and counselling. A substantial Proportion of the American literature derives from private practice, with quite different social classes represented in its case-load, and a quite different degree of professional autonomy than in the case of the British local authority social work. In seeking the psychology that is transmitted to our social workers in their professional socialisation one must therefore be prepared for an unformulated and amorphous body of knowledge, with perhaps little apparent relationship to the demands of their practice. One must also he prepared for a very different understanding of the word 'psychology'. To most psychologists it presumably retains its primary meaning of the scientific study of human thinking, development, behaviour, etc. (whilst most psychologists would be prepared to dispute amongst themselves over the latter part of such a definition, few would quibble over the former). To many social workers, however, perhaps to most, it is the secondary, informal or colloquial meaning of the word 'psychology' that assumes primacy, its use to connote 'the mental make-up of people that causes them to act as they do', Above all, it is about 'feelings'.

Psychoanalytic theories, often in vitiated form, are still a component of many social work training courses, where they occupy an important place in understanding child development (often co-existing incongruously with separate courses on sociology and on behaviour modification). Theories are taught without the concept of experimental test, and the student is left with the impossible task of forming his or her own personal synthesis according to personal preferences or pressures within the given course. Without the concept of experiment there can be no objective test of rival theories, and no evaluation of the resultant practices, The social worker's 'psychology' is rich in ideas, and very thin indeed on demonstrable techniques.

Denied a clear concept for psychology (other than that it must somehow be important) the social worker may then be left to make it up as (s)he goes along. The culture of the area office and the expectations of other professions may well influence the social worker to attach great value to such matters as 'insight', 'threat', and 'relationships'. The social worker's own supervision by the senior or team leader may be conducted in these terms, providing a most powerful force for continuing socialisation into this ethos for those amenable to it. As a result the social worker's professional expertise may turn out to comprise no more than a tangled mass of professional ideology, common assumptions and personal experiences and prejudices.

Presumably a further legacy from the 'psychiatric' background of professional social work is the continuing emphasis upon 'assessment' or 'diagnosis' and upon 'treatment'. The by now extensive (and uniformly unfavourable) American literature on effectiveness research in fields analogous to British social services work has been reviewed by Fischer (1978): the limited British literature closely parallels this (Sutton, 1981). Especially in the field of child care the social work establishment has made enormous claims of professional competence, and has received wide-ranging authority over clients' lives and a substantial share of public resources in return.

## New Waves

Amongst social workers and other social services personnel one reaction to the increasingly apparent failure of their professionalism has been a disillusion with psychology. Another has been to seek new psychologies. Over the last decade two altogether separate different approaches have been looked to. Again, both are largely transatlantic in origin, and again, because of the catholicity of social work, it is possible to find both approaches co-existing, apparently without stress, within the ideas of a single professional.

The 'radical' or 'alternative' approach to psychology in social work may be epitomised by the sources presented in a counter-course for social work students (SCANUS, 1976). Essential readings recommended to link psychology with social control were the writings of Reich, Laing, Fanon and Freud, 'who each contribute important elements towards an understanding of the psychology of oppressed social life'. In the section on 'psychology, psychiatry and child development', Goffman was recommended for his classic study of asylums, and Szasz for his critical essays on psychiatry. So too was Fromm for an upto-date critique of Freud; Berne, for games people play; Janov, for primal screams; Rogers, for encounter groups; Pens, for Gestalt Therapy; and perhaps surprisingly Kohler, for Gestalt Psychology. The study of Reich was also recommended. A much larger section on the 'experiential sciences' was largely devoted to the works of Laing Cooper and their commentators, which expressed a reaction to 'the established behavioural schools of thought in psychology, psychiatry and sociology'. Though the works of the writers suggested in the counter-course, along with those from other sectors of the Personal Growth Movement, have certainly contributed to the thinking and life-style of many social services entrants, there are as yet no clearly documented effects of such ideas' having any discernible effect upon local authority practice.

On the contrary it was behaviourism and the various practical techniques stemming from it that emerged as a discernible new force within social work at the end of the seventies. Within social work itself, in fieldwork, in day care and in residential provision, there are those who would seek to behaviouralise social work. Social services workers are urged to join the British Association for Behavioural Psychotherapy and the Association for Behaviour Modification with Children, and a Behavioural Social Work Group has been recently formed. And almost for the first time there are psychologists with a common and explicit approach, apparently eager to share their skills to generate new forms of practice (e.g. Brown, 1978a). Perhaps we are mow set for a steady 'behavioural drizzle' in social work.

## THE PSYCHOLOGISTS

The history of psychology is much shorter than that of the Poor Law, shorter even than that of voluntary social work, though child psychology antedated the introduction of psychiatric social work and its psychoanalytic orientation into this country. Until recently, however, psychologists' contact with the issues presently dealt with by social services departments have been slight. Burt (1925) took an early interest in delinquent children, their investigation and upbringing. He advocated a detailed investigation of the individual child and of his physical and social circumstances, and a careful check upon the effects achieved by any treatment recommended. Much of the former seems implicit in present-day social services assessment procedures (though many modern practices in this field fall short of Burt's suggestions): his experimental approach is not apparent. Burt's work seems now largely forgotten in social work circles, and whether it has indeed had my direct, linear influence on present-day practices remains to be documented.

In England and Wales (though not in Scotland) the educational psychologists who went to work in the new child guidance clinics from the late twenties onwards found themselves in the main tinder psychiatric domination, their functions 'limited to the cognitive 'aspects of the mind, i.e. the application of intelligence and educational tests, together with the coaching of children who present specific difficulty in any school subject' (Keir, 1952). Psychology as a whole comprised only a small workforce, clinical psychology had yet to emerge as a discrete entity, and the psychiatric deluge assured those within social work that all was well in their world as far as professional theory and technique were concerned. There was little change until the major expansion of the social services departments and of psychology in the seventies.

## Educational Psychologists in Observation and Assessment Centres

Over the sixties and into the start of the new decade four local authority departments (later social services departments) established their own psychological provisions, though only one of them, in Newham, survived the major local government reorganisations that followed. In the mid-seventies, however, the enlarged local education authorities' school psychological services undertook the routinised provision of reports to the juvenile courts, this becoming a regular practice in most, perhaps all local authorities. Their provision is made through the courts departments and assessment services of the social services departments. On the basis of a recent national survey of educational psychologists in England and Wales (Wedell and Lambourne, 1979) it may be estimated that around 200 educational psychologists now visit social services departments' observation and assessment centres, mainly for the purposes of providing psychological reports for the courts. Their efforts represent not only the major input by psychologists into the English judicial system, they also comprise a massive contribution of psychologist-hours to the routine child care work of social services departments. Despite the scale of their work there has been little examination of what they actually do there. There are a variety of ways whereby a psychologist might find himself reporting upon a child or family involved with a social services department, or working on the operations of a social services establishment, but the routine provision of psychological assessments to observation and assessment centres has probably been the major single point of contact. The Children and Young Persons Act (1969) had stipulated that every regional plan for child care should include proposals:

> *...for the provision of facilities for the observation of the physical and mental condition of children in the care of the relevant authorities and for the assessment of the most suitable accommodation and treatment for these children.*

The local authorities' interpretation of this requirement has been largely the establishment of residential *centres* where children are 'observed and assessed'. The Association of

Educational Psychologists (1976) has proposed that 'One of the most specific requirements [of the 1969 Act] is that children who are made the subject of Care Orders should have their personal needs assessed by a multi-disciplinary team which includes a psychologist.' The two interpretations have perhaps more in common with each other than with the Act.

Despite educational psychologists' extensive commitment to work in observation and assessment centres there has been only one account of how they might proceed in such work. Edwardson (1973) offered early guidelines for practice according to a school which may (perhaps unfairly) be summarised as a little testing, a little common sense and a lot of consultation. Psychometrically dependent approaches persisted in a major course on psychologists' work for social services departments organised by the Division of Educational and Child Psychologists of the British Psychological Society in 1978. Opposition to the whole concept of 'observation and assessment', particularly its residential form, has been advanced only by Cooper (1975; 1976); Brookes (1977) has enthusiastically supported it, Clayton (1979) would like the observation and assessment, but without its residential aspect. There seems reason to regard the primary purpose of observation and assessment centres to be structural to the child care system, rather than dependent on either the requirements of the 1969 Act or on the 'needs' of the children (however defined). It is hard not to view the wholesale involvement of educational psychologists in these centres as structural to the needs of their own professional systems rather than dependent upon, say, the unique contributions that a psychologist might make to problems of observing and of assessing children, or upon the psychological evaluation of the validity of residential procedures.

As far as one can tell (Brown and Sawyer, 1978; Moss and Sutton, 1980) the role filled by many educational psychologists in the observation and assessment centres has been mainly psychometric and legitimating. By 'psychometric' is meant the administration of intelligence and reading tests, and the interpretation of the child's behaviour under test to explain wider aspects of his life. By 'legitimating' is meant: first, the provision of a nominally independent expert opinion to back up the individual recommendations of the observation and assessment centre; and secondly, reassurance that all is well in what is being done, simply from the active collaboration of yet another 'expert' in the system.

There may exist, perhaps in considerable numbers, educational psychologists who have undertaken innovative psychological work and made significant changes in their local observation and assessment systems, if so they have yet to publish their Work. There are certainly educational psychologists who have been grossly dissatisfied with the constraints upon their own work at such centres and with the quality of the 'observations' and 'assessments' made there, and have withdrawn from the work altogether. And there are certainty educational psychologists who have taken a third course: unable or unwilling either to innovate or withdraw, they have stayed on, producing mediocre work or even outrightly bad psychological practice.

Psychologists who deprecate the 'psychology' of certain social workers that they meet, or wonder at the antipathy or suspicion that they themselves meet from many others, should remember that the most substantial contact that social services departments have yet had with psychologists has been with a branch of psychology which has shared some of the recent professional problems of social work itself. Educational psychology, too, has had to establish itself as 'a profession' within local government (Sutton, 1976), and within the compromise of its own bureau-professionalism it has perhaps been experiencing its own recognition of the progressive supremacy of managerial over scientific considerations.

2

# Industrial and Organizational Psychology

Industrial and organizational psychology applies psychology to organizations and workplaces. These organizations and workplaces include for-profit businesses, non-profits, government agencies, colleges, universities, and graduate and professional school programs. Industrial-organizational psychologists contribute to an organization's success by improving the performance and well-being of its people. An I-O psychologist researches and identifies how Behaviours and attitudes can be improved through hiring practices, training programs, and feedback systems. In the academic context, an I-O psychologist's research might similarly focus on improving admissions systems, learning outcomes, academic achievement, degree completion, and teaching and assessment methodologies.

## NATURE OF INDUSTRIAL PSYCHOLOGY

Industrial psychology is a relatively new branch of psychology that was created for corporations and organizations that needed more structure. Industrial psychology is able to provide this structure by evaluating employee behaviour for the good of the company. It is often referred to as *organizational psychology* because of its emphasis on analysing individuals who work for various organizations.

Essentially, industrial psychologists study the behaviour of employees in a work setting. Although industrial psychology didn't begin until the 1920's, the discipline has evolved rapidly and revolutionized the workplace within the last century. Because the workplace is a social system, the application of industrial psychology is useful in understanding its complexity.

For years, psychologists have studied how human beings have interacted with their environments and each other, but industrial psychology begins to evaluate the interaction between people and their jobs. Industrial psychologists can be used to improve job satisfaction as well as company productivity and is becoming vital to the success of many organizations.

There are certain things that industrial psychologists focus on when evaluating the relationship a person has with their work. They analyse the way a person works, their skills, duties, obligations, and general satisfaction with their job on a day-to-day basis. This information is extremely helpful to human resources departments and company overseers who must create training programs, feedback and rewards systems, and make hiring decisions as well as engage in recruitment practices. Most companies use industrial psychologists to train their own staff so that the organizations can run smoothly and at peak capacity.

One of the most interesting aspects of industrial psychology is how employee behaviour affects others individuals on the job and organization in general. Industrial psychology can be used to reduce counterproductive behaviour, enhance team effectiveness, and boost morale. It is also vital in conflict resolution. Many individuals find the brunt of their work dissatisfaction rooted in their relationships with managers and colleagues. Fortunately, industrial psychology provides solutions for this.

Although industrial psychology is a mixture of anthropology, counselling, sociology and industrial management, there are key components used in this type of psychology. Some of the key components include the evaluation of employee's personalities, perceptions, as well the biological side of their behaviour. By documenting these key points, industrial psychologists have the ability to help organizations improve their functionality and set up a system that promotes growth for the company and employees. Industrial psychology also helps CEOs and executives adjust heir way of thinking and their management style, which can impact the stress levels of the employees that they manage. By using psychology, many companies are able to retain their employees because they understand how to keep them happy. Organizations with a low retention rate and employee dissatisfaction benefit from the work and assessment of industrial psychologists.

## Overview of Industrial Organizational Psychology

Guion (1965) defines I-O psychology as "the scientific study of the relationship between man and the world of work:... in the process of making a living". Blum and Naylor (1968) define it as "simply the application or extension of psychological facts and principles to the problems concerning human beings operating within the context of business and industry". I-O psychology has historically subsumed two broad areas of study, as evident by its name, although this distinction is largely artificial and many topics cut across both areas. It has roots in social psychology; organizational psychologists examine the role of the work environment in performance and other outcomes including job satisfaction and health. I-O psychology is also represented by Division 14 of the American Psychological Association. Sometimes, I-O psychology is considered a sister field or branch of organizational studies, organizational science, organizational Behaviour, human resources, and/or management, but there is no universally accepted classification system for these related fields.

Common research and practice areas for I-O psychologists include:

- Job performance
- Job analysis/competency modeling
- Personnel recruitment and selection
- Student/educational selection and assessment
- Judgment and decision making
- Performance appraisal/management
- Individual assessment (knowledge, skills, and ability testing, personality assessment, work sample tests, assessment centres)

- Psychometrics
- Compensation
- Training and training evaluation
- Employment law
- Work motivation
- Job attitudes (e.g., job satisfaction, commitment, organizational citizenship, and retaliation)
- Occupational health and safety
- Work/life balance
- Human factors and decision making
- Organizational culture/climate
- Organizational surveys
- Leadership and executive coaching
- Ethics
- Diversity
- Job design
- Human resources
- Organizational development (OD)
- Organizational Research Methods
- Technology in the workplace
- Group/team performance.

I-O psychologists are trained in the "scientist-practitioner" model. The training enables I-O psychologists to employ scientific principles and research-based designs to generate knowledge. They use what they have learned in applied settings to help clients address workplace needs. I-O psychologists are employed as professors, researchers, and consultants. They also work within organizations, often as part of a human resources department where they coordinate hiring and organizational development initiatives from an evidence-based perspective.

## History

The "industrial" side of I-O psychology has its historical origins in research on individual differences, assessment, and the prediction of performance. This branch of the field crystallized during World War I, in response to the need to rapidly assign new troops to duty stations. After the War the growing industrial base in the US added impetus to I-O psychology. Walter Dill Scott, who was elected President of the American Psychological Association (APA) in 1919, was arguably the most prominent I-O psychologist of his time, although James McKeen Cattell (elected APA President in 1895) and Hugo Münsterberg (1898) were influential in the early development of the field. Organizational psychology gained prominence after World War II, influenced by the Hawthorne studies and the work of researchers such as Kurt Lewin and Muzafer Sherif.

## RESEARCH METHODS IN I-O PSYCHOLOGY

As described above, I-O psychologists are trained in the scientist-practitioner model. I-O psychologists rely on a variety of methods to conduct organizational research. Study designs employed by I-O psychologists include surveys, experiments, quasi-experiments, and observational studies. I-O psychologists rely on diverse data sources including human judgments, historical databases, objective measures of work performance (e.g., sales volume), and questionnaires and surveys.

I-O researchers employ both quantitative and qualitative research methods. Quantitative methods used in I-O psychology include both descriptive statistics and inferential statistics (e.g., correlation, multiple regression, and analysis of variance). More advanced statistical methods employed by some I-O psychologists include logistic regression, multivariate analysis of variance, structural equation modeling, and hierarchical linear modeling (HLM; also known as multilevel modeling). HLM is particularly applicable to research on team-and organization-level effects on individuals. I-O psychologists also employ psychometric methods including methods associated with classical test theory (CTT), generalizability theory, and item response theory (IRT). In the 1990s, a growing body of empirical research in I-O psychology was influential in the application of meta-analysis, particularly in the area of the stability of research findings across contexts. The most well-known meta-analytic approaches are those associated with Hunter and Schmidt, Rosenthal, and Hedges and Olkin. With the help of meta-analysis, Hunter and Schmidt advanced the idea of validity generalization, which suggests that some performance predictors, specifically cognitive ability tests have a relatively stable and positive relation to job performance across all jobs. Although not unchallenged, validity generalization has broad acceptance with regard to many selection instruments (e.g., cognitive ability tests, job knowledge tests, work samples, and structured interviews) across a broad range of jobs. Qualitative methods employed in I-O psychology include content analysis, focus groups, interviews, case studies, and several other observational techniques. I-O research on organizational culture research has employed ethnographic techniques and participant observation to collect data. One well-known qualitative technique employed in I-O psychology is John Flanagan's Critical Incident Technique, which requires "qualified observers" (e.g., pilots in studies of aviation, construction workers in studies of construction projects) to describe a work situation that resulted in a good or bad outcome. Objectivity is ensured when multiple observers identify the same incidents. The observers are also asked to provide information about what the actor in the situation could have done differently to influence the outcome. This technique is then used to describe the critical elements of performance in certain jobs and how worker Behaviour relates to outcomes. Most notably, this technique has been employed to improve performance among aircraft crews and surgical teams, literally saving thousands of lives since its introduction. An application of the technique in research on coping with job stress comes from O'Driscoll and Cooper.

I-O psychologists sometimes use quantitative and qualitative methods in concert. For example, when constructing behaviorally anchored rating scales (BARS), a job analyst may use qualitative methods, such as critical incidents interviews and focus groups to collect data bearing on performance. Then the analyst would have SMEs rate those examples on a Likert scale and compute inter-rater agreement statistics to judge the adequacy of each item. Each potential item would additionally be correlated with an external criterion in order to evaluate its usefulness if it were to be selected to be included in a BARS metric.

## Organizational Structure

An organizational structure is a description of the types of coordination used to organize the actions of individuals and departments that contribute to achieving a common aim. Many organizations have hierarchical structures, but not all. Organizations are a variant of clustered entities. An organization can be structured in many different ways, depending on their objectives. The structure of an organization will determine the modes in which it operates and performs.

Organizational structure allows the expressed allocation of responsibilities for different functions and processes to different entities such as the branch, department, workgroup and individual. Individuals in an organizational structure are normally hired under time-limited work contracts or work orders, or under permanent employment contracts or program orders.

# TOPICS IN INDUSTRIAL-ORGANIZATIONAL PSYCHOLOGY

## Job Analysis

Job analysis is often described as the cornerstone of successful employee selection efforts and performance management initiatives. A job analysis involves the systematic collection of information about a job. Job-analytic methods are often described as belonging to one of two approaches. One approach, the task-oriented job analysis, involves an examination of the duties, tasks, and/or competencies required by a job. The second approach, a worker-oriented job analysis, involves an examination of the knowledge, skills, abilities, and other characteristics (KSAOs) required to successfully perform the work. These two approaches are not mutually exclusive. Various adaptations of job-analytic methods include competency modeling, which examines large groups of duties and tasks related to a common goal or process, and practice analysis, which examines the way work is performed in an occupation across jobs.

Job-analytic data are often collected using a variety of quantitative and qualitative methods. The information obtained from a job analysis is then used to create job-relevant selection procedures, performance appraisals and criteria, or training programs. Additional uses of job-analytic information include job evaluations for the purpose of determining compensation levels and job redesign.

## Personnel Recruitment and Selection

I-O psychologists typically work with HR specialists to design (a) recruitment processes and (b) personnel selection systems. Personnel recruitment is the process of identifying qualified candidates in the workforce and getting them to apply for jobs within an organization. Personnel recruitment processes include developing job announcements, placing ads, defining key qualifications for applicants, and screening out unqualified applicants.

Personnel selection is the systematic process of hiring and promoting personnel. Personnel selection systems employ evidence-based practices to determine the most qualified candidates. Personnel selection involves both new hires and individuals who can be promoted from within the organization. Common selection tools include ability tests (e.g., cognitive, physical, or psychomotor), knowledge tests, personality tests, structured interviews, the systematic collection of biographical data, and work samples. I-O psychologists must evaluate evidence regarding the extent to which selection tools predict job performance, evidence that bears on the validity of selection tools.

Personnel selection procedures are usually validated, i.e., shown to be job relevant, using one or more of the following types of validity: content validity, construct validity, and/or criterion-related validity. I-O psychologists adhere to professional standards, such as the Society for Industrial and Organizational Psychology's (SIOP) *Principles for Validation and Use of Personnel Selection Procedures* and the Standards for Educational and Psychological Testing. The Equal Employment Opportunity Commission's *Uniform Guidelines* are also influential in guiding personnel selection although they have been criticized as outdated when compared to the current state of knowledge in I-O psychology.

I-O psychologists not only help in the selection and assessment of personnel for jobs. I-O psychologists also assist in the selection of students for admission to colleges, universities, and graduate and professional schools as well as the assessment of student achievement, student aptitude, and the performance of teachers and K-12 schools. Increasingly, I-O psychologists are working for educational assessment and testing organizations and divisions.

## Performance Appraisal/management

Performance appraisal or performance evaluation is the process of measuring an individual's work Behaviours and outcomes against the expectations of the job. Performance appraisal is frequently used in promotion and compensation decisions, to help design and validate personnel selection procedures, and for performance management. Performance management is the process of providing performance feedback relative to expectations and improvement information (e.g., coaching, mentoring). Performance management may also include documenting and tracking performance information for organization-level evaluation purposes.

An I-O psychologist would typically use information from the job analysis to determine a job's performance dimensions, and then construct a rating scale to describe each level of performance for the job. Often, the I-O psychologist would be responsible for training organizational personnel how to use the performance appraisal instrument, including ways to minimize bias when using the rating scale, and how to provide effective performance feedback. Additionally, the I-O psychologist may consult with the organization on ways to use the performance appraisal information for broader performance management initiatives.

## Individual Assessment and Psychometrics

Individual assessment involves the measurement of individual differences. I-O psychologists perform individual assessments in order to evaluate differences among candidates for employment as well as differences among employees. The constructs measured pertain to job performance. With candidates for employment, individual assessment is often part of the personnel selection process. These assessments can include written tests, physical tests, psychomotor tests, personality tests, work samples, and assessment centres.

Psychometrics is the science of measuring psychological variables, such as knowledge, skills, and abilities. I-O psychologists are generally well-trained in psychometric psychology.

## Remuneration and Compensation

Compensation includes wages or salary, bonuses, pension/ retirement contributions, and perquisites that can be converted to cash or replace living expenses. I-O psychologists may be asked to conduct a job evaluation for the purpose of determining compensation levels and ranges. I-O psychologists may also serve as expert witnesses in pay discrimination cases when disparities in pay for similar work are alleged.

## Training and Training Evaluation

Most people hired for a job are not already versed in all the tasks required to perform the job effectively. Similar to performance management, an I-O psychologist would employ a job analysis in concert with principles of instructional design to create an effective training program.

A training program is likely to include a summative evaluation at its conclusion in order to ensure that trainees have met the training objectives and can perform the target work tasks at an acceptable level. Training programs often include formative evaluations to assess the impact of the training as the training proceeds. Formative evaluations can be used to locate problems in training procedures and help I-O psychologist make corrective adjustments in the while the training is ongoing.

## Motivation in the Workplace

Motivation is a positive drive that enables a person to reach a set goal. In a workplace, the manager or supervisor has to know the needs or drive of an individual, and motivate according to it. In an organization, when an employee is doing good job or production is increased by him, he must be rewarded with respect to his needs.

## Organizational Culture

Organizational culture can be described as a set of assumptions shared by the individuals in an organization that directs interpretation and action by defining appropriate Behaviour for various situations. There are three levels of organizational culture: artifacts, shared values, and basic beliefs and assumptions. Artifacts comprise the physical components of the organization that relay cultural meaning. Shared values are individuals' preferences regarding certain aspects of the organization's culture (e.g. loyalty, customer service). Basic beliefs and assumptions include individuals' impressions about the trustworthiness and supportiveness of an organization, and are often deeply ingrained within the organization's culture.

In addition to an overall culture, organizations also have subcultures. Examples of subcultures include corporate culture, departmental culture, local culture, and issue-related culture. While there is no single "type" of organizational culture, some researchers have developed models to describe different organizational cultures. Organizational culture has been shown to have an impact on important organizational outcomes such as performance, attraction, recruitment, retention, employee satisfaction, and employee well-being. Also, organizations with an adaptive culture tend to perform better than organizations with an unadaptive culture.

## Group Behaviour

Group Behaviour is the interaction between individuals of a collective and the processes such as opinions, attitudes, growth, feedback loops, and adaptations that occur and change as a result of this interaction. The interactions serve to fulfil some need satisfaction of an individual who is part of the collective and helps to provide a basis for his interaction with specific members of the group.

A specific area of research in group Behaviour is the dynamics of teams. Team effectiveness refers to the system of getting people in a company or institution to work together effectively. The idea behind team effectiveness is that a group of people working together can achieve much more than if the individuals of the team were working on their own.

## JOB SATISFACTION AND COMMITMENT

Job satisfaction reflects an employee's overall assessment of their job particularly their emotions, Behaviours, and attitudes about their work experience. It is one of the most heavily researched topics in industrial/organizational psychology with several thousand published studies. Job satisfaction has theoretical and practical utility for the field of psychology and has been linked to important job outcomes including attitudinal variables, absenteeism, employee turnover, and job performance. For instance, job satisfaction is strongly correlated with attitudinal variables such as job involvement, organizational commitment, job tensions, frustration, and feelings of anxiety. Job satisfaction also has a weak correlation with employee's absentee Behaviours and turnover from an organization with employees more likely to miss work or find other jobs if they are not satisfied. Finally, research has found that although a positive relationship exists between job satisfaction and performance, it is moderated by the use of rewards at an organization and the strength of employee's attitudes about their job.

## PRODUCTIVE BEHAVIOUR

*Productive Behaviour* is defined as employee Behaviour that contributes positively to the goals and objectives of an organization. When an employee begins a new job, there is a transition period during which he or she is not contributing positively to the organization. To successfully transition from being an outsider to a full-fledged member of an organization, an employee typically needs job-related training as well as more general information about the culture of the organization. In financial terms, productive Behaviour represents the point at which an organization begins to achieve some return on the investment it has made in a new employee. There are three common forms of productive Behaviour in organizations: job performance, organizational citizenship Behaviour (OCB), and innovation.

### Job Performance

Job performance represents Behaviours employees engage in while at work which contribute to organizational goals.

These Behaviours are formally evaluated by an organization as part of an employee's responsibilities. In order to understand and ultimately predict job performance, it is important to be precise when defining the term. Job performance is about Behaviours that are within the control of the employee and not about results (effectiveness), the costs involved in achieving results (productivity), the results that can be achieved in a period of time (efficiency), or the value an organization places on a given level of performance, effectiveness, productivity, or efficiency (utility).

To model job performance, researchers have attempted to define a set of dimensions that are common to all jobs. Using a common set of dimensions provides a consistent basis for assessing performance and enables the comparison of performance across jobs. While there is disagreement about the exact dimensions of job performance, there is agreement on two major categories of job performance: in-role (technical aspects of a job) and extra-role (non-technical abilities such as communication skills and being a good team member).

To assess job performance, reliable and valid measures must be established. The most commonly used measures are ratings of employee performance on specific tasks and on overall job performance. While there are many sources of error with performance ratings, error can be reduced through rater training and through the use of behaviorally anchored ratings scales. Such scales can be used to clearly define the Behaviours that constitute poor, average, and superior performance. Additional factors that complicate the measurement of job performance include the instability of job performance over time and the restriction of variation in individual performance by organizational forces.

The determinants of job performance consist of factors having to do with the individual worker as well as environmental factors in the workplace. According to Campbell's Model of The Determinants of Job Performance., job performance is a result of the interaction between declarative knowledge (knowledge of facts or things), procedural knowledge (knowledge of what needs to be done and how to do it), and motivation (reflective of an employee's choices regarding whether to expend effort, the level of effort to expend, and whether to persist with the level of effort chosen). Regardless of the job, three determinants stand out as predictors of performance: (1) general mental ability (especially for jobs higher in complexity), (2) job experience (although there is a law of diminishing returns), and (3) the personality trait of conscientiousness (people who are dependable and achievement oriented, who plan well). These determinants appear to influence performance largely through the acquisition and usage of job knowledge and the motivation to do well.

## ORGANIZATIONAL CITIZENSHIP BEHAVIOUR

Organizational citizenship Behaviour (OCB) refers to productive Behaviours that are not part of an employees' formal job description. There are five categories of organizational citizenship Behaviours: (1) altruism, (2) courtesy, (3) sportsmanship, (4) conscientiousness, and (5) civic virtue.

There are three different explanations for why employees engage in organizational citizenship Behaviour. The first has to do with positive affect, an overall positive mood increases the frequency of helping Behaviour. The second explanation, which stems from the equity theory, is that employees reciprocate fair treatment that they have received from the organization. The third explanation is that some employees have personality traits that predispose them to participate in organizational citizenship Behaviour. There are also employees who will perform organizational citizenship Behaviour to influence how they are viewed within the organization. While these Behaviours are not formally part of the job description, performing them can certainly influence performance appraisals.

### Innovation

Innovation is a form of productive Behaviour that employees exhibit when they come up with novel ideas that further the goals of the organization. Innovation at an individual level is dependent on task-relevant skills (general mental ability and job specific knowledge), creativity-relevant skills (ability to concentrate on a problem for long periods of time, to abandon unproductive searches, and to temporarily put aside stubborn problems), and task motivation (internal desire to perform task and level of enjoyment). There are things that organizations can do in order to breed innovation in the workplace. Some of these items include providing creativity training, having leaders encourage and model innovation, allowing employees to question current procedures and rules, seeing that the implementation of innovations had real consequences, documenting innovations in a professional manner, allowing employees to have autonomy and freedom in their job roles, reducing the number of obstacles that may be in the way of innovation, and giving employees access to resources (whether these are monetary, informational, or access to key people inside or outside of the organization).

## COUNTERPRODUCTIVE WORK BEHAVIOUR

Counterproductive work Behaviour can be defined as employee Behaviour that goes against the goals of an organization. These Behaviours can be intentional or unintentional and result from a wide range of underlying causes and motivations. It has been proposed that a person-by-environment interaction can be utilized to explain a variety of counter-productive Behaviours (Fox and Spector, 1999). For instance, an employee who steals from the company may do so because of lax supervision (environment) and underlying psychopathology (person) that work in concert to result in the counterproductive Behaviour.

The forms of counterproductive Behaviour with the most empirical examination are ineffective job performance, absenteeism, job turnover, and accidents. Less common but potentially more detrimental forms of counterproductive Behaviour have also been investigated including theft, violence, substance use, and sexual harassment.

### Leadership

Leadership is a process of influencing and supporting and motivating others to work enthusiastically or effectively towards achieving the objectives or goal. A leader acts as a catalyst, who identifies the potential of a worker and tries to put that into reality. A leader can be a positive leader or a negative leader.

A leader's influence within an organization or group has been said to stem from two primary sources, that person's personal characteristics and their position within the organization. Personal power, also made up of two factors called expert power and referent power, is derived from elements like an individual's personality, their knowledge base, their ability to effectively interact with others, and their demonstrated level of effort. Positional power, also often referred to as legitimate power, is derived from the leader's position within the organization, and the authority imbued in them either directly or indirectly by the organization's controlling parties to provide either rewards or sanctions for performance.

The leader's role is to use this influence to encourage those within the organization to focus their actions toward the accomplishment of the organization's goals. Distinction should be noted between management v. leadership. Managers process administrative tasks that organize work environments. Leaders conduct those same tasks while also inspiring and motivating the workforce for which they oversee. Managers cope with complexity, leaders cope with change. Managers participate in stepwise tasks of planning and budgeting, organizing and staffing, and controlling and problem solving. In contrast, leaders approach these stages of business development through equivalent tasks of setting a direction or vision, aligning people or communication, and motivating and inspiring, respectively.

## ORGANIZATIONAL CHANGE/DEVELOPMENT

### Relationship to Occupational Health Psychology

A separate but related discipline, occupational health psychology (OHP) is a relatively new field that combines elements of industrial-organizational psychology, health psychology, and occupational health. Unlike I-O psychology, the primary emphasis in OHP is on the physical and mental health and psychological well-being of the person.

## TRAINING AND OUTLOOK

### Graduate Programs

A comprehensive list of US and Canadian master's and doctoral programs can be found at the web site of the Society for Industrial and Organizational Psychology (SIOP). Some helpful ways to learn about graduate programs include visiting the web sites on the SIOP list and speaking to I-O faculty at the institutions listed. Admission into I-O psychology Ph.D. programs is highly competitive given that many programs accept a small number of applicants every year.

There are graduate degree programs in I-O psychology outside of the US and Canada. The SIOP web site also provides a comprehensive list of I-O programs in many other countries.

## Job Outlook

According to the Bureau of Labour Statistics (2007), the job outlook for industrial-organizational psychologists is promising. Businesses enlist the services of these psychologists in order to retain employees and maintain a good work ethic. I-O psychologists specializing in research often conduct studies within companies to aid in marketing research.

## Personnel Psychology

Every organization has to make decisions about personnel selection, training, promotion, job transfer, lay-off, termination, compensation, and so on. In each case, the characteristics of both workers and jobs must be assessed. In job selection, for example, the personnel psychologist must be able to determine what are the demands of the job in question and which human abilities are required to meet these demands, and then find the most suitable candidate. Similarly, training (or retraining) requires knowledge of the job demands and the current skills levels of an employee. The personnel psychologist's task is to minimize the discrepancy between demands and skills levels. Other decisions, such as promotion or changes in amount of compensation, represent the same basic challenge for the personnel psychologist: to match the environmental characteristics with the individual's.

The personnel psychologist uses various tools, the two most common being job analysis and psychological aptitude testing. Job analysis helps to determine the most important and/or frequently occurring tasks in a particular job as well as the associated knowledges, skills, abilities and personal characteristics which support performance of those tasks. It may involve surveys, observations, interviews or combinations of these techniques, and data from current incumbents and supervisors are an important source of information. Psychological aptitude testing tries to identify the capacities and limitations of the candidates in meeting the demands of the job in question.

In the past, popular methods were short tests of intellectual ability, particularly verbal and arithmetic skills. Two of the most popular tests of this kind are the Wonderlic Personnel Test and the Otis Intelligence Test. Since 1960 special ability tests, such as the Differential Aptitude Test Battery and the Flanagan Aptitude Classification Tests have been more prominent. Psychological testing implies a standardized sample of behaviour.

The sample may be gathered by means of a standardized paper-and-pencil test with specific questions and limited alternative answers. Alternatively the sample might include broad questions and open-ended answers, with structure imposed by the respondent rather than by the test or test administrator. The sample could also include motor performance, interview behaviour, and even physiological measures, for example, resting heart rate or tests of vulnerability to stress factors in the work environment.

## Industrial/social or Industrial/clinical Psychology

This area of IO psychology concerns the reciprocal adjustment between the person and the environment, the emotional capacities of the individual and the environmental climate being the key factors under investigation.

The individual worker is assessed on the following criteria: adjustment, motivation, satisfaction, level of performance, tendency to remain within the organization and absenteeism rates. The organizational characteristics which are looked at include, for example, efforts to facilitate a positive emotional climate, reward systems used, leadership styles, and the actual structure and operation of the organization. Most adjustment strategies involve real or imagined others: this is the province of industrial social psychology. The industrial/clinical aspect considers the employee's psychological well-being, and the fact that poor adjustment often creates stress and occasionally transient abnormal behaviour.

## Human Factors or Human Engineering Psychology

This area makes assumptions which are just the opposite to those of the personnel psychologist. The problem is still the same: accomplishing a match between the individual and the job. But the human factors psychologist assumes that the person is constant and the job is variable. The psychologist must arrange or design the environment in such a way that it is more compatible with the capacities and limitations of human operators. In order to effect a better match, the job must be changed, which usually involves modifications in operations or equipment according to the capacities of the operators. These capacities could be sensory (for example, visual acuity), or cognitive (for example, information processing time). The information input and output system is emphasized: display devices (digital read-out devices, gauges or dials, and so on) and control devices (such as knobs, levers and switches) are examined and modified if found to have a negative effect on performance.

The three areas of IO are seldom, if ever, independent of one another: they are all components of an interrelated system. Selection strategies will define the capacities and shortcomings of the operators. This will yield a range for equipment design and modification. Similarly, available equipment will determine desirable capacities and characteristics of applicants. Finally, the interaction of worker characteristics, equipment and task design, and administrative practices will influence adjustment.

## DEFINITION OF INDUSTRIAL PSYCHOLOGY

Industrial psychology, currently known as industrial-organizational psychology or I-O psychology, is defined by the Society for Industrial and Organizational Psychology (SIOP) as "the scientific study of the workplace." As a type of applied psychology, I-O psychology assists organizations in selecting personnel with a focus toward how to maximize human capital.

### Ethics

There is some contentious ground with how I-O psychology is viewed. Historically, I-O psychology specialists have looked at ways to manipulate the Behaviour of workplace personnel in order to maximize productivity. The question of ethics has always squatted on the horizon since the I-O psychologist is necessarily being paid by the organization, which is served by increased production, not necessarily by increased personnel well-being. Financial considerations do not always align with good ethical practices.

## Considerations

Descriptions of toxic or dysfunctional workplace environments are common, before and after I-O psychologist intervention. For SIOP to use the term human capital in its brochure is an unfortunate choice because it continues to conflate the employees as assets used for the production of more assets. Workplace personnel whose welfare is a primary concern for their employer, work for their employer. Working for suggests collaboration and mutual respect with a shared common goal. The word capital means to be used by. For SIOP to choose to describe personnel from the state of being used, demonstrates a lack of care toward working personnel, and suggests an orientation away from worker welfare. SIOP, as a representative organization, in this way fails to allay the concerns of working personnel that I-O psychology is being used fairly and in the interest and welfare of employees.

## Ideals

The idea of I-O psychology is for the psychologist to contribute psychological insight and knowledge to an organization such that the organization improves both its productive performance and the well-being of its personnel.

## History

Although I-O psychology has been around since the 1890s, it came into public view with the work of Henry Landsberger in 1955 when he re-examined studies done at Hawthorne Works (a company outside of Chicago). These studies looked at illumination, changing worker schedules and other variables to see what differences these changes had on worker productivity. Emerging from this study was an unexpected result that later came to be known as the Hawthorne effect. People under observation produce more quickly. Harry

Braverman in his book "Labour and Monopoly Capital" argued that, "the Hawthorne effect demonstrated that the workplace was a system of power, of class antagonisms."

## Challenges

While I-O psychologists research and identify how the workplace can be improved through feedback systems, hiring practices, training and more, they continue to struggle with ethical considerations in how they apply psychology to the environments where so many people spend so much of their lives. The discipline of I-O psychology is challenged by other disciplines in fields, such as human resources and business management, where success may be measured by an organizations productivity gains rather than on its workplace culture.

## CONTRIBUTIONS OF INDUSTRIAL ORGANIZATIONAL PSYCHOLOGY

Industrial/organizational psychology (I/O psychology) is a branch of psychology that explores the principles of psychology in relation to the workplace. Psychology principles applicable to the work setting are those mentioned in learning theory and aspects of social psychology as well as motivational and emotional principles. All of these principles can be used by counselling professionals to develop training and incentive programs, to form work groups and solve interpersonal problems, and to motivate and satisfy employees. Like counselling psychology, Industrial organizational psychology is based on the scientist-practitioner model. This model guides Industrial organizational psychologists in two ways: (a) conducting research and understanding the scientific principles in working with organizations, which is the scientific portion, and (b) providing the basis for high quality and effectiveness for the organization, which is the practitioner component. This entry discusses the history of I/O psychology, the services Industrial organizational psychologists perform, and the relationship between I/O psychology and counselling.

## History and Major Contributions

It is not known exactly when Industrial organizational

psychology began; however, in 1897,W. L. Bryan discussed how telegraphers learn the skill of sending and receiving Morse code messages. Six years later, Walter Dill Scott wrote A Theory of Advertising in which he applied psychology to business. Lillian Mollen Gilbreth announced in 1908 that human beings are the most important factors in industry and that they were not being acknowledged in the manner that they should. In 1911, engineer Frederick W. Taylor became conscious of how redesigning the workplace can achieve both higher efficiency within a company and higher compensation for employees. These people were the pioneers of the industry and contributed immensely to the world of Industrial organizational psychology and to how it is used today.

Although these individuals set the tone for the field, the onset of World War I had the first great impact on Industrial organizational psychology. Developed by then-American Psychological Association (APA) president Robert Yerkes and others, Army Alpha and Army Beta tests were used to determine the general intelligence of recruits so they could be placed in the appropriate positions, signifying the role of psychologists in work placement. The Alpha test was used for recruits who could read, and the nonverbal Beta test was used for those who could not read at all or who could not read English. These tests were used in placing recruits into appropriate positions.

As the war ended, it seemed that the use of Industrial organizational psychology was ending too. However, in 1920 the Hawthorne studies propelled I/O psychology by suggesting that employees' productivity improved because of the attention they were receiving from managers and employers, not the effects of the workplace lighting as the original research question suggested. This idea, referred to as the Hawthorne effect, had a significant impact in the history of Industrial organizational psychology, as it encouraged psychologists to focus more on human relations in the workplace and boosted the importance of this area of psychology.

As psychologists in the field polished their techniques on employee selection and placement, the Army again requested that psychologists develop a test that would divide recruits into groups based on their ability to learn the duties and responsibilities needed to be a soldier. Psychologists met this request by developing the Army General Classification Test (AGCT); other methods for selecting recruits for officer training, proficiency tests, and aptitude tests were also developed. As World War II continued, Industrial organizational psychologists also used their skills to keep the nation's workforce productive to support the war need. Industries were finally realizing that techniques and principles learned from social psychology were applicable in business in areas such as selection, training, and machine design.

As the United States evolved during the 1950s and 1960s, the civil rights movement made its impact on the field of psychology in general and specifically on Industrial organizational psychology. With the passage of the Civil Rights Act, business and industry came under scrutiny because they employed disproportionately few minority psychologists; however, because the law enforced the issue of discrimination in employment, the need for I/O psychologists increased. Industrial organizational psychology advanced greatly during the 1980s and 1990s, as more sophisticated research tools assisted psychologists in generating more information about psychology and the work world and in developing new tools such as the Armed Services Vocational Aptitude Battery to assist in personnel selection and classification.

Another important factor in the development of Industrial organizational psychology is the changing demographics in the workforce. The number of employed women, Latino/as, and Asian Americans continues to increase, and more individuals, such as customers, workers, and vendors, have English as their second language.

In addition, minorities such as women are entering higher level managerial positions. Industrial organizational psychologists are needed to help promote diversity in the work environment and to educate employees about navigating diverse environments and resolving conflict that may arise among different groups. With movements toward flexible, family friendly work schedules and policies, Industrial organizational psychology has come to be a cornerstone in keeping an organization running smoothly and efficiently.

## What Industrial Organizational Psychologists Do

Industrial organizational psychology is relatable to human resource management (HRM) in selecting employees and managing the work environment. Although there are similarities in that both are involved in employee selection, Industrial organizational psychology focuses more on the use of psychological principles, psychological tests, behavioural interviews, work samples, bio data, and assessment centres rather than the use of unstructured interviews and reference checks that HRM professionals employ. Further, I/O psychology places more emphasis on the people of an organization (e.g., motivating and retaining, enhancing productivity) instead of the technicalities of actually running the organization (e.g., policy and procedure enforcement, worker benefits). Finally, a misconception of I/O psychologists is that they provide psychotherapy for employees. Although there are psychologists who do provide in house psychotherapy to employees with a range of problems, such as those who work in Employee Assistance Programs (EAPs), I/O psychologists do not; instead, they often employ research and interventions with specific organizations to increase effectiveness of that organization.

Industrial Organizational psychologists provide several different services for those with whom they work, including selection and placement of employees, training and development, developing and evaluating performance appraisal systems, organizational development, enhancing quality of work life, and evaluating ergonomics to name a few. I/O psychologists who provide selection and placement services focus on methods for selection, placement, and promotion of employees by choosing and developing tests aimed at assisting clients in accomplishing these tasks. For example, a psychologist may use testing information to help a company choose who to hire for a manager position. In providing training and development services, I/O psychologists determine what skills and methods are needed to improve employees' job performance. For example, a psychologist may work with a company to implement a leadership development program for managers and potential managers. Those who provide performance appraisal services create ways to determine how well employees are actually performing their job. Last, I/O psychologists who provide services in relation to ergonomics are concerned with the equipment and machinery related to human skills as well as with how the organization is designed. These psychologists usually work with engineers and others in the technical profession to help make the workplace safer and enable employees to be more resourceful.

In addition to these areas, there are several services I/O psychologists provide that relate to the field of counselling psychology. These include (a) enhancing employee motivation; (b) improving organizational communication; (c) addressing group Behaviour, team management, and conflict, (d) addressing employee satisfaction, and (e) executive coaching. These services are discussed in more detail below.

## Motivation

In addressing motivation, Industrial Organizational psychologists call on psychological theories such as consistency theory and Maslow's hierarchy of needs to examine individual predispositions related to motivation. Factors that contribute to a motivated predisposition include self-esteem, intrinsic motivation tendency, and a need for power and achievement. More specifically, employees who have a high self evaluation will work harder so that their behavioural outcomes match their expectancies. Although individuals with high self-esteem may be likely to perform better than those with low self esteem, this may be true only in cultures where superior job performance is socially valued. Individuals who are intrinsically motivated are those who receive satisfaction in accomplishing a goal or task in and of itself and not just in the rewards gained from doing so.

An individual's predisposition for motivation may also be affected by her or his need for achievement and power. For example, Michael Stahl found that individuals who scored high on both need for achievement and power on the Job Choice Exercise could be classified as having a high level of managerial motivation. Thus, individuals with a high need for power and achievement are more likely than those with a low need for power and achievement to be motivated to work for promotions that place them in a position of control and influence. Other factors that contribute to employee motivation include whether or not an individual's needs are being met, achievability of goals, and the incentives received for meeting work goals.

In addressing motivation, I/O psychologists may conduct assessment related to predisposing factors of motivation as mentioned above and assess employees' goals or help employees develop achievable goals. Further, I/O psychologists may work with organizations to develop and assess evaluation and feedback systems and reward systems.

## Organizational Communication

An important aspect of any group of individuals is communication. Within an organization, effective communication can increase employee satisfaction and commitment and can actually help increase the effectiveness of the organization itself. Within an organization, smaller social and functional groups exist in which communication occurs both within and between groups. Types of groups that exist include work teams, levels of management, committees, and social groups. Communication varies in the ways it is both sent and received depending on which groups or individuals are communicating.

Michael Aamodt defined four types of organizational communication: upward, downward, business, and informal communication. Upward communication is that which goes from subordinates to superiors, while downward communication goes from superiors to subordinates. Business information is the relay of information that is business-related and can occur among customers as well as managers and employees. The fourth type is informal communication and consists of unofficial information that is transmitted through groups of workers or the organization itself.

Just as communication occurs within and between groups, another important component is interpersonal communication. Interpersonal communication occurs from one person to another and includes actual spoken words as well as nonverbal cues such as body language and use of space. It is also important to note that much of interpersonal communication is greatly influenced by one's culture. While some cultures value an expressive style of communicating, others pay more attention to the factuality of what is stated.

Industrial Organizational psychologists address communication issues by assessing the current forms of organization communication through surveys, interviews, and reviews of materials such as manuals and memos. Further, I/O psychologists will work with organizations to improve communication, providing feedback on current communication systems and recommendations for improvement such as incorporating different forms of communication systems. In addition, I/O psychologists may provide training relating to communication skills, such as telephone and e-mail etiquette, interpersonal communication, and verbal and nonverbal communication.

## Croup Behaviour, Teams and Croup Conflict

In order for individuals to be considered a group, they must meet the following four criteria: Members must see themselves as a unit, rewards must be provided to members, something that affects one member in turn affects the entire group, and members of the group must share a common goal. One of the factors that may affect group performance is group cohesion. An important component of group cohesion is having a shared set of attitudes and beliefs. Typically, members in a group perceive themselves as being more similar to other group members than to individuals not included in the group.

Similar to groups is the concept of teams. Teams are groups of three or more individuals who work together to achieve a specific work related task or goal. Work teams are distinguished from one another by their specific objectives. Susan Cohen and Diane Bailey defined four different types of teams. Work teams are fairly stable teams that have the objective of producing goods or providing a service. Within work teams, there are no supervisors; rather, each member plays an equal role in contributing to the goal of increasing product or service quality. Parallel teams are representative of different departments or units and are indeed parallel to the organization as a whole. The objective of parallel teams is to work as a problem solving unit and to provide feedback or recommendations to superiors within the organization. The next type of team is project teams. These teams are formed for a limited time basis with the objective of completing one task or goal for the organization. Management teams are responsible for overseeing the work of units below them. For example, a group of managers of an organizational department may be responsible for supervising employees within that department to ensure optimal performance of the department.

Just as conflict occurs among individuals, it also occurs within and between groups. Conflict is a reaction that occurs when someone interferes with an individual's need to achieve a goal or accomplish a task, when rights have been violated, or when expectancies of a relationship are broken. Conflict can be either functional or dysfunctional. Dysfunctional conflict is harmful to the working environment and prevents goals from being achieved, while functional conflict can increase competition as well as prevent larger conflicts later on. Because conflict is unavoidable, the most important aspect of conflict is how it is dealt with. Members of a group should determine early on what attitudes toward conflict will be and how conflict should be handled.

In working with groups and teams, the I/O psychologist will assess the current functioning of the group in relation to its structure and function (e.g., leaders and followers; how work is accomplished), cohesion, communication, and conflict. The I/O psychologists may provide services such as communication skills training, feedback, and recommendations to enhance group functioning, activities to build group or team cohesion, and instruction and facilitation of conflict resolution.

## Employee Satisfaction and Commitment

Organizational commitment and employee satisfaction are important aspects of an organization that affect employee Behaviour. Organizational commitment is the amount of allegiance felt by an individual toward an organization and can be broken down into three components: affective, continuance, and normative commitment. Affective commitment deals with the emotional ties to an organization and the extent that an individual cares about the organization. Continuance commitment is an employee's decision to stay with an organization due to time and effort already expended for the company. Normative commitment is commitment based on feelings of obligation toward an organization. The levels of each type of commitment may vary among individuals, and different combinations of strengths and types (affective, continuance, and normative) of commitment will result in differing employee Behaviours.

Along with organizational commitment, job satisfaction plays a major role in employee attitudes and Behaviours. Job satisfaction is influenced both by individual characteristics and the actual organization as well as by whether or not an individual is a good fit for an organization. Timothy Judge, Edwin Locke, and C. C. Durham proposed four personality characteristics that may contribute to a higher level of job satisfaction: emotional stability, self-efficacy, self-esteem, and an external locus of control. In order for an individual to be an appropriate fit with an organization, it is important that the values, skills, interests, personality, and lifestyle of the individual are similar to those of the organization. Because a great deal of satisfaction and commitment is related to personal characteristics, counselling psychologists can play an important role in helping assess an individual's wants and needs and in determining how they can contribute to job satisfaction.

## COUNSELLING AND INDUSTRIAL ORGANIZATIONAL PSYCHOLOGY

Similar to I/O psychology, counselling psychology's historical roots are tied to the military and the world of work, helping individuals to make the most out of their potential and to develop throughout their work careers. As a specialty of psychology, counselling involves a philosophy and working approach that resemble those of many areas of I/O psychology. For example, Sandra Shullman identified many overlaps between counselling psychology and consultation, a service often provided by I/O and counselling psychologists, such as recognizing and building on strengths, assisting individuals to achieve optimal functioning, identifying and addressing the impact of systems, and empowering consultees or clients to foster change. Counselling psychologists, trained as professional psychologists, develop competency in (a) gathering information and making conclusions or diagnoses; (b) consulting at the individual, group, and system levels to solve problems; (c) providing interventions to address problems; and (d) developing new knowledge through designing, implementing, and evaluating research. These foundational and functional competencies of professional psychology provide the groundwork on which counselling psychologists can offer services, as counselling psychology continues to expand to areas outside of traditional practice arenas and allows counselling psychologists to provide consultation services in areas such as health care, equal employment opportunity, safety, workers compensation, employee assistance programs, labour relations, employee outplacement, and recruitment. Clyde Crego notes that this overlap and generalization of competencies suggests that it is highly likely that counselling psychologists and students in training to become counselling psychologists can, with appropriate training, adapt their skills in order to provide I/O related services in a variety of settings.

# 3

# Social Aspects of Organizational Behaviour

Organizational Behaviour is an academic discipline concerned with describing, understanding, predicting, and controlling human Behaviour in an organizational environment. The field is particularly concerned with group dynamics, how individuals relate to and participate in groups, how leadership is exercised, how organizations function, and how change is effected in organizational settings. When organizational Behaviour theory is directed specifically at ways in which management can control an organization, it is sometimes known as *organizational Behaviour management,* or OBM.

Organizational Behaviour is a fairly new discipline, dating back to the early 20th century, although some experts suggest that it came into existence right after the U.S. Civil War. Organizational Behaviour has evolved from early classical management theories into a complex school of thought, and it continues to change in response to the dynamic workforce in which today's businesses operate.

## THE CLASSICAL MANAGEMENT SCHOOL

In 1911, Frederick W. Taylor's book, *Principles of Scientific Management,* was published. This book marked the first serious attempt to publish the results of scientific management studies aimed at motivating workers to produce more. Taylor was the best known of a group of people, primarily mechanical engineers, who applied time-and-motion study concepts in the workplace. These engineers focused on the task concept to show that workers could be motivated to produce more, especially if they were offered an incentive to do so.

The task concept centred around the idea that if managers planned workers' tasks at least one day in advance, production would increase. Taylor devised a differential piece-rate system based on two different rates of pay. His system was simple: workers who did less than the expected output received a low rate of pay. Those who exceeded the standard earned more money. That was a radical idea for the time. It separated the worker from the machine and indicated that employees could control how much they produced. Taylor also suggested in his approach that money motivated workers. This, too, was a unique idea. This approach became known as Theory X, and it would later be distinguished from other theories that took a different view of worker motivation and human nature. What Taylor did not do, however, was take into account group Behaviour. He, like most classical managers, had no concept of the importance of workers as members of groups. The next wave of theorists, the human relations experts, addressed the issue of group Behaviour.

## The Hawthorne Experiments

Human relationists tried to add a human dimension to classical theory in their studies. They did not try to refute the classical management proponents. Rather, they introduced the idea that workers would be willing to accept as part of their reward humane treatment, personal attention, and a chance to feel wanted. To prove their point, human relationists embarked on a series of experiments.

Perhaps the most significant experiments were the Hawthorne experiments. The studies began in 1924 at the Hawthorne Works, part of the Western Electric Company, located in Cicero, Illinois. The researchers' original goal was to measure the effect of illumination on output. In simplified terms, what they actually learned was that an individual's work performance, position, and status in an organization are determined not only by the individual, but by group members, too. They also learned that workers formed cliques that affected their production and that there were certain codes of conduct members of individual cliques were expected to follow. The

Hawthorne studies opened the door to more experiments by other human relationists.

## Human Resources Theory

The next group to take centre stage in the organizational Behaviour arena postulated that a manager's role was not to control workers, but to facilitate employee performance. According to human resources experts, people work to make a living, but their efforts go far beyond just laboring. They also work to fulfil certain needs, e.g., contributing to organizational objectives, attaining a feeling of accomplishment, and using their creativity in the work environment.

Managers were well advised to keep all these needs in mind when dealing with workers. According to the human resources theorists, managers should apply mutual goal-setting and problem-solving approaches to their workforce members Their approach has been termed Theory Y. Managers were encouraged to make use of whatever training was necessary to ensure maximum performance.

The training could take a variety of forms, i.e., technical, human, or conceptual. They were also advised to open communication lines in all directions to promote organizational effectiveness. After all, the theorists emphasized, workers welcome self-direction and self-control and will perform well when managers take an interest in their lives. In short, the human resources advocates said, managers should place their primary emphasis on using workers as if they are important human assets.

## THE SYSTEM APPROACH TO ORGANIZATIONAL BEHAVIOUR

Modem theorists apply a five-part system approach to organizational Behaviour:

- the individual
- the formal organization
- the informal organization
- the fusion process, in which the first three modify and shape one another
- the physical environment.

Each part is essential. None can exist alone in the system. This system approach is the basis for modem organizational theory, which is founded on behavioural science studies.

## The Behavioural Sciences

There are three behavioural sciences: psychology (the study of individual Behaviour), sociology (the study of social Behaviour within societies, institutions, and groups), and anthropology (the study of the origin, cultural development, and Behaviour of humans). Each has made important contributions to the study of organizational Behaviour.

From an organizational standpoint, psychologists are concerned with the processes of learning, perception, and motivation. Sociologists study the various organizations that compose society, e.g., political, legal, business, governmental, and religious bodies. Finally, anthropologists are interested in the impact of culture on Behaviour. The three disciplines have had a major impact on the study of organizational Behaviour.

Organizational Behaviour scientists study four areas: individual Behaviour, group Behaviour, organizational structure, and organizational processes. They investigate facets of these areas like personality and perception, attitudes and job satisfaction, group dynamics, politics and the role of leadership in the organization, job design, the impact of stress on work, decision-making processes, the communications chain, and company cultures and climates. They use a variety of techniques and approaches to evaluate each facet and its impact on individuals, groups, and organizational efficiency and effectiveness.

In regard to individuals and groups, researchers try to ascertain why people behave the way they do. They have developed a variety of models designed to explain individuals' Behaviour. They investigate the factors that influence personality development, including genetic, situational, environmental, cultural, and social factors. Researchers also look at personality types such as authoritarian (people who adhere closely to conventional values) and dogmatic (people who are extremely rigid in their beliefs). They want to find out what causes a person to form either type of personality and learn whether one or the other—or neither—is a positive trait for people in the business world.

Researchers have also studied a number of concepts, including:

1. Stereotyping—the process of categorizing people based on limited information
2. Halo effect—the use of known personal traits as the basis for an overall evaluation
3. Perceptual defence—the process of screening out or distorting information that is disturbing or that people do not care to acknowledge
4. Projection—people attribute their own undesirable traits or characteristics to others.

They evaluate perception versus reality, individuals' locus of control (whether they believe they or outside forces are in control of their lives), and common problems resulting from these personality traits and characteristics. Finally, they look at an individual's attitudes and correlate them to job satisfaction and job performance.

## THE IMPORTANCE OF JOB SATISFACTION STUDIES

The study of job satisfaction is central to organizational behavioural scientists. Companies want to know why their employees are or are not satisfied. If they are not happy, executives look to the behavioural scientists for ways to improve individuals' attitudes and to suggest ways of improving the work environment. This implies that the theorists have to look well beyond the tangible factors influencing job satisfaction, such as pay, benefits, promotional opportunities, and working conditions. They have to study how groups influence the workplace and individuals' expectations.

## THE DYNAMICS OF GROUP BEHAVIOUR

Perhaps the most basic issue scholars have addressed in the area of group Behaviour is the definition of "group." They have agreed that there is no one definition. Therefore, they have looked more at why people join groups, types of groups, and group activities and goals. Studies have focused on group norms, individuals' Behaviour within groups and how it changed, their roles within groups, and what groups could accomplish that individuals could not. Many researchers believe that a group is more than the sum of the individual members, even though its goals, interactions, and performance are determined primarily by the individuals within it.

In an era when teamwork and collaboration figure prominently in many corporations' stated values, organizational Behaviour theory suggests some models for how people work together well, and conversely, how collaboration breaks down. As in most social science theories, there is no exact formula for how people collaborate in a work environment, but there are some significant social and psychological dimensions that influence these Behaviours. Many of them relate to communication styles and methods. While electronic mail has been extolled as an important tool for efficient, speedy, and inexpensive communications, some evidence (mostly anecdotal at this stage) suggests that mechanical means of communication like e-mail hinder effective group work by fostering feelings of mistrust, distance, and apathy. By contrast, removing hierarchical and personal barriers and engendering open, face-to-face discussion appear to improve group interactions.

In another important area, organizational Behaviour scientists draw a distinction between leadership and management. They define management as the process of accomplishing tasks, whereas leadership is the process of getting things done by influencing other people. Another question is whether leaders are "born or made." In order to answer that question, researchers have sought common characteristics shared by leaders. They have found a few—intelligence, dependability, responsibility, social activity, and high originality—but there appear to be too many competing variables to form any universal conclusions of common leadership characteristics.

## Power, Politics and Conflict

Organizational Behaviour scientists have identified five basic types of power managers and leaders use to influence their subordinates: reward, coercive, legitimate, referent, and expert. Reward power, which is based on an individual's expectation of receiving desired outcomes, was found to be a positive force. However, if the members of a group do not believe they will be rewarded for their efforts, the person in a position to offer rewards will not be able to influence the individuals. Similarly, managers who rely on coercive power, which is based on fear, will probably be unable to influence workers, especially group members, for a long period of time.

The other three types of power also have advantages and disadvantages. For instance, legitimate power, which exists as part of a manager's position in the hierarchy, is often ignored by workers who do not respect the individual filling the role. Referent power, which is based on the manager's charisma, influences only those individuals or group members who are swayed by the charismatic leader. Finally, expert power, which is power acquired from experience and learning, is a positive force, but only to the degree managers can convince individuals and group members that their leadership skills go beyond expertise alone.

People attempting to exercise power in the organization often resort to political tactics to do so. They blame others for mistakes, form power coalitions, praise co-workers and subordinates when they think it will help them achieve goals and reinforce their images. In short, they use every stratagem possible to win friends and influence people. In the process, however, they often create conflict. This prompted researchers to study conflict and its possible solutions.

Organizational Behaviour scientists recognize that conflict exists at both the individual and group levels. They have devised a number of ways to deal with it. Among them are mutual problem solving, compromise, and avoidance. Significantly, they discovered that conflict resolutions are most often temporary, and they have looked for ways to make them more permanent. In order to find permanent solutions, they have performed more in-depth studies of organizational structure and processes and how both affect individuals and groups.

## ORGANIZATIONAL DESIGN AND PROCESSES

Organizational Behaviour scientists have conducted extensive studies on job definitions and the tasks a job comprises. They have looked at how each job fit into different groups within the organization, a process called departmentalization.

The researchers have studied managerial spans of control, i.e., the number of people an individual manager can manage most effectively. The process required that researchers reduce to its most basic level each task performed and then find ways to perform jobs more efficiently and effectively.

Many researchers have suggested viable ways that organizations could restructure jobs and relationships to stimulate job satisfaction and productivity simultaneously. They have devised better communications programs, identified the elements that create stress, and explained how it could be better managed.

Organizational Behaviour scientists performed extensive studies on company cultures and climates with an eye to upgrading employees' quality of life in the workplace. They have sought ways to include more people in the managerial and decision-making processes. Their suggestions have included such techniques as quality circles and participative management programs.

Quality circles, which are team approaches to identifying and resolving work-related problems, became popular in some businesses. So, too, did participative management efforts, which gave a wider variety of people opportunities to comment on—and implement—new ideas in the workplace. One prominent organizational Behaviour scientist, William Ouchi, recommended that American companies integrate more Japanese management concepts into their management practices. His approach became known as Theory Z.

The ideas promulgated by organizational Behaviour scientists have caught on in managerial circles. Not surprisingly, not all of the programs can be used by all companies. If there is one thing that researchers have recognized, it is that no two companies are alike.

To compensate for the dissimilarities, behavioural scientists reformed detailed cultural profiles to determine which programs fit individual companies' needs. These profiles have illustrated the importance of culture in the field of organizational Behaviour. Researchers have examined how company cultures control individual and group Behaviour, promote innovation, foster personnel commitment, and so on.

## Organizational Change

Another subject of special interest to organizational Behaviour scholars is how change affects people in an organization and how the process of change can be managed to maximize its success and minimize unintended disruptions. Change is compelled by many sources: social and demographic trends, economic cycles, competition, technology, and politics and regulation, to name a few. Scholars distinguish between change that is incremental and ongoing, sometimes called first-order change, and change that is radical and episodic, termed second-order change. While each form can have both positive and negative consequences, radical changes are commonly seen as requiring the most caution and skill at pulling off.

For example, one of the most visible trends in corporate America since the 1980s has been the rise of sudden mass layoffs at large corporations, or downsizing. This clearly represents one of the largest kinds of changes a company might face, and its scope affects not only the workers who lose their jobs but also those who remain.

Researchers have found that downsizing can have both positive and negative effects on the employees who stay on. In some cases, for example, layoffs can induce employees to work harder and engage in other Behaviours that benefit the company. One obvious explanation is that these workers might fear losing their jobs if they don't improve their performance, but there are likely other reasons as well, such as a move to fill a performance vacuum left by the departing workers. Still, other workers may respond by diminishing their performance; they may be demoralized by the corporate policies and may lower their mental and emotional investment in their jobs.

However, studies in organizational Behaviour suggest that all of these responses aren't inevitable. Scholars have suggested that the way in which the company goes about managing the change, in this case, the events leading up to and following downsizing, can have a significant effect on how employees react. This is not to say all negative reactions can be eliminated, but that there is a good chance they can be reduced. In the downsizing example, taking actions that foster trust in the management (such as open communication or demonstrating objective and consistent criteria for decision making) and that increase employee feelings of empowerment (letting workers have a say in some aspects of change) have been posited as methods of reducing some of the negative shocks of massive organizational change. Similar principles apply to managing other forms of organizational change.

More broadly, scholars like psychologist Kurt Lewin have identified basic models for managing change in organizations. In Lewin's widely cited three-step process, outlined in his 1951 classic *Field Theory in Social Science,* management must first "unfreeze" the status quo in the organization, facilitate a move to a new set of practices or environment, and then solidify or "refreeze" the new practices or environment into a permanent state. The process of unfreezing the current status involves introducing new policies or initiatives that begin to actively move employees away from the old way of doing things and/or removing policies or practices that tie them to the old. The second step, the shift to the new practices, is the formal implementation of the changes, for example, reorganizing a division or closing a branch office. Third, during refreezing management must solidify the changes by ensuring all the policies and practices are now geared toward maintaining the new equilibrium, and not throwbacks to the supplanted practices or lingering transition measures that create an atmosphere of instability or uncertainty.

## THE FUTURE OF ORGANIZATIONAL BEHAVIOUR

The international economy has taken on added importance in organizational Behaviour circles in recent years, as international companies have special requirements and dynamics to contend with. Researchers currently are studying such things as communications between and among foreign business operations, cultural differences and their impact on individuals, language difficulties, motivation techniques in different cultures, as well as the differences in leadership and decision-making practices from country to country.

Today, organizational Behaviour scientists are dealing with a wide range of problems confronting the business world. For instance, they continue to study downsizing, career development in the global economy, social issues such as substance abuse and changes in family composition, and the global economy. They are trying to determine just what effects such factors are having on the workplace and what can be done to alleviate associated problems.

## ORGANIZATIONAL BEHAVIOUR AND SOCIAL ASPECTS

Learner Objectives :

1. Develop an understanding about individual behaviour, inter personal behaviour, group dynamics within the organization.
2. Equip the HR professionals/students in managing human behaviour in organizations.
3. Equip the students in facilitating a better understanding of the "self" and professional behaviour in relation to others.
4. Develop understanding about CSR/social responsibility of manager and its various dimensions in industrial organization.

## BEHAVIOURAL CHANGE THEORIES

Behavioural change theories and models are attempts to explain the reasons behind alterations in individuals' behavioural patterns. These theories cite environmental, personal, and behavioural characteristics as the major factors in behavioural determination. In recent years, there has been increased interest in the application of these theories in the areas of health, education, criminology and energy with the hope that understanding behavioural change will improve the services offered in these areas.

### History

Many of the original works outlining the major theories that are the basis for current knowledge about behavioural change theories were published in the 1970s and 1980s. These include Icek Ajzen's articles on the Theories of Reasoned Action and Planned Behaviour, Albert Bandura's writings on Social Cognitive Theory, and James Prochaska and Carlo DiClemente's works on the Transtheoretical Model. More recently, interest in behavioural change theories has arisen due to their apparent application in areas like health, education, and criminology, leading to further research backed by institutions like the National Institutes of Health and the UK Prime Minister's Strategy Unit. With this renewed interest, however, there is also a shift towards research into understanding the maintenance of behavioural change in addition to broadening the research base for revising current theories that focus on initial change.

## General Theories and Models

Each behavioural change theory or model focuses on different factors in attempting to explain behavioural change. Of the many that exist, the most prevalent are the learning theories, Social Cognitive Theory, Theories of Reasoned Action and Planned Behaviour, Transtheoretical Model and the Health Action Process Approach. Research has also been conducted regarding specific elements of these theories, especially elements like self-efficacy that are common to several of the theories.

## Self-efficacy

Self-efficacy is an individual's impression of their own ability to perform a task such as going to the shops. This impression is based upon factors like the individual's prior success in the task or in related tasks, the individual's physiological state, and outside sources of persuasion. Self-efficacy is thought to be predictive of the amount of effort an individual will expend in initiating and maintaining a behavioural change, so although self-efficacy is not a behavioural change theory per se, it is an important element of many of the theories, including the Health Belief Model, the Theory of Planned Behaviour and the Health Action Process Approach.

## BEHAVIOUR ANALYTIC THEORIES OF CHANGE

From behaviourists like Burrhus Frederic Skinner come the learning theories, which state that complex behaviour is learned gradually through the modification of simpler behaviours. Imitation and reinforcement play important roles in these theories, which state that individuals learn by duplicating behaviours they observe in others and that rewards are essential to ensuring the repetition of desirable behaviour. As each simple behaviour is established through imitation and subsequent reinforcement, the complex behaviour develops. When verbal behaviour is established the organism can learn through rule-governed behaviour and thus not all action needs to be contingency shaped.

Skinner (1957) was one of the first psychologists to recognise the critical role of imitation (what he termed "echoic behaviour") in the learning of language. Behaviour analytic theories of change have been quite effective in improving the human condition.

## Social Cognitive Theory

According to the social learning theory, which is also known as the social cognitive theory, behavioural change is determined by environmental, personal, and behavioural elements. Each factor affects each of the others. For example, in congruence with the principles of self-efficacy, an individual's thoughts affect their behaviour and an individual's characteristics elicit certain responses from the social environment. Likewise, an individual's environment affects the development of personal characteristics as well as the person's behaviour, and an individual's behaviour may change their environment as well as the way the individual thinks or feels. Social learning theory focuses on the reciprocal interactions between these factors, which are hypothesised to determine behavioural change.

## Theory of Reasoned Action

The Theory of Reasoned Action assumes that individuals consider a behaviour's consequences before performing the particular behaviour. As a result, intention is an important factor in determining behaviour and behavioural change. According to Icek Ajzen, intentions develop from an individual's perception of a behaviour as positive or negative together with the individual's impression of the way their society perceives the same behaviour. Thus, personal attitude and social pressure shape intention, which is essential to performance of a behaviour and consequently behavioural change.

## Theory of Planned Behaviour

In 1985, Ajzen expanded upon the theory of reasoned action, formulating the Theory of Planned Behaviour, which also emphasises the role of intention in behaviour performance but is intended to cover cases in which a person is not in control of all factors affecting the actual performance of a behaviour. As a result, the new theory states that the incidence of actual behaviour performance is proportional to the amount of control an individual possesses over the behaviour and the strength of the individual's intention in performing the behaviour. In his article, Ajzen further hypothesises that self-efficacy is important in determining the strength of the individual's intention to perform a behaviour.

## Stages of Change Model

According to the Transtheoretical Model, which is also known as the Stages of Change Model, behavioural change is a five-step process. The five stages, between which individuals may oscillate before achieving complete change, are precontemplation, contemplation, preparation, action, and maintenance. At the precontemplation stage, an individual may or may not be aware of a problem but has no thought of changing their behaviour. From precontemplation to contemplation, the individual develops a desire to change a behaviour. During preparation, the individual intends to change the behaviour within the next month, and during the action stage, the individual begins to exhibit new behaviour consistently. An individual finally enters the maintenance stage once they exhibit the new behaviour consistently for over six months.

## Health Action Process Approach

The Health Action Process Approach (HAPA) is designed as a sequence of two continuous self-regulatory processes, a goal-setting phase (motivation) and a goal-pursuit phase (volition). The second phase is subdivided into a pre-action phase and an action phase. Motivational self-efficacy, outcome-expectancies and risk perceptions are assumed to be predictors of intentions.

This is the motivational phase of the model. The predictive effect of motivational self-efficacy on behaviour is assumed to be mediated by recovery self-efficacy, and the effects of intentions are assumed to be mediated by planning. The latter processes refer to the volitional phase of the model.

## Applications

Behavioural change theories have potential applications in many areas. Prominent areas of application include healthcare, education, criminal and energy consumption behaviour. These issues are important to societal functionality and policy-making, resulting in recent renewed interest in these theories.

## Health

In the interest of promoting healthy lifestyle development, behavioural change theories have gained recognition for their possible effectiveness in explaining health-related behaviours and providing insight into methods that would encourage individuals to develop and maintain healthy lifestyles. Specific health applications of behavioural change theories include the development of programs promoting active lifestyles and programs reducing the spread of diseases like AIDS. In addition, the National Institutes of Health has, in recent years, funded research to broaden the information base for behavioural change theories.

Models specific to health applications include the Health Belief/Health Action Model, Relapse Prevention Model, the Health Action Process Approach and the I-Change Model. The Health Belief Model, also known as the Health Action Model, states that individuals will alter health-related behaviour according to the perceived severity of the threat to their health. The Relapse Prevention Model concentrates on promoting prolonged healthy behaviour by making distinctions between lapses and relapses in an attempt to encourage individuals to maintain healthy lifestyles. The I-Change Model, the Integrated Model for explaining motivational and behavioural change, is derived from the Attitude – Social influence – Self-Efficacy Model. This model can be considered as an integration of ideas of Ajzen's Theory of Planned Behaviour, Bandura's Social Cognitive Theory, Prochaska's Transtheoretical Model, the Health Belief Model, and goal setting theories. Previous versions of this model (referred to as the ASE-model) have been used to explain a variety of types of health behaviour. In a similar way, the Health Action Process Approach represents an integration of self-efficacy theory and volition theories.

## Education

Behavioural change theories can be used as guides in developing effective teaching methods. Since the goal of much education is behavioural change, the understanding of behaviour afforded by behavioural change theories provides insight into the formulation of effective teaching methods that tap into the mechanisms of behavioural change. In an era when education programs strive to reach large audiences with varying socioeconomic statuses, the designers of such programs increasingly strive to understand the reasons behind behavioural change in order to understand universal characteristics that may be crucial to program design.

In fact, some of the theories, like the Social Learning Theory and Theory of Planned Behaviour, were developed as attempts to improve health education. Because these theories address the interaction between individuals and their environments, they can provide insight into the effectiveness of education programs given a specific set of predetermined conditions, like the social context in which a program will be initiated. Although health education is still the area in which behavioural change theories are most often applied, theories like the Stages of Change Model have begun to be applied in other areas like employee training and developing systems of higher education.

## Criminology

Empirical studies in criminology support behavioural change theories. At the same time, the general theories of behavioural change suggest possible explanations to criminal behaviour and methods of correcting deviant behaviour. Since deviant behaviour correction entails behavioural change, understanding of behavioural change can facilitate the adoption of effective correctional methods in policy-making. For example, the understanding that deviant behaviour like stealing may be learned behaviour resulting from reinforcers like hunger satisfaction that are unrelated to criminal behaviour can aid the development of social controls that address this underlying issue rather than merely the resultant behaviour.

Specific theories that have been applied to criminology include the Social Learning and Differential Association

Theories. Social Learning Theory's element of interaction between an individual and their environment explains the development of deviant behaviour as a function of an individual's exposure to a certain behaviour and their acquaintances, who can reinforce either socially acceptable or socially unacceptable behaviour. Differential Association Theory, originally formulated by Edwin Sutherland, is a popular, related theoretical explanation of criminal behaviour that applies learning theory concepts and asserts that deviant behaviour is learned behaviour. Jeffery's reexamination of Sutherland's original theory adds that because of the necessity of temporal proximity between punishment and behaviour for conditioning to occur, the legal system's application of punishment is more likely to generate law evasion rather than to correct deviant behaviour.

## Energy

Recent years have seen an increased interest in energy consumption reduction based on behavioural change, be it for reasons of climate change mitigation or energy security. The application of behavioural change theories in the field of energy consumption behaviour yields interesting insights. For example, it supports criticism of a too narrow focus on individual behaviour and a broadening to include social interaction, lifestyles, norms and values as well as technologies and policies- all enabling or constraining behavioural change. Intervention programmes aimed at the change of energy consumption patters need to take into account that behavioural change is best achieved and maintained if supported by tailored information and changes in context, for example supportive social networks, policies or technologies.

## Objections

Behavioural change theories are not universally accepted. Criticisms include the theories' emphases on individual behaviour and a general disregard for the influence of environmental factors on behaviour. In addition, as some theories were formulated as guides to understanding behaviour while others were designed as frameworks for behavioural interventions, the theories' purposes are not consistent. Such criticism illuminates the strengths and weaknesses of the theories, showing that there is room for further research into behavioural change theories.

## UNDERSTANDING WORKPLACE BEHAVIOUR

One of the greatest challenges facing managers and leaders is to understand people's motives. If we know why people do the things they do we can develop greater understanding, better relationships at work, a happier environment and improved individual, team and organisational performance. This, of course, leads to bottom-line benefits.

Over a period of 25 years I have tried to develop behavioural models that can help leaders assign jobs, put together effective teams, motivate staff and deliver outstanding results. The Pyramid of Workplace Behaviour shows the three levels that build a complete picture of the different ways that people approach work.

### Values

Values are fundamental concepts or beliefs which people use to guide their behaviour in the workplace. Values will drive our decision making and cause us to summon up energy to preserve what we believe in. Values go beyond specific situations and determine how we view people, behaviour and events. Often major sources of conflict and disillusionment are due to mismatched values. Whereas we are often willing to work on tasks that we dislike, we are much less likely to compromise when our values are under threat.

Values are difficult to observe in others, as they are inner concepts often buried in the human psyche and not readily accessible by the conscious mind. When these values are violated, the conscious mind takes over and appropriate behaviour occurs to defend this attack.

Workplace values can be measured by the author's Window on Work Values. This is a model that groups values together in clusters of eight 'value types' which are depicted as window panes, rather like those in the rose windows of many European cathedrals. The value types close to one another in the window are related, whereas those on opposite sides of the window are unrelated. The Window on Work Values has two independent axes. Running east-west through the window is the axis which focuses on either the self or the group. The self-focus value types govern the dominance of personal over group goals. The defining motivations for the self-focus value types are actions that further individual gain and foster a hierarchy of differentiation within an organisation. The group-focus value types have defining goals where the individual is subordinated to the wishes, needs and goals of the group. Although many people can do both, the results suggest that most people will have a bias one way or the other. Running north-south through the model is the axis defining the organisational environment that people value. On the north side are the values associated with organisational constraint, while on the south side are the values associated with organisational freedom.

Organisational constraint as a motivational type is derived from the prerequisite for some groups to ensure smooth interaction and group survival, thereby developing a prescriptive set of norms for group members to restrain impulses and inhibit actions that might hurt others. Organisational freedom, on the other hand, is a motivational type with defining goals of independence of thought and action, where individual behaviour is unrestricted and people are free to choose their pathways, unfettered by organisational constraints.

As such these two value types are unlikely to share equal portions of the human psyche, as the behaviours associated with each are conflicting. The Window on Work Values helps explain why problems exist within any group of people working together. Value types define core frameworks that people hold and for which they are prepared to expend considerable energy in either promoting or defending.

Most people will hold three or four of the values reasonably strongly. Because of the structure of the model, these values are more likely to be concentrated in one particular section, giving rise to key value patterns which are useful in understanding and predicting individual and group behaviour.

## RISK ORIENTATION

The middle layer of the Workplace Behaviour Pyramid addresses the way people approach risk. The behaviours associated with this operate at the middle level of the human psyche. They are not so fundamental as values, as they can be influenced to some extent by the work environment and the attitudes of colleagues.

All through our life we are faced with opportunities and obstacles; they crop up in every project we undertake no matter how much forward planning is done. What determines people's risk profiles is the different emphasis they place on either 'seeing the opportunities' or 'seeing the obstacles'. Some people treat obstacles as an opportunity to take a new direction, whereas others use them as an excuse to give up. Some people treat obstacles as a stumbling block, but for others they are stepping-stones to the future.

## The Risk-orientation Scale

The risk-orientation scale enables us to measure someone's approach to risk. At one extreme, people can focus most of their energy on seeing opportunities. They are always positive when new ideas are presented and will look optimistically at most situations. The downside is the energy they assign to seeing obstacles. They don't always see potential difficulties and this can cause them to misjudge situations.

At the other end of the scale, people may focus most of their energy on seeing obstacles. When working on a project, they are more likely to put a lot of effort into looking at all the things that might go wrong. When faced with potential opportunities they may well ignore them, presenting cogent arguments to support their view that the risks are too great.

## Opportunities versus Obstacles

The Opportunities-Obstacles Quotient is a useful measure to quantify a person's position on the risk-orientation scale. It is defined as the ratio of the energy put into seeing opportunities to the ratio of the energy put into seeing obstacles. It is measured by a 50-item questionnaire which assesses people's responses to various statements. People who map strongly towards the 'opportunities side' of the scale have a high 'moving towards goals' energy; that is, they set challenging goals and regularly achieve them. When difficulties occur or blockages to their goals arise, they are quick to generate alternative pathways and move around the blockage, still focusing on the goal. As well, they are generally optimistic and full of hope that everything will turn out for the best. They tend to put less energy into finding faults with proposals, projects and people and usually have a positive attitude that can enthuse those around them. For them, the future is a rosy place and one they want to be part of, because it is likely to be better than where they are now. People who are strongly at the 'seeing obstacles' end of the scale have a lower energy and are less able to generate pathways around obstacles. When blockages occur they are more likely to keep pressing forward down the same pathway and will quickly give up when their energy is expended.

As well, they tend to be more pessimistic and will anticipate the worst scenario when problems arise. They will usually put a lot of effort into fault finding, and this can be both a strength and a weakness. When faced with a new idea they are more likely to identify all the difficulties that might prevent the idea from becoming a reality. 'Seeing-obstacles' people are also more comfortable with the present and past. To them the future is not a rosy place but one that is fraught with difficulties. Some hanker for 'the good old days' when life was much better than it is now.

## Preferences

We all approach our work in different ways—we think in different ways, we plan in different ways and we communicate in different ways. Some aspects of our work might interest us more than others and therefore we will tend to place more emphasis on these activities. Preferences are another name for what we like doing. We value our preferences but they are not 'values'.

Preferences guide our behaviour, but if we have to work outside them at various times then we can usually cope. Values, on the other hand, are deep-seated determinants of behaviour and we are more likely to react negatively when these values are violated.

Preferences are usually transparent and are often the first thing we notice in others: 'He's rather quiet, isn't he?' or 'She never stops talking'. Some people prefer to think things through on their own, whereas others need to talk out loud to clarify their ideas. Preferences are at the apex of the pyramid because they are readily visible to others and are usually the basis of first impressions. They are also subject to a degree of variability, depending on the situations faced.

## UNDERSTANDING HUMAN BEHAVIOUR AND ITS EXISTENCE

We may be more effective counsellors if we can more adequately understand human nature. Human Behaviour and its existence can be more fully understood by viewing ourselves as biological, psychological, sociological, humanistic, and spiritual entities. By understanding ourselves and our existence we may also live to fully experience what it is to be human. In one regard, we may view a human as a biological organism consisting of a complex structure of chemical components while possessing thoughts and feelings through integrated electrical-chemical reactions. Furthermore, the human organism has evolved through time to reflect the environmental and social obstacles placed on it through the process of evolutionary selection. We can also distinguish ourselves as psychological and social entities. From a very early age we learn from those around us and develop particular comfort zones in which we develop our personality. From our personality and our place in life we develop our identity of ourselves.

Recognizing an individual in a humanistic light has been a major step toward understanding the total being. The humanistic system of thought centres on the person and their values, capacities, and worth. In addition, it is concerned with the interests, needs, and welfare of human beings.

Finally, the spiritual ideology distinguishes us apart from bodily or worldly existence and its concerns. It is not to be confused with one's memory of a loved one, nor a supernatural occurrence appearing in a storybook. It is a concept of us that reaches beyond finite existence.

We can not fully describe or understand human Behaviour, human experience, or human existence with just a single model. Conversely, these ways of viewing the human being are not mutually exclusive yet may be viewed from a variety of constructs. Likewise, human Behaviour can be more fully understood using various co-existing models: Chemical, Biological, Psychological, Sociological, and Spiritual.

## PERSONALITY DEVELOPMENT

From a very early age we learn from our environment and those around us. We start by imitating our parent's Behaviours. We are conditioned to focus on selected stimuli in our environment. Our Behaviour is influenced by not only events around us but biological predisposition as well. Circumstance and individual choice also dictate Behaviour and conversely, the development of holistic health in general. As children we also develop comfort zones in which we develop our personality. As we engage in social interactions, reflect on feelings, ponder on thoughts, and display mannerisms we learn to become more proficient in those Behaviours we practice. Furthermore, as we experience these Behaviours we tend to favor particular patterns and degrees of social interaction, feelings, and thoughts, and mannerisms. It is speculated this favouritism toward a particular personality is shaped by observation, imitation, positive reinforcement, and finally, generalization.

From our personality and our place in life we develop our identity of ourselves. From the perception our identity come our self-worth, self-concept, and consequently, our self-esteem.

### Development of Maladaptive Behaviour

The holistic health concept includes developing and maintaining physical, mental, emotional, mental, social, and spiritual growth. Although it is optimal to develop all components of holistic health equally, sometimes the development a just few of these components may be enough to bring about the degree of self-worth or happiness necessary for a seemingly normal life. Often, a weak development of one or more of these components may adversely affect other components of holistic health. Sometimes this weak link may be felt as a void or unquenchable thirst in ones life. Conversely, discontent is experienced when what occurs does not match with what was expected. This void or discontentment may bring about several exaggerated needs that may stagnate the development of holistic health.

Individuals may futilely attempt to satisfy these exaggerated needs by implementing particular Behaviours. A perception of at least temporary satisfaction is sometimes enough to reinforce this Behaviour for a life long pattern. In most cases, we can implement this Behaviour within socially acceptable boundaries. In some cases, though, this Behaviour may be socially unacceptable or self-destructive.

Modern values have compromised our being. We rationalize day care, divorce, and the materialistic world in which we live with no real understanding of our selfishness, insecurities, and the consequences of our Behaviours. We have alienated our lives, our children lives, and ultimately our society. This has threatened all aspects of our individual holistic health: physical, mental, emotional, mental, social, and spiritual.

Throughout the day, we have relative stranger look after our kids, feed them refined foods, encourage them to sit down and be quiet, feed them more slop, tell them we're to busy or tired, and try to discipline them with threats or reward them with treats. After all this we wonder why our children are obese and have Behaviour problems. Authorities speculate modern amenities have some way affected the minds of the young and old alike. TV competes with studies, physical activity, and social interaction. Moreover, until recently, we remained active by walking, lifting, hunting, and working. As a result, our bodies and minds no longer have the physical stimulation it once thrived on. In addition, our transient society has challenged social ties to ones family and friends, inviting isolation and feelings of loneliness. Furthermore, the advent of the telephone and, more recently, the computer has, in many instances, altered the way we socialize. Finally, the society's sensationalization of the good life has replaced worshiping "all that is non-materialistic and everlasting" with worshiping "all that is materialistic and lasting a finite time".

Emotional highs and lows are always present throughout ones life. As reality therapy illustrates, emotionally adjusted individuals remain in a more positive mood states for longer durations as compared to less emotionally adjusted individuals. Furthermore, it seems that more emotionally adjusted individuals possess more emotional resilience than others when in a lower emotional state.

## UNDERSTANDING OF ORGANISATIONAL BEHAVIOUR

In order to understand organisational behaviour, one must develop an understanding of the term organisation. According to Robbins and Barnwell an organisation is 'a consciously coordinated social entity, with a relatively identifiable boundary, that functions on a relatively continuous basis in order to achieve a common goal or set of goals' (2002). In the broad spectrum of the term organisation, one may see that they 'exist to achieve goals and objectives' (Forrest and Johnstone 2004). For example the health organisation Nepean Hospital can be seen as an organisation, because all its members (employees) work in a consciously coordinated social entity, in order to perform the continuous function to achieve the common goal, of providing health for the general public.

Organisational behaviour is the study of what the people who make up an organisation think, feel and do in and around organisations. It explores individual emotions and behaviour, team dynamics and the systems and structures of organisations. Organisational behaviour seeks to provide an understanding of the factors necessary for managers to create an organisation that is more 'effective' than its competitors. Through a study of organisational behaviour managers may attempt to develop organisational citizenship within its employees. According to Robbins, Millett and Waters-Marsh organisational behaviour is 'a field of study that investigates the impact that individuals, groups and structure have on behaviour within organisations for the purpose of applying such knowledge towards improving an organisation's effectiveness' (2004).

This concept attempts to understand three specific determinants of organisational behaviour: individuals, groups and structure (Robbins et al 2004). In the organisation Nepean Hospital the mission statement is 'to improve health outcomes of the general public' (Sydney Western Area Health Service Mission Statement 2005) and all three of these determinants of organisational behaviour may be seen. The individual employees may include the nurses, doctors, wardspersons, ward clerks, cleaners, managers, and staff specialists. The groups may include the medical teams, neurosurgical, renal, medical emergency teams, groups of nurses, nurses and wardspersons.

The structure, in this case is a matrix design. According to Montgomery the matrix design 'includes both a vertical and a horizontal chain of command' (2002). Thus, the Nurse Unit Manager has her own direct senior, in her own vertical line of command; however, concerning 'infection control,' 'public health,' 'mental health' or 'drug and alcohol' issues the directors of these areas are also her 'direct' senior (from the side). This design is helpful as the expert on each subject is near to hand, yet the day to day individual service delivery to clients is the responsibility of the Nurse Manager and his or her staff.

By developing an understanding of organisational behaviour, managers of organisations are better equipped and capable of managing people so that they physically want to do all that they can to further increase the efficiency and effectiveness of the organisation.

# 4

# Theory and Behaviour of Organizational Psychology

## ORGANIZATIONAL THEORIES

There are several theories which explain the organization and its structure (EXHIBIT 1). Classical organization theory includes the *scientific management approach,* Weber's *bureaucratic approach,* and *administrative theory.*

The *scientific management approach* is based on the concept of planning of work to achieve efficiency, standardization, specialization and simplification. The approach to increased productivity is through mutual trust between management and workers. Taylor (1947) proposed four principles of scientific management:

- science, not rule-of-thumb;
- scientific selection of the worker;
- management and labour cooperation rather than conflict; and
- scientific training of workers.

Show EXHIBIT 2 and discuss these principles.

Weber's *bureaucratic approach* considers the organization as a part of broader society. The organization is based on the principles of:

- structure;
- specialization;
- predictability and stability;

- rationality; and
- democracy.

Show EXHIBIT 3, and discuss Weber's bureaucratic approach. Observe that this approach is considered rigid, impersonal, self-perpetuating and empire building.

*Administrative theory* was propounded by Henry Fayol and is based on several principles of management (EXHIBIT 4). In addition, management was considered as a set of planning, organizing, training, commanding and coordinating functions.

Neoclassical theory emphasizes individual or group behaviour and human relations in determining productivity. The main features of the neoclassical approach are individual, work group and participatory management. Show EXHIBIT 5 and discuss the principles.

Show EXHIBIT 6 on a modern approach to organization characteristics. Modern theories are based on the concept that the organization is an adaptive system which has to adjust to changes in its environment. Discuss the important characteristics of the modern approach to organizations. Modern theories include the *systems approach,* the *socio-technical approach,* and the *contingency or situational approach.*

The *systems approach* considers the organization as a system composed of a set of inter-related-and thus mutually dependent-sub-systems. Thus the organization consists of components, linking processes and goals (EXHIBIT 7).

The *socio-technical approach* considers the organization as composed of a social system, technical system and its environment. These interact among themselves and it is necessary to balance them appropriately for effective functioning of the organization.

The *contingency or situational approach* recognizes that organizational systems are inter-related with their environment and that different environments require different organizational relationships for effective working of the organization.

Ask participants whether they consider the research organization as a social system. Since scientists constitute the core resource in a research organization, their growth is as important as the growth of the organization. A social organization is characterized by complexity, degrees of interdependence between sub-systems, openness, balance and multiplicity of purposes, functions and objectives. Show EXHIBIT 8 and discuss each of these characteristics.

Now move to goal setting in an organization. Ask participants "Why should goals be set?" Goals are set to increase performance and provide control. Show EXHIBIT 9 and discuss how goal setting improves performance. How are goals set? Following management by objectives, the process of goal setting involves five steps (EXHIBIT 10). First, the overall objectives of the organization are set and then an action plan is evolved. The second step is to prepare members in the organization for successful implementation of the action plan. Individual goals are set in the third step. Periodic appraisal and feedback is the fourth step, to ensure smooth implementation of the action plan. Finally, an appraisal of performance by results takes place.

Now discuss the concept of integration and coordination in the organization. These are controlling mechanisms for smooth functioning of the organization. Organizational differentiation is the unbundling and re-arranging of the activities. Integration is re-grouping and re-linking them. The need for integration arises in the face of environmental complexity, diversity and change. Show EXHIBIT 11 and discuss some of the important reasons which necessitate integration.

How is integration achieved? Obviously, the structure of the organization should facilitate proper coordination and integration of different specialized units. What could happen were the organizational structure not proper? Integration is achieved through vertical coordination along the hierarchy, decision making levels, and span of control (EXHIBIT 12). There are several methods to improve integration. These include rules and procedures and professional training.

Next discuss the process in the organization, which involves the concept of power, decision making and communication. Power refers to the ability to get an individual or group to do something or to change in some way. Power could emanate from position, economic status, knowledge, performance, personality, physical or ideological traits. Observe that power is one of the strongest motives, and affects setting of objectives and availability of resources in an organization. Next discuss the concept, and the various types of organization-based power (EXHIBIT 13). Communication is another important process in the organization and is a key mechanism for achieving integration and coordination of the activities of specialized units at different levels in the organization. Communication can be horizontal, downward or upward (EXHIBIT 14).

Finally, discuss decision making in an organization. It begins with goal setting, identification and evaluation of alternatives and the choice of criteria. Show EXHIBIT 15 and discuss the important steps involved in decision making. There are several models of decision making (EXHIBIT 16).

## READING NOTE: ORGANIZATIONAL THEORIES

Organizational theories which explain the organization and its structure can be broadly classified as classical or modern.

### Classical Organization Theory

Classical organization theories deal with the formal organization and concepts to increase management efficiency. Taylor presented scientific management concepts, Weber gave the bureaucratic approach, and Fayol developed the administrative theory of the organization. They all contributed significantly to the development of classical organization theory.

### Taylor's Scientific Management Approach

The scientific management approach developed by Taylor is based on the concept of planning of work to achieve efficiency, standardization, specialization and simplification. Acknowledging that the approach to increased productivity was through mutual trust between management and workers, Taylor suggested that, to increase this level of trust,

- the advantages of productivity improvement should go to workers,
- physical stress and anxiety should be eliminated as much as possible,
- capabilities of workers should be developed through training, and
- the traditional 'boss' concept should be eliminated.

Taylor developed the following four principles of scientific management for improving productivity:

- *Science, not rule-of-thumb* Old rules-of-thumb should be supplanted by a scientific approach to each element of a person's work.
- *Scientific selection of the worker* Organizational members should be selected based on some analysis, and then trained, taught and developed.
- *Management and labour cooperation rather than conflict* Management should collaborate with all organizational members so that all work can be done in conformity with the scientific principles developed.
- *Scientific training of the worker* Workers should be trained by experts, using scientific methods.

## Weber's Bureaucratic Approach

Considering the organization as a segment of broader society, Weber (1947) based the concept of the formal organization on the following principles:

- *Structure* In the organization, positions should be arranged in a hierarchy, each with a particular, established amount of responsibility and authority.
- *Specialization* Tasks should be distinguished on a functional basis, and then separated according to specialization, each having a separate chain of command.
- *Predictability and stability* The organization should operate according to a system of procedures consisting of formal rules and regulations.
- *Rationality* Recruitment and selection of personnel should be impartial.
- *Democracy* Responsibility and authority should be recognized by designations and not by persons.

Weber's theory is infirm on account of dysfunctions (Hicks and Gullett, 1975) such as rigidity, impersonality, displacement of objectives, limitation of categorization, self-perpetuation and empire building, cost of controls, and anxiety to improve status.

## Administrative Theory

The elements of administrative theory (Fayol, 1949) relate

to accomplishment of tasks, and include principles of management, the concept of line and staff, committees and functions of management.

- *Division of work or specialization* This increases productivity in both technical and managerial work.
- *Authority and responsibility* These are imperative for an organizational member to accomplish the organizational objectives.
- *Discipline* Members of the organization should honour the objectives of the organization. They should also comply with the rules and regulations of the organization.
- *Unity of command* This means taking orders from and being responsible to only one superior.
- *Unity of direction* Members of the organization should jointly work toward the same goals.
- *Subordination of individual interest to general interest* The interest of the organization should not become subservient to individual interests or the interest of a group of employees.
- *Remuneration of personnel* This can be based on diverse factors such as time, job, piece rates, bonuses, profit-sharing or non-financial rewards.
- *Centralization* Management should use an appropriate blend of both centralization and de-centralization of authority and decision making.
- *Scalar chain* If two members who are on the same level of hierarchy have to work together to accomplish a project, they need not follow the hierarchy level, but can interact with each other on a 'gang plank' if acceptable to the higher officials.
- *Order* The organization has a place for everything and everyone who ought to be so engaged.
- *Equity* Fairness, justice and equity should prevail in the organization.
- *Stability of tenure of personnel* Job security improves performance. An employee requires some time to get used to new work and do it well.

- *Initiative* This should be encouraged and stimulated.
- *Esprit de corps* Pride, allegiance and a sense of belonging are essential for good performance. Union is strength.
- *The concept of line and staff* The concept of line and staff is relevant in organizations which are large and require specialization of skill to achieve organizational goals. Line personnel are those who work directly to achieve organizational goals. Staff personnel include those whose basic function is to support and help line personnel.
- *Committees* Committees are part of the organization. Members from the same or different hierarchical levels from different departments can form committees around a common goal. They can be given different functions, such as managerial, decision making, recommending or policy formulation. Committees can take diverse forms, such as boards, commissions, task groups or *ad hoc* committees. Committees can be further divided according to their functions. In agricultural research organizations, committees are formed for research, staff evaluation or even allocation of land for experiments.
- *Functions of management* Fayol (1949) considered management as a set of planning, organizing, training, commanding and coordinating functions. Gulick and Urwick (1937) also considered organization in terms of management functions such as planning, organizing, staffing, directing, coordinating, reporting and budgeting.

## NEOCLASSICAL THEORY

Neoclassical theorists recognized the importance of individual or group behaviour and emphasized human relations. Based on the Hawthorne experiments, the neoclassical approach emphasized social or human relationships among the operators, researchers and supervisors (Roethlisberger and Dickson, 1943). It was argued that these considerations were more consequential in determining productivity than mere changes in working conditions. Productivity increases were achieved as a result of high morale, which was influenced by the amount of individual, personal and intimate attention workers received.

## Principles of the Neoclassical Approach

The classical approach stressed the formal organization. It was mechanistic and ignored major aspects of human nature. In contrast, the neoclassical approach introduced an informal organization structure and emphasized the following principles:

*The individual* An individual is not a mechanical tool but a distinct social being, with aspirations beyond mere fulfilment of a few economic and security works. Individuals differ from each other in pursuing these desires. Thus, an individual should be recognized as interacting with social and economic factors.

*The work group* The neoclassical approach highlighted the social facets of work groups or informal organizations that operate within a formal organization. The concept of 'group' and its synergistic benefits were considered important.

*Participative management* Participative management or decision making permits workers to participate in the decision making process. This was a new form of management to ensure increases in productivity.

Note the difference between Taylor's 'scientific management'-which focuses on work-and the neoclassical approach-which focuses on workers.

## Modern Theories

Modern theories tend to be based on the concept that the organization is a system which has to adapt to changes in its environment. In modern theory, an organization is defined as a designed and structured process in which individuals interact for objectives (Hicks and Gullet, 1975). The contemporary approach to the organization is multidisciplinary, as many scientists from different fields have contributed to its development, emphasizing the dynamic nature of communication and importance of integration of individual and organizational interests. These were subsequently re-emphasized by Bernard (1938) who gave the first modern and comprehensive view of management. Subsequently, conclusions on systems control gave insight into application of cybernetics. The operation research approach was suggested in 1940. It utilized the contributions of several disciplines in problem solving. Von Bertalanffy (1951) made a significant contribution by suggesting a component of general systems theory which is accepted as a basic premise of modern theory. Some of the notable characteristics of the modern approaches to the organization are:

- a systems viewpoint,
- a dynamic process of interaction,
- multilevelled and multidimensional,
- multimotivated,
- probabilistic,
- multidisciplinary,
- descriptive,
- multivariable, and
- adaptive.

Modern understandings of the organization can be broadly classified into:

- the systems approach,
- socio-technical theory, and
- a contingency or situational approach.

## The Systems Approach

The systems approach views organization as a system composed of interconnected-and thus mutually dependent-sub-systems. These sub-systems can have their own sub-sub-systems. A system can be perceived as composed of some components, functions and processes (Albrecht, 1983). Thus, the organization consists of the following three basic elements (Bakke, 1959):

(i) *Components.* There are five basic, interdependent parts of the organizing system, namely:

- the individual,
- the formal and informal organization,
- patterns of behaviour emerging from role demands of the organization,
- role comprehension of the individual, and
- the physical environment in which individuals work.

(ii) *Linking processes.* The different components of an organization are required to operate in an organized and correlated manner. The interaction between them is contingent upon the linking processes, which consist of communication, balance and decision making.

- *Communication* is a means for eliciting action, exerting control and effecting coordination to link decision centres in the system in a composite form.
- *Balance* is the equilibrium between different parts of the system so that they keep a harmoniously structured relationship with one another.
- *Decision analysis* is also considered to be a linking process in the systems approach. Decisions may be to produce or participate in the system. Decision to produce depends upon the attitude of the individual and the demands of the organization. Decision to participate refers to the individual's decisions to engross themselves in the organization process. That depends on what they get and what they are expected to do in participative decision making.

(iii) *Goals of organization.* The goals of an organization may be growth, stability and interaction. Interaction implies how best the members of an organization can interact with one another to their mutual advantage.

## Socio-technical Approach

It is not just job enlargement and enrichment which is important, but also transforming technology into a meaningful tool in the hands of the users. The socio-technical systems approach is based on the premise that every organization consists of the people, the technical system and the environment (Pasmore, 1988). People (the social system) use tools, techniques and knowledge (the technical system) to produce goods or services valued by consumers or users (who are part of the organization's external environment). Therefore, an equilibrium among the social system, the technical system and the environment is necessary to make the organization more effective.

## The Contingency or Situational Approach

The situational approach is based on the belief that there cannot be universal guidelines which are suitable for all situations. Organizational systems are inter-related with the environment. The contingency approach suggests that different environments require different organizational relationships for optimum effectiveness, taking into consideration various social, legal, political, technical and economic factors.

## THE RESEARCH ORGANIZATION AS A SOCIAL SYSTEM

An organization is a continuing system, able to distinguish and integrate human activities. The organization utilizes, transforms and joins together a set of human, material and other resources for problem-solving (Bakke, 1959). The main function of an organization is to satisfy specific human needs in interaction with other sub-systems of human activities and resources in the given environment. In a research organization, individual needs of researchers are more often in conflict with organizational needs than in any other organization. Therefore, growth of the organization should concurrently also promote growth of the individual.

### Characteristics of the Research Organization

Social organizations are characterized by their complexity, degree of inter-dependence between sub-systems, openness, balance, and multiplicity of purposes, functions and objectives.

*Complexity* A research organization consists of a number of individuals, groups, or departments, each of which is a sub-system within the total system. The prevalence of these sub-systems makes the organization complex.

*Degree of inter-dependence of sub-systems* The various sub-systems of the research organization are inter-dependent which makes it further complex, as each sub-system has its way of working, requirements, behaviour, etc.

*Openness of the social organization* Research organizations operate in the wider environment of a larger organization or system, and are therefore open. They have to function in harmony with environmental requirements, goals and functions. This may cause conflicts in the organization unless the sub-systems are appropriately balanced.

*Balance and the social organization* Social organizations are highly dynamic. Forces such as researchers, managerial hierarchy and various inputs from within and outside the organization have to be balanced for the smooth functioning of the organization.

*Multiplicity of purpose, functions and objectives* Most research organizations have a multiplicity of sub-systems, each of which has dynamic interactions with others. In the research organization, a researcher can be viewed as a sub-system with specific needs, goals and functioning, although those needs, goals and functioning may sometimes not match those of the organization.

## Goal Setting

In an organization, goal setting is one of the control systems, a component of the appraisal process and an effective tool for human resource management.

The concept of goal setting is now used to increase the performance of the organization as well as the individual through management by objectives. Drucker (1954) suggested that management by objectives can be useful for managers for effectively managing the future direction of the organization.

## Importance of Goal Setting

Well specified and clear goals improve performance in an organization by:

- making clear what people have to do;
- solving specific problems related to the work as they emerge during the process of goal setting;
- reducing ambivalence in the assigned work and thus encouraging increasing efforts;
- supporting people to find a connection between their work and the achievements of the organization;
- assisting individuals in allocating their time, efforts and personal resources to important areas;
- giving a feeling of accomplishment and contentment when specified goals are achieved; and
- providing some control over the people and their work in an organization. Goals are an objective way of assessing performance in the organization.

There is a definite linkage between goal setting and performance. Latham (1981) reported that

- specified goals are better than vague or general goals,
- difficult and challenging but attainable goals are better than relatively easy goals,
- goals evolved through participation and accepted by workers are preferred to assigned goals, and
- objective and timely feedback about progress toward goals is better than no feedback.

## The Process of Goal Setting

Peter Drucker suggested thirty years ago that a systematic approach to goal setting and appraising by results leads to improved organizational performance and employee satisfaction. This concept of goal setting is now widely used in most organizations. The process of goal setting (or management by objectives as it is often called) involves several steps (Luthans, 1985):

(i) The first step in the process is setting general organizational objectives and preparing an action plan. Goal setting is based on a top-down approach, and involves:
   - identifying key result areas in the organization,
   - identifying measures of performance,
   - stating objectives, and
   - evolving agreement between members of top management on the objectives and goals set.

(ii) Once goals are formulated, the second step is to activate the system for implementation. For successful implementation of such a system, it is essential to prepare the members in the organization.

(iii) The third step is to set individual goals. Individual goals are decided jointly by superiors and subordinates. Once goals are finalized, an action plan is developed for implementation.

(iv) The fourth step involves:
   - ensuring that work is carried out in the right direction,

- identifying obstacles, and
- making adjustments to eliminate obstacles.

(v) Finally comes appraisal of performance of the individual against the set targets. An appraisal and feedback system is an important part of goal setting. The individual is given feedback on his or her performance, and provided with suitable rewards and motivation.

## Integration and Coordination

Integration and coordination refer to integration of the objectives and activities of specialized units or sub-systems in order to achieve the organization's overall strategic objectives. Coordination and integration are necessary controlling mechanisms to ensure placid functioning, particularly when organizations become large and complex. Integration aims at ensuring that different sub-systems work towards common goals.

Integration of the organizational sub-systems relates to differentiation and division of labour in the organization. Organizational differentiation means un-bundling and re-arranging of activities. Re-grouping and re-linking them is organizational integration (Lawrence and Lorsch, 1967). When different units are assigned different tasks and functions, they set independent goals for performing the assigned tasks and function accordingly. In such situations, integration of the activities of different sub-systems is necessary to facilitate smooth working and to bridge communication gaps. In research organizations, integration of research units and administrative units is very important for the smooth functioning of research activities.

## Need for Integration

Integration and coordination is necessary for several reasons (Anderson, 1988):

- As the organization encounters environmental complexity, diversity and change, it requires more and more differentiation of its units. Need for integration also increases with increase in structural dimensions.
- Different specialized units are required to achieve broad strategic objectives rather than only individual

objectives. For the purpose of achieving these strategic objectives, a research manager has to coordinate different units.

- A research manager has to settle conflicts and disputes between different specialized units. When different units are assigned different goals and tasks, conflicts are inevitable. A manager needs to integrate and coordinate the work of different sub-units to effectively resolve conflicts.
- Managers also need to coordinate and integrate independent units or research stations to ensure that their objectives and functioning are in consonance with overall organizational goals and strategies.
- The necessity for coordination increases with increased specialization, because increases in specialized functions leads to decision making in specialized units or sub-units. This may cause conflict.

## Methods of Integration

Within any large organization it is important to have proper communication systems to enable different sub-systems to coordinate various activities and avoid obstacles in the work environment. Lack of proper coordination often causes conflicts in an organization. To ensure proper coordination in research organizations, the research manager has to take care of behavioural dimensions (such as motivation and conflicts) while ensuring an efficient overall structure.

## Achieving Integration

The structure of a research institution needs to be suitably designed to facilitate proper coordination and integration of different specialized units. A poorly designed structure may:

- hinder coordination and integration,
- cause conflicts, and
- lead to poor performance.

## COORDINATING VERTICALLY THROUGH HIERARCHY

Work is assigned to specialized units and coordinated by a manager. A hierarchy (vertical) of authority evolves from lower to higher levels. A manager can use the following principles of hierarchy of authority for integrating specialized units:

- The *unity of command* principle. Every worker should report to only one manager.
- The *scalar* principle. Decision making authority (and a chain of command) should be from the top to lower levels.
- *Responsibility* principle. A manager is accountable for the performance of his or her subordinates. In turn, subordinates are responsible to their manager for their performance.

## Determining the Decision Making Level

A manager has to decide about the levels at which decisions are to be taken, and this would depend upon the type, impact and values of decisions.

## Deciding the Span of Control

Span of control refers to the number of specialized activities or personnel supervised by one manager. There is no optimal number for a span of control and number of levels in the hierarchy. In fact, span of control and hierarchy levels are inter-related and depend on situational factors (Barkdull, 1963). Some of the important situational factors are:

- Similarity of functions.
- Complexity of supervised functions.
- Direction and control needed by subordinates.
- Coordination required by the manager.
- Planning required by the manager.
- Organizational help received by the manager.

## Methods to Improve Integration

There are several ways to improve integration, the most common being through a hierarchy of authority. For this, specialized units whose activities are inter-related could be put under one manager.

Coordination can also be improved through

- developing rules and procedures wherever possible,
- providing professional training,

- liaison roles, and
- use of professional committees involving managers from different specialized units.

Using committees to improve coordination is more difficult than other methods, as it requires considerable skills in group dynamics and technical knowledge on the part of the chairperson of the committee. The person who takes this role must not be involved directly in the work, but tries to assist managers in improving integration.

## PROCESS IN THE ORGANIZATION

Norms for proper functioning of the organization are evolved through organizational processes. These relate to power, decision making, communication, motivation and leadership. Socialization also plays a significant role.

### Power in the Organization

Power refers to the ability to get an individual or group to do something or to change in some way. Politics is a process to achieve power. Power is inter-related with authority and influence. Bernard (1938) defined authority in terms of 'legitimate power.' Power is considered as an essential element in any human organization so as to engender order and coordinate various activities. Power provides one of the strongest motivations (Galbraith, 1952). It also affects the setting of objectives and the distribution of resources in an organization. The source of power can be positional, economic, knowledge, performance, personality, physical or ideological (Hicks, 1975). Organization-based power refers to the power beyond the range of legitimate authority because of the position which a person has in the organization (Milgram, 1974). This power can be controlled and transferred by the organization.

Four categories of organizational power can identified, according to source (French and Raven, 1959):

- *Reward power* This refers to the control over rewards desired by others. This is given by persons at a higher level or by decision-makers.
- *Coercive power* This is the power to give punishment. This too is given by persons at a higher level or by decision-makers.

- *Expert power* This is based on personal skills, knowledge, training, experience, etc. It cannot be transferred by the organization since it is person-specific.
- *Charismatic power* This derives from the sensitivity of the owner. This facilitates association with others.

In research organizations, as in other organizations, power plays a significant role. It influences the organization's strategies, recruitment of competent scientists, behavioural control system and changes in the organizational structure.

## COMMUNICATION IN THE ORGANIZATION

Communication is a basic element in organizational structure and functioning. It is the key mechanism for achieving integration and coordination of the activities of specialized units at different levels in the organization. The communication process consists of seven steps (Shannon and Weaver, 1949): message, encoding, transmitting, receiving, decoding, understanding and feedback. Organizational communication can be horizontal, upward, and downward:

- *Horizontal (lateral) communication* aims at linking related tasks, work units and divisions in the organization. The importance of horizontal communication increases with task specialization and diversity in organizational structure. The need for lateral or horizontal communication was first stressed by Fayol (1949), when he suggested a 'gang plank' between similar hierarchical positions.
- *Downward communication* provides information from higher levels to lower levels. Being superior-subordinate communication, it follows the chain of command through the line of authority. Downward communication can be of four types (Katz and Kahn, 1966):
- communication designed to provide job rationale to produce understanding of the task and its relation to other organizational tasks;
- communication about organizational procedures and practices;
- feedback to the subordinate about his or her performance; and

- communication to foster inculcation of organizational goals.
- *Upward communication* serves as a control system for the organization.

In an agricultural research organization, a suitable blending of lateral, downward and upward communication is required to effectively coordinate and integrate activities of individual subsystems. The effectiveness of research results greatly depends upon proper communication links among scientists, between scientists and agricultural extension workers, and between extension workers and farmers.

In an agricultural research organization, there are several specialized sub-systems which need to be integrated through horizontal communication. Downward communication facilitates transmission of research results to actual users. Upward communication enables flow of information from lowers level to the top level: farmers Þ extension workers Þ scientists Þ research manager Þ DG and policy-makers

## Organizational Decision Making

Decision making is choosing among alternatives. It starts with goal setting in the organization, and entails searching for alternatives, analysing alternatives and choosing criteria. Decisions may pertain to

- broad policies or plans for the organization,
- programmes and projects to achieve goals, or
- operations of programmes and management systems.

The process of decision making involves nine steps:

(i) Setting organizational goals.
(ii) Establishing performance criteria.
(iii) Classifying and defining the problem.
(iv) Developing criteria for a successful solution.
(v) Generating alternatives.
(vi) Comparing alternatives to criteria.
(vii) Choosing an alternative.
(viii) Implementing the decision.
(ix) Monitoring the decision and getting feedback.

## Models of Decision Making

There are five major models for decision making in an organization (Gortner, Mahler and Nicholson, 1987). They are:

- The *economic* or *rational choice* model, as used in bureaucratic organizations. It is based on rational choice among well reasoned and logical alternatives.
- *Incremental bargaining,* commonly used in resolving conflicts through negotiation.
- Simon's *bounded rationality* model, which is used as an aggregative model in administrative practices. This model is suitable as a consultant-assisted method for policy making.
- Peters and Waterman's *well managed* model (also called the *garbage can* or *non-decision making* model) aims at formulating a descriptive model of choice which focuses on the expressive character of decision making in the organization. It does not consider rationality and incrementation. This method is based on an empirical perception of how successful organizations are being run.
- *Quantitative techniques of decision making.* Decisions have to be made under varying conditions of certainty or uncertainty, with different degrees of risk (Luthans, 1985).

Certainty decisions are largely made by managers at lower levels under known conditions with known outcomes. For such decisions, nearly complete information is available. Quantitative techniques are not usually required to make certainty decisions. However, calculus and a few mathematical programming techniques can be useful.

Risk decisions are more difficult to make than certainty decisions because of limited information and the possibility of several outcomes for each alternative. Most risk decisions are taken at higher levels. For risk decisions, probability techniques (objective and subjective probability) are widely used.

Decisions under uncertainty are the most intricate. For such decisions, probability techniques are of limited help. However, minimax analysis and Bayes's procedure can be used in refining the decision making process under conditions of uncertainty. Minimax analysis attempts to calculate the worst outcome that can occur for each alternative, whereas Bayes's procedure is based on the concept of expected value and assumes that each possible outcome has an equal chance of occurring.

## ORGANIZATIONAL THEORY AND BEHAVIOUR

### Classical Organization Theory

Classical organization theory evolved during the first half of this century. It represents the merger of scientific management, bureaucratic theory, and administrative theory.

Frederick Taylor (1917) developed scientific management theory (often called "Taylorism") at the beginning of this century. His theory had four basic principles: 1) find the one "best way" to perform each task, 2) carefully match each worker to each task, 3) closely supervise workers, and use reward and punishment as motivators, and 4) the task of management is planning and control.

Initially, Taylor was very successful at improving production. His methods involved getting the best equipment and people, and then carefully scrutinizing each component of the production process. By analysing each task individually, Taylor was able to find the right combinations of factors that yielded large increases in production.

While Taylor's *scientific management theory* proved successful in the simple industrialized companies at the turn of the century, it has not faired well in modern companies. The philosophy of "production first, people second" has left a legacy of declining production and quality, dissatisfaction with work, loss of pride in workmanship, and a near complete loss of organizational pride.

Max Weber (1947) expanded on Taylor's theories, and stressed the need to reduce diversity and ambiguity in organizations. The focus was on establishing clear lines of authority and control. Weber's *bureaucratic theory* emphasized the need for a hierarchical structure of power. It recognized the importance of division of labour and specialization. A formal set of rules was bound into the hierarchy structure to insure stability and uniformity. Weber also put forth the notion that organizational Behaviour is a network of human interactions, where all Behaviour could be understood by looking at cause and effect.

*Administrative theory* (i.e., principles of management) was formalized in the 1930's by Mooney and Reiley (1931). The emphasis was on establishing a universal set of management principles that could be applied to all organizations.

Classical management theory was rigid and mechanistic. The shortcomings of classical organization theory quickly became apparent. Its major deficiency was that it attempted to explain peoples' motivation to work strictly as a function of economic reward.

## Neoclassical Organization Theory

The human relations movement evolved as a reaction to the tough, authoritarian structure of classical theory. It addressed many of the problems inherent in classical theory. The most serious objections to classical theory are that it created overconformity and rigidity, thus squelching creativity, individual growth, and motivation. Neoclassical theory displayed genuine concern for human needs.

One of the first experiments that challenged the classical view was conducted by Mayo and Roethlisberger in the late 1920's at the Western Electric plant in Hawthorne, Illinois (Mayo, 1933). While manipulating conditions in the work environment (e.g., intensity of lighting), they found that any change had a positive impact on productivity. The act of paying attention to employees in a friendly and nonthreatening way was sufficient by itself to increase output. Uris (1986) referred to this as the "wart" theory of productivity. Nearly any treatment can make a wart go away—nearly anything will improve productivity. "The implication is plain: intelligent action often delivers results" (Uris, 1986).

The Hawthorne experiment is quite disturbing because it cast doubts on our ability to evaluate the efficacy of new management theories. An organization might continually involve itself in the latest management fads to produce a continuous string of Hawthorne effects. "The result is usually a lot of wheel spinning and cynicism" (Pascale, 1990). Pascale believes that the Hawthorne effect is often misinterpreted. It is a "parable about researchers (and managers) manipulating and 'playing tricks' on employees." Erroneous conclusions are drawn because it represents a controlling and manipulative attitude toward workers.

Writing in 1939, Barnard (1968) proposed one of the first modern theories of organization by defining organization as a system of consciously coordinated activities. He stressed in role of the executive in creating an atmosphere where there is coherence of values and purpose. Organizational success was linked to the ability of a leader to create a cohesive environment. He proposed that a manager's authority is derived from subordinates' acceptance, instead of the hierarchical power structure of the organization. Barnard's theory contains elements of both classical and neoclassical approaches. Since there is no consensus among scholars, it might be most appropriate to think of Barnard as a transition theorist.

Simon (1945) made an important contribution to the study of organizations when he proposed a model of "limited rationality" to explain the Hawthorne experiments. The theory stated that workers could respond unpredictably to managerial attention. The most important aspect of Simon's work was the rigorous application of the scientific method. Reductionism, quantification, and deductive logic were legitimized as the methods of studying organizations.

Taylor, Weber, Barnard, Mayo, Roethlisberger, and Simon shared the belief that the goal of management was to maintain equilibrium. The emphasis was on being able to control and manipulate workers and their environment.

## Contingency Theory

Classical and neoclassical theorists viewed conflict as something to be avoided because it interfered with equilibrium. Contingency theorists view conflict as inescapable, but manageable.

Chandler (1962) studied four large United States corporations and proposed that an organization would naturally evolve to meet the needs of its strategy — that form follows function. Implicit in Chandler's ideas was that organizations would act in a rational, sequential, and linear manner to adapt to changes in the environment. Effectiveness was a function of management's ability to adapt to environmental changes.

Lawrence and Lorsch (1969) also studied how organizations adjusted to fit their environment. In highly volatile industries, they noted the importance of giving managers at all levels the authority to make decisions over their domain. Managers would be free to make decisions contingent on the current situation.

## Systems Theory

Systems theory was originally proposed by Hungarian biologist Ludwig von Bertalanffy in 1928, although it has not been applied to organizations until recently (Kast and Rosenzweig, 1972; Scott, 1981). The foundation of systems theory is that all the components of an organization are interrelated, and that changing one variable might impact many others. Organizations are viewed as open systems, continually interacting with their environment. They are in a state of dynamic equilibrium as they adapt to environmental changes. Senge (1990) describes systems thinking as: understanding how our actions shape our reality. If I believe that my current state was created by somebody else, or by forces outside my control, why should I hold a vision? The central premise behind holding a vision is that somehow I can shape my future, Systems thinking helps us see how our own actions have shaped our current reality, thereby giving us confidence that we can create a different reality in the future.

A central theme of systems theory is that nonlinear relationships might exist between variables. Small changes in one variable can cause huge changes in another, and large changes in a variable might have only a nominal effect on another. The concept of nonlinearity adds enormous complexity to our understanding of organizations. In fact, one of the most salient argument against systems theory is that the complexity introduced by nonlinearity makes it difficult or impossible to fully understand the relationships between variables.

## Organizational Structure

Until recently, nearly all organizations followed Weber's concept of bureaucratic structures. The increased complexity of multinational organizations created the necessity of a new structure that Drucker called (1974) "federal decentralization". In federal decentralization, a company is organized so that there are a number of independent units operating simultaneously. "Each unit has its own management which, in effect, runs its own autonomous business." This structure has resulted in large conglomerates which have diversified into many different fields in order to minimize risk.

The project management organizational structure has been used effectively in highly dynamic and technological environments (French, Kast and Rosenzweig, 1985). The project manager becomes the focal point for information and activities related to a specific project. The goal is to provide effective integration of an organization's resources towards the completion of a specific project. Impementing a project management approach often involves dramatic changes in the relationships of authority and responsibility.

The matrix organizational structure evolved from the project management form (Kolodny, 1979). It represents a compromise between the traditional bureuacratic approach and the autonomous project management approach. A matrix organization has permanently established departments that provide integration for project management. The matrix form is superimposed on the hierarchical structure, resulting in dual authority and responsibilities. Permanent functionality departments allocate resources to be shared among departments and managers.

Systems theory views organizational structure as the "established pattern of relationships among the parts of the organization" (French, Kast, and Rosenzweig, 1985, p. 348). Of particular importance are the patterns in relationships and duties. These include themes of 1) integration (the way activities are coordinated), 2) differentiation (the way tasks are divided), 3) the structure of the hierarchical relationships (authority systems), and 4) the formalized policies, procedures, and controls that guide the organization (administrative systems).

The relationship between the environment and organizational structure is especially important. Organizations are open systems and depend on their environment for support.

Generally, more complex environments lead to greater differentiation. The trend in organizations is currently away from stable (mechanistic) structures to more adaptive (organic) structures. The advantage is that organizations become more dynamic and flexible. The disadvantage is that integration and coordination of activities require more time and effort.

The relationship between an organization and its environment is characterized by a two-way flow of information and energy. Most organizations attempt to influence their environment. Advertising campaigns and lobbying efforts are two examples. Some theorists believe that "... environments are largely invented by organizations themselves. Organizations select their environments from ranges of alternatives, then they subjectively perceive the environments they inhabit" (Starbuck, 1976). Strategic decisions regarding product lines and distribution channels contribute to the selection of the organizational structure and the environment.

It is a commonly held tenant that people are less satisfied with their work in highly structured organizations. Many research studies have been conducted to examine the relationship between organizational structure and employee Behaviour (e.g., satisfaction, performance, and turnover). However, the results of these studies are contradictory. Structural deficiencies can result in low motivation and morale, decisions lacking in timeliness or quality, lack of coordination and conflict, inefficient use of resources, and an inability to respond effectively to changes in the environment.

One enduring and controversial debate about organizational structure is whether or not there is a maximum desirable size for an organization, after which there will be declining effectiveness. Does an organization become increasingly dysfunctional as it exceeds its "ideal" size? Several researchers have hypothesized that organizational growth is beneficial only up to a point. Most researchers support a curvilinear growth theory. Pfeffer and Salancik (1978) found that profitability increases with size and then tapers off. Warwick (1975) reported that the growth in the U.S. State Department resulted in decreased flexibility and responsiveness, even though specific steps had been taken to abate these problems. There are several theories to explain these findings. The most common explanation is based on the fact that an organization's size is usually positively correlated with age. Older (i.e., larger) organizations have become more rigid in their ways and they are less able to adapt to change. Another popular theory is that in larger organizations, workers' jobs become more specialized. The lack of variety creates a less motivating environment. Other theories have proposed that excessive size creates crippling coordination problems.

## ORGANIZATIONAL BIRTH AND GROWTH

Clearly, one of the most dominant themes in the literature has been to define organizations from the perspective of their position on a growth curve. Cameron and Whetten (1983) reviewed thirty life-cycle models from the organizational development literature. They summarized the studies into an aggregate model containing four stages. The first stage is "entrepreneurial", characterized by early innovation, niche formation and high creativity. This is followed by a stage of "collectivity", where there is high cohesion and commitment among the members. The next stage is one of "formalization and control", where the goals are stability and institutionalization. The last stage is one of "elaboration", characterized by domain expansion and decentralization. The striking feature of these life-cycle models is that they did not include any notion of organizational decline. They covered birth, growth, and maturity, but none included decline or death. The classic S-curve typifies these life-cycle models. Whetten (1987) points out that these theories are a reflection of the 1960s and 1970s, two highly growth oriented decades.

Land and Jarman (1992) have attempted to redefine the traditional S-curve that defines birth, growth, and maturity. The first phase in organizational growth is the entrepreneurial stage. The entrepreneur is convinced that their idea for a product or service is needed and wanted in the marketplace. The common characteristic of all entrepreneurs and new businesses is the desire to find a pattern of operation that will survive in the marketplace. Nearly all new businesses fail within the first five years. Land and Jarman (1992) argue that this is "natural", and that even in nature, cell mutations do not usually survive. This phase is the beginning of the S-curve. The second phase in organizational growth is characterized by a complete reversal in strategy.

Where the entrepreneurial stage involves a series of trial and error endeavors, the next stage is the standardization of rules that define how the organizational system operates and interacts with the environment. The chaotic methods of the entrepreneur are replaced with structured patterns of operation. Internal processes are regulated and uniformity is sought. During this phase, growth actually occurs by limiting diversity. "Management procedures, processes, and controls are geared to maintain order and predictability" (Land and Jarman, 1992). This phase is the rapid rise on the S-curve.

Organizational growth does not continue indefinitely. An upper asymptopic limit can be imposed by a number of factors. Land and Jarman (1992, p. 258) identify the most common reasons why organizations reach upper growth limits:

- Rapidly increasing internal and market place complexity in such areas a product proliferation and market divisions
- Internal competition for resources
- Increasing cost of manufacturing and sales
- Diminishing returns
- Declining share of the market
- Decreasing productivity gains
- Growing external pressures from regulators and influence groups
- Increasing impact of new technologies
- New and unexpected competitors.

The transition to the third phase involves another radical change in an organization. Most organizations are not able to make these changes, and they do not survive. "The organization must open up to permit what was never allowed in to become a part of the system, not only by doing things differently, but by *doing different things*". The organization needs to continue its core business, while at the same time engaging in inventing new business. This bifurcation is necessary because the entrepreneurial environment (of inventing business) is incompatible with the controlling environment of the core business.

The goal is a continuing integration of the new inventions into the mainstream business, where a re-created organization emerges. The core business is changed by the inventions it assimilates, and the organization takes on a new form. Land and Jarman (1992) believe that the greatest challenge facing today's organizations is the transition from phase two to phase three. "Organizations defeat their best intentions by continuing to operate with essential beliefs that automatically perpetuate the second phase."

There are several factors that contribute to organizational growth (Child and Kieser, 1981). The most obvious is that growth is a by-product of another successful strategy. A second factor is that growth is deliberately sought because it facilitates management goals.

For example, it provides increased potential for promotion, greater challenge, prestige, and earning potential. A third factor is that growth makes an organization less vulnerable to environmental consequences. Larger organizations tend to be more stable and less likely to go out of business. Increased resources make diversification feasible, thereby adding to the security of the organization.

Child and Kieser (1981) suggest four distinct operational models for organizational growth. 1) Growth can occur within an organization's existing domain. This is often manifest as a striving for dominance within its field. 2) Growth can occur through diversification into new domains. Diversification is a common strategy for lowering overall risk, and new domains often provide fertile new markets. 3) Technological advancements can stimulate growth by providing more effective methods of production. 4) Improved managerial techniques can facilitate an atmosphere that promotes growth. However, as Whetten (1987) points out, it is difficult to establish cause and effect in these models. Do technological advancements stimulate growth, or does growth stimulate the development of technological breakthroughs? With the lack of controlled experiments, it is difficult to choose between the chicken and the egg.

## Organizational Decline

Until recently, most theories about organization development viewed decline as a symptom of ineffective performance. Well-managed organizations were expected to grow year after year. Implicit in these theories was the idea that organizational growth is synonymous with expansion. These theories reflected what scholars observed in the business world. Organizational growth was an indicator of successful management.

Kenneth Boulding (1950) proposed a biological model of economics, characterized by birth, maturation, decline, and death. He argued that in all organisms, there is an "inexorable and irreversible movement towards the equilibrium of death." Many organizational theorists took strong exception to Boulding's biological determinism theory. They maintained that organizations are not constrained by a defined life cycle, and there is no indication that all organizations need to die.

The 1980's ushered in a new era where organizational decline was apparent everywhere. Management strategies involved reducing employees, salary freezes and reductions, cutting administrative overhead, and consolidating operations. It became clear that the traditional S-curve model was incomplete and did not address the issues of declining organizations.

One of the problems in the literature is that it is difficult to agree on a precise definition of organizational decline. Is a company in decline when it cuts back the number of employees in order to become more profitable? A common definition of decline is a decrease in profit or budget. Most theorists agree that decline negatively impacts individuals and the organization as a whole. Cameron, Whetten, and Kim (1987) argue that decline results in decreased morale, innovativeness, participation, leader influence, and long-term planning. They associate decline with, conflict, secrecy, rigidity, centralization, formalization, scapegoating, and conservatism.

Nystrom and Starbuck (1984) attribute organizational decline to over-confidence. According to this theory, a successful past can lure an organization to become over-confident in its ability to prosper. This leads to a lackadaisical attitude towards new innovations, quality, and customer satisfaction. Another theory is that large size promotes rigidity, which makes it cumbersome for an organization to respond to environmental changes (Whetten, 1987).

In applying the biological life-cycle model to organizations, Wilson (1980) identified two different types of organizational decline: "k" and ""r" extinction. When an organization has reached the upper asymptopic limit defined by carrying capacity of its niche, it declines because of k-extinction. The organization has exhausted its environmental resources, or other organizations have begun competing for limited resources. When an organization falls short of its upper asymptopic limit, and begins declining without reaching its maximum potential, it is called r-extinction. Bad management or a failure to remain competitive are the most common reasons for r-extinction.

Bibeault (1982) proposed a four-stage model to describe the process of turning around an organization in decline. The key to the process was to replace the top personnel. Bibeault argued that only way to reverse a decline is to 1) change the management, the rationale being that "problem causers have little credibility as problem solvers" (Whetten, 1987). Chaffee (1984) also stressed the symbolic value of changing administrative personnel. Change in management is followed by 2) an evaluation stage, 3) implementing emergency actions and stabilization procedures, and finally, 4) a return to growth.

A different approach for describing organizational turnaround was proposed by Zammuto and Cameron (1985). Their model was based on the idea that turnaround could be accomplished by addressing five process domains. 1) The defence domain involves strategies for protecting the organization from a hostile environment.

An example would be an organization that forms a common-purpose coalition with other organizations. 2) The offense domain involves expanding on the activities that the organization already does well. 3) Creating new domains consists of diversification activities. 4) The consolidation domain involves reducing the scope of activities by cutting back to core products and services. 5) The substitution domain involves replacing one set of activities with another.

In contrast to these theories, Harrigan (1980, 1981, 1982) and Porter (1980) have looked at how organizations respond to decline as a result of environmental limitations (i.e., k-extinction). Organizational activities often involve attempts to focus on a specific market niche in which the organization might have a competitive advantage. Another approach is to rapidly liquidate the organization, and extract as much remaining value as possible, although Harrigan (1982) notes that there are often financial, legal, structural, and emotional obstacles to this strategy.

The most common response to organizational decline is retrenchment. Whetten (1987) identifies three sequential stages involved in the process. The first is one of identification. Management must be sensitive to problems when they first appear, and be able to meet the problems head on. The second is one of communication. Management must communicate a clear message of the organization's situation and instill confidence in its ability to meet the crisis. The third stage involves the implementation of a downsizing program.

Sutton (1983) surveyed managers to examine their beliefs regarding how employees would react to an organizational closing. It was found that managers had several inaccurate perceptions. For example, managers' incorrectly believed that productivity and quality would plummet, employee sabotage and theft would increase, and there would be increases in conflict. On the other hand, Sutton's study did offer evidence that rumors were abundant, the best employees sought different employment, and that employee's had trouble accepting the closing.

## THE LEARNING ORGANIZATION

Peter Senge (1990) defines learning as enhancing ones capacity to take action. "So learning organizations are organizations that are continually enhancing their capacity to create." Senge believes that organizations are evolving from controlling to predominantly learning.

Senge (1990) discusses learning disabilities in companies One of the most serious disabilities is when people form a strong identification with their position. What they do becomes a function of their position. They see themselves in specific roles, and are unable to view their jobs as part of a larger system. This often leads to animosity towards others in the organization, especially when things go wrong. Another disability is that we are slow to recognize gradual changes and threats.

Senge (1990) refers to several other learning disabilities as "myths". He discusses the "myth of proactiveness", where "proactiveness is really reactiveness with the gauge turned up to 500%." Another myth is that we "learn from experience". Senge maintains that we actually only learn when the experience is followed by immediate feedback. Another myth is that management teams can provide creative and beneficial solutions. Senge maintains that the result of management teams is "skilled incompetence, where groups are highly skilled at protecting themselves from threat, and consequently keeping themselves from learning."

Senge (1990) believes that new organizations can be built by adopting a set of disciplines, where a discipline is defined as a "particular theory, translated into a set of practices, which one spends one's life mastering." Thus, mastering a discipline becomes a life-long learning process.

According to Senge, there are five disciplines important to the learning organization. The first discipline is "building a shared vision". "Building" involves an ongoing process, and "shared" implies that the vision is held in common by individuals. A second discipline of "personal mastery" demonstrates a commitment to the vision. A third discipline involves the idea of mental models, where we construct internal representations of reality. An important element of using mental models is the need to balance inquiry and advocacy. A fourth discipline in that only shared mental models are important for organizational learning. The fifth discipline is a commitment to a systems approach.

## Community

Gozdz (1992) believes that learning organizations are centred around the concept of community. "An organization acting as a community is a collective lifelong learner, responsive to change, receptive to challenge, and conscious of an increasingly complex array of alternatives." Communities provide safe havens for its members and foster an environment conducive to growth. Gozdz describes the community as group of people who have a strong commitment to "ever-deepening levels of communication."

M. Scott Peck (1987) describes the process of building a community in *The Different Drum*. An organization goes through a four-stage process. The first stage is one of denial. Group members ignore differences in power, and pretend that they are a community. Decision-making processes go unchallenged. The next stage occurs when differences between members become apparent. Attempts are made to restore the situation to what has worked in the past by eliminating differences. An organization enters the third stage when members realize that their efforts to control differences have failed. They begin communicating and true collaborative efforts emerge. In the final stage, there is the true spirit of community. Differences are embraced. Decisions are made collectively. Learning and innovation comes from the group as a whole

Many organization experience brief periods of community, but they are not able to sustain those periods. Gozdz (1992) describes this failure as a lack of discipline and commitment.

There is an illusion that once a sense of community occurs within an organization it will remain constant. This is not the case. The sense of community or flow state is repeatedly lost. It can be deliberately regained at ever greater levels of organizational maturity, but only when sustaining community is seen and accepted as a path to developing mastery. This path is community as a discipline.

According to Gozdz (1992), the job of the leaders in the process of community building is to keep peoples' attention focused on the process. The four stages of community development are repeated over and over again. New situations and contingencies arise that initiate new cycles in the growth process.

## ORGANIZATIONAL MORALITY

The classical view of organizational responsibility is best illustrated by Adam Smith's (1937) belief that an "invisible hand" directs all activities towards the public good, and that the responsibility of an organization was only to maximize profits within the constraints of the law. The free market system was seen as a self-controlling mechanism, whereby an organization producing the best goods and services would prosper. Any interference with the free market system was viewed as an affront against the best interests of society.

The accountability concept states that organizations receive their charter from society as a whole, and therefore their ultimate responsibility is to society. Environmental and worker protection laws reflect the belief that maximization of profits is secondary to the health of society. The extensive proliferation of laws restricting business demonstrates a growing skepticism concerning the morality and ethics of corporate management.

Some theorists believe that organizations have the social responsibility "to take actions which protect and improve the welfare of society as a whole along with their own interests". Others take a more narrow approach, and believe that social responsibility extends only to "social problems caused wholly or in part by the corporation".

Linda Stark (1989) discusses the five stages of corporate moral development, although she is quick to point out that progression through the stages is neither linear or one direction. An amoral corporation pursues profit at any cost. A legalistic corporation follows the letter of the law, but not the spirit. A responsive corporation makes ethical decisions based on long-term economic decisions. An emergent ethical corporation recognizes its social responsibility and balances ethics and profitability. The ethical corporation places social responsibility at its centre and bases its existence on ethics.

Environmental awareness has evolved to become a major ethical consideration in many corporations. During the 1950's, science and technology were viewed as the answer to the world's problems. The ecological ramifications of that era became apparent in the 1960's. The 1970's began with the organization of the first Earthday. The Environmental Protection Agency (EPA) and the Occupational Safety and Health Administration (OSHA) were created to monitor the environment and worker safety. During the 1980's, many corporations began to take proactive conservation measures. Environmental considerations began to be addressed at the manufacturing level so that harmful materials and waste were minimized or removed from the production process. Citizen action groups became increasingly effective in forcing corporations to examine their environmental impact. In the 1990's, many corporations have adopted the policy of "sustainable development." The key issue is that environmental protection is one of the highest priorities of every business.

## ORGANIZATIONAL BEHAVIOUR IN HISTORICAL PERSPECTIVE

### The Taming of Emotions

Theory and practice of organizational Behaviour bring us many promising concepts and skills: Coaching, transactional analysis, one-minute management, self-managing teams, authentic self-presentation, 360° feed-back, etc.. Also a wide arsenal of skill-training has been developed: Problem solving, feed-back skills, decision making, negotiating, effective leadership; to name only a few.

In all these areas the handling of emotions seems rather neglected. I will describe how a few centuries ago emotions in the workplace could not be neglected; emotions were very visible. People experienced great difficulties in coping with fierce even outrageous impulses. We have tamed these impulses. But they are still of critical importance for organizational behaviour. Moreover our manners and standards of emotion management show a close relation with patterns of power and dependency. This is another neglected area for authors and trainers concerned with skill-training. How realistic are the insights of organizational Behaviour when neglecting the overriding importance of power relations? How helpful is modern skill-training in its disregard of emotional drives, power differences and dependency relations? I will explore these questions by applying a historical perspective.

In this article I will describe how over the past 600 years behavioural standards in the West have changed in close relation to changing patterns of power and dependency. In doing so I am building on the work of Elias (1939) and Wouters (1990). One characteristic of this development is the increasing control and curbing of emotions. Another more recent characteristic concerns the process of informalization.

This contribution starts with the Behaviour in meetings of rulers and authorities in the Middle Ages. In part 2 'Increasing discipline ánd informalization' I will address Behaviour in modern organizations. Both parts will conclude with some suggestions to improve our understandig of Behaviour in the workplace.

## STRUGGLING WITH VIOLENCE

The Dutch historian Huizinga (1924) writes about the more ferocious and rather unpredictable shifts of Behaviour in medieval Europe. There undoubtedly were norms and agreements to regulate mutual interaction, but *"time after time the fierce roughness breaks through the embellished forms"*.

"At the coronation banquet of Charles VI, in 1380, the Duke of Burgundy seeks, by force, to take the place to which he is entitled, as doyen of the peers, between the king and the Duke of Anjou. Already the train of the Duke begins to thrust aside their opponents; threatening cries arise, a scuffle is breaking out when the king prevents it, by doing justice to the claims of the Duke of Burgundy".

According to an observer at the peace conference at Atrecht in 1435, the participants *"throw themselves on the ground, sobbing and groaning"*. The relatively refined life at the court is characterized as *"continual noise and disorder, swearing and quarrels, jealousies and injuries, in short, the court is an abyss of sins, the gate of hell"*. A ferocious fight can erupt at any time over anything, whether it be a game of chess or a ceremonial funeral.

### Even-temperedness

To my knowledge, the earliest publication in Europe to propagate other rules of conduct among authorities is a treatise by Bernard du Rosier (1404-1475), also known in his days by the more commonly used Latin name Bernardus de Rosergio. His treatise was written at the court of the King of Castile. Central to the text is 'equanimitas'-even-temperedness. What does it refer to? Well, as the term itself suggests, it refers to keeping emotions under control continuously. Two examples:

*"... although offended, surmount these injuries of the heart and rise up to the most exalted attitude... suppress emotions and show oneself in command".*

*"Let outrage yield to friendliness, impetuosity to wisdom, rigidity to adaptability and curtness to approachability. Remain distinguished and unmoved to those whose responses are less pleasant or negative,.........".*

Rosier keeps on repeating the necessity to temper and control all kinds of apparently normal and powerful affects. For example:

- being inflated with supercilious, conceited arrogance
- tyrannical Behaviour, clinging to greed
- brazen and presumptuous forcing one's own way
- mocking religious matters
- committing foul acts, being choleric or malicious
- pursuing fame based on vanities.

Recent advice for administrators and managers lacks such colourful references to untamed Behaviour. In our days containment of these strivings is obviously more matter-of-course.

## Restraint en Regulation

Despite of periods of stagnation, Behaviour at the European courts gradually became more restrained and refined. Also, next to the courtly military-aristocratic elites, merchant and artisan guilds, predecessors of modern work-organizations emerged which tried to regulate interaction. In the 15th and 16th century guild regulations we find the precursors of current meeting procedures. The bakers' apprentices guild's register of 1404 states: *"Someone who uses violence, spills beer or utters offensive language, will be fined..."*..

These regulations describe in detail what is not allowed: swearing, breaking glassware, delivering blows, attacking someone with knife drawn. Furthermore, one must be on time and wear decent clothing. The fines imposed to enforce this Behaviour were considerable. In 1457 the guilds-dominated town council of Utrecht in the Netherlands even issued a regulation that addressing other issues than those on the agenda during a meeting was punishable by death.

## EARLY CAPITALISM AND INCREASING DISCIPLINE

In our first industrial organizations only the company-owners and their immediate environment had been part of the development described above. The workers had to be coerced to toe the line through rules that closely resemble those in the 15th century guild registers. In his description of the emergence of the factory regime in the 19th century, Van Iterson (1992) wrote:

"The problems for the manufacturers were first of all problems of discipline and coordination. Factory regimes are based on a tangled combination of i) coercion (from the side of the manufacturers) and ii) willingness or motivation (on the workers' part)."

The discipline which seems so natural to us now, was not in evidence then:

"Bringing together men, women and children in one space implied the danger that people would get in each other's way, that arguments could erupt, sexual relations engaged in, or that they would 'overindulge' in other activities which were considered debauched (drinking) or idle (games).

Labourers also had to learn to control their language: subversive and obscene utterances also posed a threat to orderly labour and they were fined heavily. The same dangers also existed outside the factory, especially in combination with alcohol consumption. So conformance with the industrial regime was indirectly threatened by 'corruption of the morals' in their free time." (Van Iterson, 1992)

This can be illustrated by the case of the earthenware industry of Josiah Wedgwood (1730-1790), a liberal reformer in public affairs and a patriarchical factory owner in eighteenth century England. During his lifetime he transformed a local pottery, with a dozen men at work, into an international firm.

### Waste and Idleness

Wedgwood had to fight a long local tradition of 'customs in common', in particular the 'stoppages for Wakes', (a local annual feast lasting several days and nights which were spent eating and drinking intemperately and 'fornicating'), but he also had to combat 'waste', 'idleness', 'the bane of drinking', 'working by the rule of thumb', 'inefficiency', 'arbitrariness', 'irregularity' (McKendrick, 1961).

His own personal control over his men was effective enough. But he was 'forced with increasing frequency to leave them 'without any head to look after them' (McKendrick, 1961). There was no tradition of supervision in his factory in his absence. For instance, when he put an older worker in charge, it turned out that this man lacked authority due to his familiarity with colleagues. The resulting informality 'lapsed too easily to irregularity'. As Wedgwood describeds:

" Daniel does pretty well at work and I am here every day, but he often leaves the work and drinks two or three days together, and has no taste to direct at any time" (McKendrick, 1961).

## Supervision and Regulations

Wedgwood formalized his disciplinary rules by writing them down in the Potters Instructions (1780) and in the 'Common Place Book'. Some examples of the rules and sanctions for enhancing one's self-control:

"Any person seen throwing within the yard of this manufactory forfits 2s.6d,..", "any workman strikeing or otherwise abuseing an overlooker to lose his or there place..", any workman conveying Ale or Licquor into the manufactory in working hours forfits 2s...", "any person playing at fives against any of the walls where there are windows forfits 2s.." (McKendrick, 1961).

## The Scientific Method

Taylor, the founder of scientific organizational design (1856-1915), made a contribution to organizational science that fits well into this perspective. His methods were largely intended to impose discipline on the activities of subordinates, something which was sorely needed as far as Taylor was concerned. He gave many descriptions of how employees managed to restrict production by 'soldiering or loafing'.

He repeatedly stated that his 'scientific method', using individual training, separation, special reward systems and other measures, could gradually overcome these tendencies. Taylor vividly described his experiences as a foreman in a steelworks:

"No one who has not had this experience can have an idea of the bitterness which is gradually developed in such a struggle.... And there are few foremen indeed who were able to stand up against the combined pressure of all the men in the shop.... If the writer had been one of the workmen, and had lived where they lived, they would have brought such social pressure to bear upon him that it would have been impossible to have stood out against them."

From these tumultuous experiences Taylor distilled his, as he called it, 'scientific management'. His experiences provide a good impression of how personal power can be replaced by more 'neutral' mechanisms of control. Despite the strong resistance Taylor encountered, his methods were introduced on a large scale. This was possible because of the much greater power of management. At the same time management was forced to exploit this power surplus due to the fierce competition with other companies. Taylor's own intentions were entirely different. He believed that the interests of employers and workers were essentially the same. 'The great mental revolution which occurs under scientific management' would do away with contention and antagonism and replace them with 'friendly co-operation and mutual helpfulness'. Maybe we can see this idealistic dream as a precursor of more recent images of the learning organization, empowerment and shared values.

The examples in this article illustrate the struggle to discipline and control organizational Behaviour. Very central is the need to tame strong emotional impulses to raise the chances on a reliable flow of products. The current high degree of self-discipline and control looks sometimes quite natural and seems self-understood. It definitely is not.

1. Changes in patterns of emotion management as described for instance by Rosier, take many generations. Nearly three centuries after Rosier, Callières writes "show no contempt", "do not utter threats immediately",

"control your temper", "It is better not to appoint gamblers and drunkards to high positions". Félice writes towards the end of the 18th century: "Men are moved by feelings alone. Master your emotions or you will be off on false adventures". It seems as if the development was frozen for all those centuries. But despite all kinds of stagnation and counter-movements the development towards different patterns of emotion management is unmistakable. At first in small groups at the junctions of commerce and politics (Elias, 1994). Groups whose continuity sometimes lasted only a few generations before they perished in battle and confusion. Only a long-term perspective reveals how, gradually, more and more segments of the population acquired this different psychological make-up. The pace at which this development will continue is unsure.

2. *Standards of social skills are related to patterns of power and dependency*. Many social configurations do not foster the abilities of emotion management which apply to some of our modern organizations. *Current standards of social skills propagated in textbooks and training programmes have to be seen in relation to networks of dense interdependencies and rather flat power balances.* These networks are to be found mainly in those parts of the West which because of their economic and political position are quite able to propagate their standards on a global level. Let us not forget that in many societies and organizations other ways of emotion management are needed simply to survive. *Also within our Western societies there are many organizations resembling steep power pyramids. Workers feel very dependent on their superiors. Other behavioural rules and forms of emotion management apply in these organizations! For instance the skills of open communication and personal feedback may not be experienced as very appropriate. They may even endanger one's position in the organization.*
3. Ways of emotion management are *not naturally given or fixed traits of the personality structure* of human beings. The historical perspective shows the changing ways in which people deal with emotions. It concerns

a painstaking struggle which took centuries. Becoming an adult person means that we go through this same learning process in close relation with the dependencies as experienced by us. The skills of emotion management have to be relearned by each new generation. Abilities as described by Rosier once took generations of efforts to develop. Many people in our society already master them in their teens. But many people in our society have a different personal history; they have learned to survive in other patterns of power and dependency. They have not developed the kind of self-organisation and discipline others may take for granted. Misunderstanding, personal tensions and conflicts are the result.

## CHANGING BALANCES OF POWER AND INFORMALIZATION

Forms of communication between people are related to changing relations of power and dependency. The interdependency networks existing today force us to develop more informal manners. One might speak of being forced into the informal. Paradoxically this more informal Behaviour makes higher demands on our control than the more standardized Behaviours which were once linked with the hierarchy. It presupposes such a degree of natural self-control, that more spontaneous and direct Behaviour becomes possible without the risk of losing all restraints or clamming up. This applies to many areas of social interaction. Elias describes the very conventional ritual which regulated relationships between men and women in the early twentieth century. This ceremonial has lost its function of guidance and external constraint. So, no fixed ritual to provide security; the burden of shaping life together lies on the shoulders of the individuals concerned. This demands a more complicated management of affect and Behaviour. Elias quotes Time Magazine when describing the resulting insecurity.

*"A man seated on the downtown bus might endure agonies of self-examination before offering his seat to a woman. The male has to learn to size up the female by age, education and possibly ferocity of feminism before opening a door for her:*

*would the courtesy offend her? It makes for ambiguity: if a man studiously refuses to open a door for a women, is he sexually liberated? Or just an ill-bred slob?"*

This informalization brings with it stronger demands on one's own judgment and responsibility. Will this informalization lead an undisciplined mess? In some parts of our society this will be the case but in situations where people are compelled to sustain regular working relationships the development towards stronger discipline and stricter standards goes on. A few examples of behavioural standards in the office:

*'Never, ever come into a place in a hurry. Better to walk in cool and collected and be ten minutes late, than being on time and out of breath. Panting indicates: this person does not have his affairs under control'.*

*'Whatever you do, don't take too many notes. Writing a lot indicates: this person is afraid to forget things. Or: this person has no authority, he/she has to report back in detail'.*

*'Watch for the man whose eyes wander to an attractive secretary during important meetings, he's vulnerable'.*

This is according to a column on the do's and don'ts of organizational Behaviour in a business magazine. Detailed, and actually quite sharp rules of conduct and at the same time relaxed and informal Behaviour, is that combination possible? Apparently it is! We see here a being forced into the informal, including (albeit in a different way than in the past) various 'small' showdowns between people to demonstrate that they understand, that they belong. Status competition is often the driving force behind changes in organizational Behaviour.

## Other ways of Emotion Management

The curbing and control of emotions solved many problems with regard to interaction. Sure, but these problems have been replaced by new problems. I will let J. Heller (1975) speak about company-life in his famous novel 'Something happened', the chapter entitled: 'The office in which I work'.

"People in the company, for example, do their best to minimize friction (we are encouraged to revolve around each other eight hours a day like self-lubricating ball bearings, careful not to jar or scrape) and to avoid quarrelling with each other openly. It is considered a much better form to wage our battles sneakily behind each other's back than to confront each other directly with any semblance of complaint. (The secret attack can be denied, lied about, or reduced in significance, but the open dispute is witnessed and has to be dealt with by somebody who finds the whole situation deplorable.) We are all on a congenial, first name basis, especially with people we loathe (the more we loathe them, the more congenial we try to be), and our wives and children are always inquired about familiarly by their first names, even by people who have never met them or met them only once".

"Andy Kagle, as head of our Sales Department, has a very powerful position with the company and is now afraid of losing it. He may be right. His name is all wrong. (Half wrong. Andrew is right, but Kagle?) So are his clothes. He shows poor judgment in colors and styles, as well as in fabrics, and his suits and coats and shirts do not fit him well enough.....

Kagle has ability and experience, but they don't count anymore. What does count is that he has no tone. His manners are no good.....

*He knows he is awkward. He is not a hearty extrovert; he is a nervous extrovert, the worst kind (especially to other nervous extroverts), and so he may be doomed".*

*In these two quotations we see how ways of emotion management play a role in the mutual power game, as demonstrated in references like "we are all on a congenial first name basis", "wrong judgment in colours en styles", "his manners are no good", "he is a nervous extrovert, so he may be doomed". This latter observation is especially interesting because it refers directly to 'wrong' emotion management. If you can't manage the right manners and right tone, you are 'doomed'.*

Jealousy, even hatred, disappointment, triumph, anger, dejection, gossip and frustration preoccupy many people in organizations. Then why in management literature, must we do with bloodless constructions like the informal organization, the unwritten rules of the game, dissatisfiers, role-conflict and cultural analysis? What kind of covering up is this? Our first industrialists such as Wedgwood and Regout still testify to the need to control violence and other wild and untamed Behaviour in their factories. Have our offices and factories now become graveyards of emotional tranquility and neutrality? The explanation for this disregarding of emotions lies perhaps in the risk we feel when we let go even a little. It has taken us centuries to reach the current level of trust in ourselves and others. The rationalization of interaction in our modern organizations makes us handle emotions irrationally. They are gone, disappeared into the periphery of eccentrics, the helpless, cultural minorities and the maladjusted. Whom we sometimes treat heartlessly because they express what we are trying to keep down in ourselves.

## Five Implications

The emotional aspect of organizations requires much more attention. Otherwise important issues remain unaddressed. A few implications will be briefly elaborated here:

1. Much literature and much training on enhancing skills like problem-solving, negotiating, meeting-skills, empathy and feedback provide us with all kinds of sensible dos and don'ts. These dos and don'ts give us something to go on, but they can only be effective if they are internalised, integrated in the psychology of the person, and become 'second nature'. This is a much neglected aspect in current training and literature. The do's and don'ts are fairly simple to understand and to practise by means of specially designed exercises in a learning group. It is my observation that these lessons fade away very quickly under the strife and tensions of real life. Then 'fiery' emotions move in. *So, the learning of skills cannot be separated from one's style of emotion management.* Do's and don'ts are all right but they have to be combined with an awareness of emotional styles and agility in dealing with emotions.
2. What about jealousy, aggression and nasty status competion as described for instance by Heller? It is highly improbable that emotions connected to pride, anger, inferiority, disorientation, envy, triumph, superiority, sexual attractiveness and racial origin will ever disappear from work relations. We have learned over the ages, to control related impulses like direct

aggression, outbursts of physical and sexual violence, open humiliation and flight. This control also implied endless gossiping, vicious buried frictions, ghastly manipulations, cynicism, stereotyping, distrust and fear. Increasing interdependencies no longer go with these kinds of emotion management. On the contrary, a high level of flexibility and open communication are becoming important success factors. *"Revolving around each other on a congenial, first name basis, especially with people we loathe" saps these abilities.* Feedback on bothersome Behaviours, openness about one's own moods but also more awareness of 'hidden' aggressive impulses, are helpful. Therefore it makes sense to become more consious of the emotional games we play. This implies that emotions are much more admitted into our consciousness and can be discussed in a constructive, even playful way among the people involved. Emotions gain acceptance as important guides for Behaviour. We have to increase our ability to differentiate among them and to tolerate these impulses in our awareness. This means that emotions come under a more conscious but less rigid control.

3. In organizations of high interdependencies between units, people are forced to become more adaptable, manoeuvrable and flexible. This implies also changing ways of emotion management. Playful teasing, controlled feed-back on Behaviour, smooth but direct reactions on the impact of posture and non-verbal signs, light-hearted exaggeration of destructive Behaviour: all these are examples of ways to raise our emotional agility. To cope with the demands of closer interdependence we have to stretch our abilities in emotion management.

   This will not only be a matter of informalization (more agile, playful and relaxed, higher tolerance for all kinds of impulses), but also a matter of more discipline. *Rules of emotion management will be introduced.* The rules of constructive feedback as described in many textbooks on communication (talk about the effects of Behaviour in terms of your own feelings, do not become defensive, do not justify or judge attitudes or personalities, focus on concrete behavioural incidents) are good examples. The importance of empathy as the ability to sustain good working relationships with people because one has a better understanding of the other person is another example. Also the spirals of 'harmful' emotion management will be more easily recognized and discussed; for instance: blaming other people for one's own actions.

4. We are compelled into a process of trial and error to develop abilities of emotion management. Closer interdependencies ask for easy communication along the chains of personal relations. Higher demands of team effectiveness force its members towards more intense and direct interaction. In many organizations in the west this is needed to improve results and to gain a competitive edge. This forces us to develop competencies to keep relations and communication open and to prevent a gradual bottling-up of negative feelings that hamper easy interaction. In these networks we cannot afford to waste our energies in stressful games of emotional cover-up and vicious frictions. In these relations emotional openness is no longer the same as taking up a vulnerable position. *On the contrary, a more formal attitude and the covering up of emotions with nice manners are the Behaviours which make people vulnerable.*
5. Let us not forget that changes in emotion management presuppose changes in the power balances between people. It concerns a precarious development. Stronger interdependencies and changing balances of power often coincide with loss of privileges and an intensification of social competition, individual stress and insecurity. The accompanying fears and conflicts provoke a hardening of feelings of aggression and escapism. If these tensions rise to high levels they feed themselves into vicious circles and changes will be blocked. History shows that changes in established patterns of emotion management are accompanied by frustration and conflict (Wouters, 1990). *Stagnation and regression are as normal as evolution.*

# 5

# Social and Personality Development

## PERSONALITY DEVELOPMENT

The concept of personality refers to the profile of stable beliefs, moods, and behaviours that differentiate among children (and adults) who live in a particular society. The profiles that differentiate children across cultures of different historical times will not be the same because the most adaptive profiles vary with the values of the society and the historical era. An essay on personality development written 300 years ago by a New England Puritan would have listed piety as a major psychological trait but that would not be regarded as an important personality trait in contemporary America. Contemporary theorists emphasize personality traits having to do with individualism, internalized conscience, sociability with strangers, the ability to control strong emotion and impulse, and personal achievement.

| Five Perspectives on Personality Development | | |
|---|---|---|
| **Perspective** | **Assumed Processes** | **Primary Outcomes** |
| Temperament | Inherent physiological mechanisms | Ease of arousal, ability to regulate emotions and impulses, energy, reaction to unfamiliar people and events, dominant mood |
| Psychoanalytic | Conflict over sexual and hostile motives | Defenses, phobias, depressed mood |
| Attachment | Relation to the caretaker in the infant years | Control of impulse, social habits, security, anger, frustration tolerance, trust in others, capacity for love |
| Self | Interpretations of experience, identification | Guilt, shame, anxiety, self-confidence |
| Observed behavior | Acquired habits | Sociability, aggressive behavior, impulsivity, shyness, obedience |

An important reason for the immaturity of our understanding of personality development is the heavy reliance on questionnaires that are filled out by parents of children or the responses of older children to questionnaires. Because there is less use of behavioural observations of children, our theories of personality development are not strong.

There are five different hypotheses regarding the early origins of personality (see accompanying table). One assumes that the child's inherited biology, usually called a temperamental bias, is an important basis for the child's later personality. Alexander Thomas and Stella Chess suggested there were nine temperamental dimensions along with three synthetic types they called the difficult child, the easy child, and the child who is slow to warm up to unfamiliarity. Longitudinal studies of children suggest that a shy and fearful style of reacting to challenge and novelty predicts, to a modest degree, an adult personality that is passive to challenge and introverted in mood.

A second hypothesis regarding personality development comes from Sigmund Freud's suggestion that variation in the sexual and aggressive aims of the id, which is biological in nature, combined with family experience, leads to the development of the ego and superego. Freud suggested that differences in parental socialization produced variation in anxiety which, in turn, leads to different personalities.

A third set of hypotheses emphasizes direct social experiences with parents. After World War II, Americans and Europeans held the more benevolent idealistic conception of the child that described growth as motivated by affectionate ties to others rather than by the narcissism and hostility implied by Freud's writings. John Bowlby contributed to this new emphasis on the infant's relationships with parents in his books on attachment. Bowlby argued that the nature of the infant's relationship to the caretakers and especially the mother created a profile of emotional reactions toward adults that might last indefinitely.

A fourth source of ideas for personality centres on whether or not it is necessary to posit a self that monitors, integrates, and initiates reaction. This idea traces itself to the Judeo-

Christian assumption that it is necessary to award children a will so that they could be held responsible for their actions. A second basis is the discovery that children who had the same objective experiences develop different personality profiles because they construct different conceptions about themselves and others from the same experiences. The notion that each child imposes a personal interpretation to their experiences makes the concept of self critical to the child's personality.

An advantage of awarding importance to a concept of self and personality development is that the process of identification with parents and others gains in significance. All children wish to possess the qualities that their culture regards as good. Some of these qualities are the product of identification with each parent.

A final source of hypotheses regarding the origins of personality comes from inferences based on direct observations of a child's behaviour. This strategy, which relies on induction, focuses on different characteristics at different ages. Infants differ in irritability, three-year-olds differ in shyness, and six-year-olds differ in seriousness of mood. A major problem with this approach is that each class of behaviour can have different historical antecedents. Children who prefer to play alone rather than with others do so for a variety of reasons. Some might be temperamentally shy and are uneasy with other children while others might prefer solitary activity.

The current categories of child psychopathology influenced the behaviours that are chosen by scientists for study. Fearfulness and conduct disorder predominate in clinical referrals to psychiatrists and psychologists. A cluster of behaviours that includes avoidance of unfamiliar events and places, fear of dangerous animals, shyness with strangers, sensitivity to punishment, and extreme guilt is called the internalizing profile.

The cluster that includes disobedience toward parent and teachers, aggression to peers, excessive dominance of other children, and impulsive decisions is called the externalizing profile. These children are most likely to be at risk for later juvenile delinquency. The association between inability of a three-year-old to inhibit socially inappropriate behaviour and later antisocial behaviour is the most reliable predictive relation between a characteristic scene in the young child and later personality trait.

## ARE THERE PERSONALITY TYPES?

We often share personality traits with others, especially members of our own family and community. This is probably due largely to being socialized in much the same way. It is normal for us to acquire personality traits as a result of enculturation. Most people adopt the traditions, rules, manners, and biases of their culture. Given this fact, it is not surprising that some researchers have claimed that there are common national personality types, especially in the more culturally homogenous societies. During the 1940's, a number of leading anthropologists and psychologists argued that there are distinct Japanese and German personalities that led these two nations to view other countries as trying to destroy them.

The concept of national personality types primarily had its origins in anthropology with the research of Ruth Benedict beginning in the 1920's. She believed that personality was almost entirely learned. She said that normal people acquire a distinct *ethos*, or culturally specific personality pattern, during the process of being enculturated as children. Benedict went on to say that our cultural personality patterns are assumed to be "natural" by us and other personality patterns are viewed as being "unnatural" and deviant. She said that such feelings are characteristic of all people in all cultures because we are ethnocentric. Benedict compared the typical personalities of the 19th century North American Plains Indians with those of the farming Pueblo Indians of the Southwest. She said that the bison hunting Plains Indians had personalities that could be typified as being aggressive, prone to violence, and seeking extreme emotional states. In contrast, she said that the typical Pueblo Indian was just the opposite—peaceful, non-aggressive, and sober in personality.

Benedict's views were especially popular in the 1930's among early feminists such as her student Margaret Mead. This was because if personality is entirely learned, it means that feminine and masculine personality traits are not biologically hard-wired in. In other words, culture rather than genes, makes women nurturing towards children and passive in response to men. Likewise, culture makes men aggressive and domineering. If this is true, these stereotypical behaviours can be altered and even reversed. Mead carried out ethnographic field work among the Polynesian and Melanesian peoples of the South Pacific to find examples of societies in which femininity and masculinity have very different and even opposite characteristics from those found in the Western World. She began her research in Samoa in 1925 where she discovered a relaxed adolescence in which sex is talked about freely by boys and girls rather than hidden or suppressed.

Most anthropologists today believe that Benedict and her students went too far in their assertions about the influence of culture on personality formation and in discounting heredity. They also tended to over simplify by defining people who did not share all of the traits of the "national personality type" as being deviants. It is more accurate to see the members of a society as having a range of personality types. What Benedict was describing was actually the modal personality. This is the most common personality type within a society. In reality, there is usually a range of normal personality types within each society.

In the early 1950's, David Riesman proposed that there are three common types of modal personality that occur around the world. He called them tradition oriented, inner-directed, and other directed personalities. The tradition-oriented personality is one that places a strong emphasis on doing things the same way that they have always been done. Individuals with this sort of personality are less likely to try new things and to seek new experiences. Those who have inner-directed personalities are guilt oriented. That is to say, their behaviour is strongly controlled by their conscience.

As a result, there is little need for police to make sure that they obey the law. These individuals monitor themselves. If they break the law, they are likely to turn themselves in for punishment. In contrast, people with other-directed personalities have more ambiguous feelings about right and wrong. When they deviate from a societal norm, they usually don't feel guilty. However, if they are caught in the act or exposed publicly, they are likely to feel shame.

Advocates of Riesman's concept of three modal personalities suggest that the tradition-oriented personality is most common in small-scale societies and in some sub-cultures of large-scale ones. Inner-directed personalities are said to be more common in some large-scale societies, especially ones that are culturally homogenous. In contrast, the other-directed personality is likely to be found in culturally diverse large-scale societies in which there is not a uniformity in socialization processes and there is considerable anonymity for city dwellers.

While Riesman's analysis of personalities was insightful, critics have pointed out that individuals may have characteristics of all three of his identified modal types. For instance, most North Americans probably do not feel guilty about exceeding speed limits when they are driving on freeways, however, they would feel very guilty hitting someone with their car and would likely call the police. In other words, for some infractions of the law they are other-directed (or shame-controlled), and for others they are inner-directed (or guilt-controlled). Likewise, many people like to do some things in the same way every day but seek new experiences in other areas of their lives. You may like to wear the same style of clothes and spend your leisure time at the same place with your friends most days. However, you may easily get bored eating the same kinds of food every day and regularly try new restaurants when you go out to eat. In other words, you are tradition-oriented for some things but not others.

## PERSONALITY AND DEVELOPMENTAL PSYCHOLOGY

*Social and Personality Development* looks at the processes by which we come to be who we are. It covers a range of topics central to personality and developmental psychology.

An individual's personality is an aggregate conglomeration of decisions we've made throughout our lives. There are inherent natural, genetic, and environmental factors that contribute to the development of our personality. According to process of socialization, "personality also colours our values, beliefs, and expectations... Hereditary factors that contribute to personality development do so as a result of interactions with the particular social environment in which people live." There are several personality types as Katharine Cook Briggs and Isabel Briggs

Myers illustrated in several personalities typology tests. These tests only provide enlightenment based on the preliminary insight scored according to the answers judged by the parameters of the test. Other theories on personality development are Jean Piaget stages of development, and personality development in Sigmund Freud's theory being formed through the interaction of id, ego, and super-ego.

## What is Personality

Personality is the supreme realization of the innate idiosyncrasy of a living being. It is an act of high courage flung in the face of life, the absolute affirmation of all that constitutes the individual, the most successful adaptation to the universal condition of existence coupled with the greatest possible freedom for self-determination."-Carl Gustav Jung, 1934.

## As We Move from Intelligence to Personality

As this course moves from intelligence (1st 5 weeks) into personality (next 10 weeks), it is worth pointing out that the relationship between intelligence and personality may be stronger than many assume.

Intelligence influences different aspects of personality in many different ways. In fact, intelligence is sometimes considered to be part of personality. This issue will probably always be debated. The main point to bear in mind is that both intelligence and personality are prominent individual differences.

Personality is not easily defined. Basically, 'personality' refers to our attempts to capture or summarize an individual's 'essence'. Personality is personality, the science of describing and understanding persons. Clearly, personality is a core area of study for psychology, if not the core. Together with intelligence, the topic of personality constitutes the most significant area of individual difference study.

No two people are exactly the same-not even identical twins. Some people are anxious, some are risk-taking; some are phlegmatic, some highly-strung; some are confident, some shy; and some are quiet and some are loquacious. This issue of differences is fundamental to the study of personality. Note also that in studying these differences we will also examine where the differences come from: as with intelligence we will find that there is a mixture of nature and nurture involved.

Perspectives on personality that we'll be examining:

- Trait Perspective
- Biological Perspective
- Psychoanalytic Perspective
- Learning Perspective
- Phenomenological Perspective
- Cognitive Perspective.

## Lay Usage of the Term "Personality"

We use the term personality frequently but what does it actually mean?

- "She has a wonderful personality."
- "He has no personality."
- "He has personality plus."
- "We seem to have a personality conflict."
- "It's just her personality."
- "She has her mother's personality."
- "He's a real personality."

## Personality Comes from the Greek Word "Persona", Meaning "Mask"

The word 'personality' derives from the Latin word 'persona' which means 'mask'. The study of personality can be understood as the study of 'masks' that people wear. These are the personas that people project and display, but also includes the inner parts of psychological experience which we collectively call our 'self'.

## "I" is for Personality

According to Adams personality is "I". Adams suggested that we get a good idea of what personality is by listening to what we say when we use "I". When you say I, you are, in effect, summing up everything about yourself-your likes and dislikes, fears and virtues, strengths and weaknesses.

The word I is what defined you as an individual, as a person separate from all others."

## "I am" Exercise

Write 10 honest endings to "I am..."

Share them with someone

Does this sum up your personality? Why or why not?

Various definitions of personality:

- "Deceptive masquerade or mimicry."
- "The entire organization of a human being at any stage of development."
- "Levels or layers of dispositions, usually with a unifying or integrative principle at the top."
- "The integration of those systems or habits that represent an individual's characteristic adjustments to the environment."
- "The way in which the person does such things as remembering, thinking or loving."
- "Those characteristics that account for consistent patterns of behaviour"
- "Personality is not an existing substantive entity to be searched for but a complex construct to be developed and defined by the observer."
- A contemporary definition for personality is offered by Carver and Scheier: "Personality is a dynamic organisation, inside the person, of psychophysical systems that create a person's characteristic patterns of behaviour, thoughts, and feelings."
    - o Dynamic Organisation: suggests ongoing readjustments, adaptation to experience, continual upgrading and maintaining Personality doesn't just lie there. It has process and it's organised.
    - o Inside the Person: suggests internal storage of patterns, supporting the notion that personality influences behaviours, etc.
    - o Psychophysical systems: suggests that the physical is also involved in 'who we are' Characteristic Patterns: implies that consistency/continuity which are uniquely identifying of an individual.

- o Behaviour, Thoughts, and Feelings: indicates that personality includes a wide range of psychological experience/manifestation: that personality is displayed in MANY ways.

Carver & Scheier suggest that the word personality "conveys a sense of consistency, internal causality, and personal distinctiveness". This issue of "personal distinctiveness is very important. There are certain universal characteristics of the human race and particular features of individuals. We all for example experience stress and the elevated cortisol that goes with it, and we all suffer the immune suppressive effects thereof. BUT each of us is unique too.

## Personality Development

Personality is defined as the enduring personal characteristics of individuals. Although some psychologists frown on the premise, a commonly used explanation for personality development is the psychodynamic approach. The term psychodynamic describes any theory that emphasizes the constant change and development of the individual. Perhaps the best known of the psychodynamic theories is Freudian psychoanalysis. Personality development is the developing a personality cult so as to create a strong positive impression about self with the targeted group, or in general; and more pertinent aspect of such personality is to maintain and prove in a long run. Ten Imp. Points for an Ultimate Personality:

- Appearance.
- Intelligence.
- Smartness.
- Trustworthy, High integrity and Responsible.
- Knowledge, in depth.
- Management.
- Efficiency.
- Economic independence.
- Morality/Character.
- Being beneficial/advantageous.

Strong negative aspects to spoil personality:

- Unhygienic

- Hurting attitude.
- Useless approach.
- Non-beneficial communication.
- Untrustworthy, Irresponsible, Lack of integrity.
- Below average performance.
- Powerless egoism.
- Financial indiscipline.
- Mismanagements.
- Uncontrolled burst of negative emotions.

The four aspects influencing personality are:

- Physical, Social, Psychological and Philosophical.
- Physical personality depends upon pleasing personality indirectly supported by health, strength and withstanding capacity.
- Social personality's main factors are: social values, communication skill, attitude and economic independence especially in relation with wealth.
- Psychological personality is in tune with personal values, approach, thinking pattern, emotional management and influenced by knowledge, intelligence and smartness.
- Philosophical personality is on account of maturity of values.

Main factors for developing a strong personality in social environment:

1. Pleasing appearance.
2. Beneficial communication.
3. Adapting and adhering to social values in interactions.
4. Developing confidence of:
   (a) Sincerity, integrity and trust.
   (b) Completing duties, fulfilling responsibilities in time.
   (c) Economic independent, but not being miser.
5. Additional spices for the best impression:
   (a) Awareness and alertness.
   (b) Useful application of: knowledge in depth, positive intelligence and defensive smartness.

(c) Self-Confidence, Initiative, dynamism, leadership qualities, will-power and self-discipline.

(d) Adaptive to moral values.

Main factors for developing a strong personality in working field:

1. Sincerity, integrity and trust.
2. Awareness, alertness and grasping capacity.
3. Beneficial communication skill.
4. Useful application of required knowledge in depth, positive intelligence and defensive smartness.
5. Non dependence of economic condition other than for rightful privileges.
6. Completing duties and fulfilling responsibilities in time and absolute accountability.
7. Pleasing appearance with good health.
8. Social interactions in tune with institutional decorum.
9. Sensible thinking inspite of emotionally charged, or embarrassing, circumstances.
10. Dynamism in positive approaches, initiative in new skills and adaptive to institutional policies.
11. Being in tune with changing times; especially so with changing technologies in the respective line.
12. Not to be with:
    (1) Creating helplessness, self satisfaction at others' cost, egoism, sadism, criticism, putting blame on others to escape, irritating communication, untrustworthiness.
    (2) Laziness, lethargic attitude, falling into helplessness, unusual attitude, useless/boom-ranging approaches, irresponsibility, ignorance, borrowings, unhygienic/disliking appearance.

Main factors for Self development:

1. Self-discipline especially against temptations.
2. Not telling lies.
3. Attainment of maturity in distinguishing good and bad, and development of discipline to do such good and will-power to stand against such bad.

4. Performance of accepted role-play with fulfilling duty, responsibility and accountability.
5. Love and gratitude.
6. Using sensibility rather than becoming emotional.
7. Listen and gather but take your own decision.
8. Don't accept failures, but rectify mistakes in such failures.
9. Skill to do, will to achieve and thrill to help.
10. Try to create happiness around you even at your own personal cost.
11. Helping should always be motto of life without expectation in return.
12. Be selfish within such level of: don't give away your owns if meant for fulfilling your duties.
13. Thinking should be positive so that your attitude and approaches will also be positive.
14. Learn useful knowledge, develop positive intelligence and equip with defensive smartness.
15. Time shall be managed to such optimum level either for usefulness, or for relaxation.
16. Have such hobbies so as to convert the remaining time to be useful.
17. Dependence should be a strategy to get the things done.

Other notable points:-

1. Favourable social interactions are possible by pleasing appearance, beneficial communication, happy creating attitude, and mutually useful approach with maturity in social values.
2. In-depth knowledge should be useful:
    - Positive intelligence should be beneficial.
    - Defensive smartness should be protective.
3. Criticism is the self-defensive mechanism to cover up one's own inefficiency.
4. Not telling a lie is not wrong but it doesn't mean to tell the truth; however, not telling truth should be for a positive aspect without absolute selfishness.

In other words, personality development depends on:

- Character and Conduct.
- Theory of relativity, Perceptions and Values.
- Awareness and alertness.
- Health, wealth, in-depth knowledge, positive intelligence and defensive smartness.
- Self-Confidence, Will-Power and Self-Discipline.
- Duty, responsibility and accountability.
- Moral Values.

## FREUD'S PSYCHOANALYTIC THEORY

### Drives

Freud believed that two basic drives—sex and aggression—motivate all our thoughts and behaviours. He referred to these as Eros (love) and Thanatos. Eros represents the life instinct, sex being the major driving force. Thanatos represents the death instinct (characterised by aggression), which, according to Freud, allowed the human race to both procreate and eliminate its enemies.

### Structure of Personality

Freud conceived the mind as only having a fixed amount of psychic energy (libido). The outcome of the interaction between the id, ego and the superego, (each contending for as much libidinal energy as possible) determines our adult personality.

### Tripartite Personality

Freud believed that personality had three parts—the id, ego, and super-ego—referring to this as the tripartite personality. The id allows us to get our basic needs met. Freud believed that the id is based on the pleasure principle, i.e. it wants immediate satisfaction, with no consideration for the reality of the situation. As a child interacts more with the world, the ego begins to develop. The ego's job is to meet the needs of the id, whilst taking into account the constraints of reality. The ego acknowledges that being impulsive or selfish can sometimes hurt us, so the id must be constrained. The superego develops during the phallic stage, as a result of the moral constraints placed on us by our parents. It is generally believed that a strong superego serves to inhibits the biological instincts of the id (resulting in a high level of guilt), whereas a weak superego allows the id more expression (resulting in a low level of guilt).

## Defence Mechanisms

The ego, having a difficult time trying to satisfy both the needs of the id and the superego, employs defence mechanisms. Repression is perhaps the most powerful of these. Repression is the act by which unacceptable id impulses (most of which are sexually related) are "pushed" out of awareness and into the unconscious mind. Another example of a defence mechanism is projection. This is the mechanism that Freud used to explain Little Hans' complex. Little Hans is said to have projected his fear for his father onto horses, which is why he was afraid of horses.

## Psychosexual Stages

Freud believed that at particular points in the child's development, a single part of the body is particularly sensitive to sexual stimulation. These euro-genous zones are the mouth, anus and the genital region. At any given time, the child's libido is focused on the primary euro-genous zone for that age. As a result, the child has certain needs and demands that are related to the euro-genous zones for that stage. Frustration occurs if these needs are not met, but, a child may also become overindulged, and so may be reluctant to progress beyond the stage. Both frustration and overindulgence may lead to fixation—some of the child's libido remains locked into that stage. If a child is fixated at a particular stage, the method of obtaining satisfaction that characterised that stage will dominate their adult personality.

### STAGES

## Oral Stage (0-18 Months)

This stage begins at birth, when the mouth is the primary source of libidinal energy. A child who is frustrated at this stage may develop an adult personality that is characterised by pessimism, envy and suspicion. The overindulged child may develop to be optimistic, gullible, and full of admiration for others.

## Anal Stage (18 Months-3 yrs)

The child's focus on pleasure on this stage is on eliminating and retaining faeces. This represents the conflict between the id, which derives pleasure from the expulsion of bodily wastes, and the super-ego which represents external pressure to control bodily functions. If the parents are too lenient in this conflict, it will result in the formation of an anal expulsive character who is disorganised, reckless and defiant. Conversely, a child may opt to retain faeces, thereby spiting his parents, and may develop into an anal retentive character who is neat, stingy and obstinate.

## Phallic Stage (3-6 yrs)

During this stage, boys develop unconscious desires for their mother and become rivals with their father for her affection. This is reminiscent with Little Hans' case study. So the boys develop a fear that their father will punish them for these feelings (castration anxiety) so decide to identify with him rather than fight him. As a result, the boy develops masculine characteristics and represses his sexual feelings towards his mother. This is known as the Oedipus complex. During recent years, it is now believed that girls go through a similar process. This is called the Electra complex. Freud believed that the resolution of this female conflict comes much later and is never truly complete.

## Latent (6 yrs-puberty)

The latency period is not a psychosexual development as such, but a stage when sexual drives lie dormant. Freud saw latency as a period of unparalleled repression of sexual desires and euro-genous impulses.

## Genital Stage (Puberty Onwards)

This stage begins at puberty, when sexual urges are once again awakened. Interest now turns to heterosexual relationships. The less fixation the child has in earlier stages, the more chance they have of developing a "normal" personality, and thus develop healthy meaningful relationships with those of the opposite sex. Although many people view Freud's descriptions of personality development as pure fantasy, his ideas have endured and have had far reaching influences both in and outside psychology. Freud has changed the way we think about the importance of childhood, and also made us aware of the unconscious elements of our psyche that are essential for development.

## Overview

***A part of personality can be defined as follows:*** A part of personality is a discretely identified, localized portion of the personality system that performs a unique function, stores information, or represents a thematic quality of the individual's mental processes.

To get a better sense of what is meant above, each key part of the definition can be further described:

***Personality:*** The system that represents the collective function of major psychological subsystems such as motives, emotions, cognitions, the self, and similar such aspects.

***Discretely identified:*** That is, using sound analytic and conceptual rules, it makes sense to identify various discrete subsystems of personality. The part is not necessarily a discrete part of the brain or mind, although that is the intention, but nonetheless can be divided for purposes of scientific exploration.

***Localized portion of the system:*** It is a portion or component of the system, and not the whole system.

***That performs a unique function:*** That is, some parts of personality are responsible for doing something that affects the operation of the personality system (e.g., short-term memory).

***Stores information:*** That is, some parts of personality store information about the self and the world (e.g., knowledge about baseball).

***Represents the thematic quality of personality processes:*** That is, some parts of personality represent identified thematic aspects or patterns of personality function (e.g., an expert in baseball).

Personality parts (or components) can be distinguished according to two broad fashions: according to their type, and their function.

## For Example

The above description of a personality part can be made clearer with some further examples of personality parts.

In the emotions area, for example, there are examples of parts that do something, store information, and represent qualities of personality. Happiness (as a part that "does something"): the capacity to respond happily involves an integrated ability to relax physically, crinkle one's eyes, smile, think positive thoughts, and share enjoyment with others.

Anxious schema (as a part that "stores information"). A mental representation of something, for example, a birthday party, that, for the individual, has various worries and concerns related to it.

Well-Being (as a part that reflects a person's pattern of operation). An individual's general subject sense that he or she is doing well.

## Personality Type

The concept of personality type refers to the psychological classification of different types of individuals. Personality types are sometimes distinguished from personality traits, with the latter embodying a smaller grouping of behavioural tendencies. Types are sometimes said to involve *qualitative* differences between people, whereas traits might be construed as *quantitative* differences. According to type theories, for example, introverts and extraverts are two fundamentally different categories of people. According to trait theories, introversion and extraversion are part of a continuous dimension, with many people in the middle. While typologies of all sorts have existed throughout time the most influential idea of psychological types originated in the theoretical work of Carl Jung, published as *Psychological Types* in 1921. Other typologies such as Socionics, MBTI, and Keirsey Temperament Sorter all have roots in Jungian philosophy.

Usage:

- One example of personality types is Type A and Type B personality theory. According to this theory, impatient, achievement-oriented people are classified as Type A, whereas easy-going, relaxed individuals are designated as Type B. The theory originally suggested that Type A individuals were more at risk for coronary heart disease, but this claim has not been supported by empirical research.

- Developmental psychologist Jerome Kagan is a prominent contemporary advocate of type theory. He suggests that shy, withdrawn children are best viewed as having an inhibited temperament, which is qualitatively different from other children.
- As a matter of convenience, trait theorists sometimes use the term "type" to describe someone who scores exceptionally high or low on a particular personality trait. Hans Eysenck refers to superordinate personality factors as *types*, and more specific associated traits as *traits*.
- Several pop psychology theories (e.g., *Men Are From Mars, Women Are From Venus*, the enneagram) rely on the idea of distinctively different types of people.

## Criticism

The term "type" has not been used consistently in psychology and has become the source of some confusion. Furthermore, because personality test scores usually fall on a bell curve rather than in distinct categories, personality type theories have received considerable criticism among psychometric researchers. One study that directly compared a "type" instrument (the MBTI) to a "trait" instrument (the NEO PI) found that the trait measure was a better predictor of personality disorders. Because of these problems, personality type theories have fallen out of favour in psychology. Most researchers now believe that it is impossible to explain the diversity of human personality with a small number of discrete types. They recommend trait models instead, such as the five factor model.

Major theories:

- DISC assessment
- Enneagram of Personality
- Four Temperaments
- Humorism
- Keirsey Temperament Theory

- Myers-Briggs Type Indicator
- Socionics
- Type A and Type B personality theory.

## NPA Personality Theory

The NPA theory of personality was developed by A.M. Benis on the basis of concepts presented over fifty years ago by psychiatrist Karen Horney. The model posits three major behavioural traits underlying personality: narcissism (N), perfectionism (P) and aggression (A), leading to the formulation of discrete *character types*. Each trait is based on a major pleiotropic gene (a gene determining several related characteristics) that follows the rules of Mendelian genetics.

The NPA model proposes that the character traits A and N are indispensable to human development, being related to the sympathetic and parasympathetic nervous systems, respectively. The trait P is also assumed to function at the level of the central nervous system and to act as a modifier of the expression of traits A and N. The NPA model proposes to clarify the genetic bases of known personality disorders, diseases related to behavioural factors ("psychosomatic diseases") and mental illnesses. An online *NPA personality test* is available in English and French versions.

## What is Personality?

Personality is a collection of emotional, thought and behavioural patterns unique to a person that is consistent over time. Although many investigators have proposed various theories of personality, no objectively testable model has emerged. The NPA model falls into the category of a trait theory of personality, its unique approach being that it is biologically based on classical human genetics.

## NPA MODEL BASED ON THREE GENETIC TRAITS

## Genetics and Environment

Although it is universally accepted that both genetic and environmental factors (or "nature and nurture") comprise personality, the relevant genes have yet to be identified. Studies of the heritability of personality factors conducted with identical and fraternal twins emphasize the importance of genetics in behaviour. The NPA model acknowledges the possible importance of environment and culture in personality but emphasizes that it is the genetic, or structural, factors that first need to be identified.

The NPA model acknowledges that the genetic bases of personality are themselves complex. It assumes at least four tiers to this genetic basis:

- male or female gender
- character type based on the three NPA traits
- temperament, or the degree of activity or excitability of an individual in the pavlovian sense
- other facets of personality, such as Raymond Cattell's 16 Personality Factors, Hans Eysenck's P-E-N model of personality, or the life style approaches of enneagram theory.

The NPA model, thus, focuses on only the second of these four tiers, acknowledging that *temperament* and *other facets of personality* may involve a large number of genes.

## Traits of Narcissism (N), Perfectionism (P) and Aggression (A)

Karen Horney advanced the concept that at maturity there exist at least three expansive character types, namely the "narcissistic", the "perfectionistic" and the "arrogant-vindictive". Extending these ideas, the NPA model posits that the human character rests primarily on the existence of three major traits: narcissism (N), perfectionism (P) and aggression (A). Each of these traits is assumed to exist as the expression of a single major pleiotropic gene. Horney considered that the traits have environmental origins, being the result of an individual's desperate search for dominance in the context of a stifling upbringing. The NPA model — in ascribing the traits to genetic origins — emphasizes biological attributes associated with the traits.

## Aggression

The behavioural trait of aggression is acknowledged to be the most labile of the three. The stereotypic acts associated with this trait involve body posturing, gestures, and eye contact of intimidation and deference, with individuals having this trait continually competing with each other on a scale of dominance and submission. The trait of aggression corresponds to a striving for power over one's environment, hence it is one main component of competitiveness in social relations, or ambition. In a pejorative connotation the trait may reveal itself in the context of sadism or sadomasochism. The facial expression is non-sanguine, i.e., tending toward sallowness or pallor in individuals of light skin colour. The hallmark of the trait of aggression is a mass discharge of the sympathetic nervous system: the "fight or flight" response or the *aggressive-vindictive rage*. During the expression of this rage, the facial complexion of pallor is accentuated.

## Narcissism

The trait of narcissism is noted to be less labile than that of aggression (where individuals may be constantly altering their character states on a scale of dominance and submission). The stereotypic acts associated with the trait include self-flaunting body posturing, expansive arm gestures, bowing, instinctive self-adornment, and a natural attraction to the limelight of personal recognition. Individuals having only this trait (of the three) are competitive but non-aggressive in their strivings for recognition.

The trait corresponds to a striving for glory in one's environment, representing the second main component of human ambition. In a pejorative connotation, the unbridled trait of narcissism may reveal itself in the context of conceit, exhibitionism, vanity or misoneism. An associated facial expression includes the radiant gingival smile (broadly exposing the gums and teeth). The facial complexion in individuals of light skin colour tends toward blood-red or ruddy. Hallmarks of the trait include blushing, flushing, and a mass discharge of the parasympathetic nervous system: the *narcissistic rage* of defence and withdrawal. During expression of this rage the normally sanguine complexion becomes even more florid.

## Perfectionism

The trait of perfectionism in the NPA model is not a basic drive of ambition and is not associated with a rage reaction.

Rather it is a mediator of the unbridled drives of aggression and/or narcissism. The stereotypic acts associated with the trait of perfectionism are obsessiveness, compulsiveness, repetition, and the maintenance of neatness, order and symmetry. A clue to the nature of the trait lies in the compulsive, repetitive mannerisms of autistic children and some adult schizophrenic individuals.

The behavioural pattern is often ritualistic and the speech characterized by echolalia. It is posited that such autistic and schizophrenic individuals are those in whom the two components of ambition, i.e. aggression and narcissism, have been suppressed by genetic or environmental factors, either congenitally, in childhood, or after maturity, thus revealing in the individual a primitive state of perfectionism.

## Character Types

The notion that humans exhibit only a limited number of discrete character types can be traced back to the time of the ancient Greeks, in particular to the theory of humours (blood, black bile, yellow bile and phlegm). The NPA model attempts to relate genetic NPA types to these character types of antiquity, as well as to the classic personality disorders of modern psychiatry.

## DOMINANCE: DOMINANT CHARACTER TYPES

In dominant types the traits A and N, if present at all, are fully expressed. The NPA model generates the following dominant character types:

### N Type

The narcissistic (N) type is found in the writings of Karen Horney and others who have developed the classic psychiatric views of narcissism. In the NPA model this type is the equivalent of the sanguine character type described by the ancients. The important attributes of this type are: expansiveness but unaggressiveness, non-perfectionism, a tendency to flamboyant self-adornment, a natural attraction to the limelight, the gingival smile of recognition and the florid narcissistic rage. In extreme forms this type appears as a self-anointed visionary, a proselytizing evangelist or a messianic personality.

## A Type

The aggressive (A) type corresponds to Horney's arrogant-vindictive type and to her concept of "moving against people". In the NPA model this is the classic choleric character type of antiquity. The main attributes of this type are: unbridled arrogance, instinctual vindictiveness, non-perfectionism, no tendency to self-adornment, a wry or sardonic grin in place of a gingival smile, and the pallid-complexioned aggressive-vindictive rage. In extreme forms this type appears as a sadistic personality, as an extroverted paranoid personality, or as the so-called antisocial or sociopathic personality.

## NA Type

The narcissistic-aggressive (NA) type is regarded to be a composite of the previously described narcissistic and aggressive types. Horney described the essence of this character type, in the female, in an article, "The over valuation of love: a study of a common present day type".

The main attributes of this type are: a sanguine complexion, synergistic merging of unbridled narcissism and aggression, hyperactivity, non-perfectionism, a tendency toward extreme self-adornment, exhibitionism in the limelight, a "flashy" extroverted smile, a tendency toward hypersexuality, and the capacity to exhibit the narcissistic, aggressive-vindictive or combined narcissistic-aggressive rages. In extreme forms this character type appears as the hypomanic, histrionic or hysterical personality.

## NP Type

The attributes of the narcissistic-perfectionist (NP) type were described by Horney in her exposition of the "perfectionist type". In the NPA model this encompasses the classic phlegmatic type known to the ancients. The main qualities of this type are: a tendency toward a sanguine complexion, industriousness, orderliness, an intense sense of duty, un-aggressiveness, stubbornness, negativism, a tendency to ruminate, perfectionistic rather than unbridled self-adornment, an uncommonly seen gingival smile of recognition, and the capacity to exhibit the florid narcissistic rage. In extreme forms this character appears as the obsessive-compulsive personality.

## PA Type

The perfectionistic-aggressive (PA) type is alluded to by Horney in her mention of aggressive types who function in the capacity of a "power behind the throne", that is, personages who utilize intellectual qualities and planning rather than overt aggression to achieve their aims. In the NPA model this is the classic non-sanguine, austere melancholic personality of the ancients. The principal qualities of this type are: a non-sanguine complexion, passive aggressiveness, dour perfectionism, vigilance, mani pulativeness, a proud bearing, haughty reservedness, a calculated vindictiveness, a lack of an innate tendency to self-adornment, a sardonic grin, and the pallid-complexioned aggressive-vindictive rage. In extreme forms this is the passive-aggressive, rebellious-distrustful, or ruminating paranoid personality.

## NPA Type

The narcissistic-perfectionistic-aggressive (NPA) type was not explicitly described by Horney, although she did note that the three traits can coexist in the same individual. The main attributes of this type are: a sanguine complexion, a loud voice, dynamism with a tendency to be overbearing, bombastic garrulity, intense eye contact, a strong sense of duty, a bent toward conventional values, unpretentious self-adornment, an outgoing smile of moderate intensity, and the capacity to exhibit the narcissistic, aggressive, or explosive narcissistic-aggressive rages. In the extreme cases this individual is the managerial-autocratic or explosive personality.

## SUBMISSION: SUBMISSIVE CHARACTER TYPES

In submissive types the trait of aggression is not fully expressed. The NPA model defines two gradations of submission: *non-compliance*, in which the individual is basically submissive but is easily activated to an energetic state of aggression, and *compliance*, in which the individual tends to remain in a profound state of submission.

In the model the state of submission most often has a genetic basis, the result of a congenital, inherited, incomplete expression of the gene for the trait A. However, the model also allows for environmental causes, the state of submission being induced during the juvenile period on the basis of environmental constraints to character development. That is, phenocopies (based on environmental factors) of a genetically disposed submissive state may exist. Also, like dominant types having full expression of the trait A, submissive types may exhibit the *aggressive-vindictive rage*.

## Non-compliant Types

The model denotes the state of *non-compliance* by *A-*, obtaining the following non-compliant submissive phenotypes:

- Aggressive (A-)
- Perfectionistic-aggressive (PA-)
- Narcissistic (NA-)
- Narcissistic-perfectionistic (NPA-).

## Compliant Types

The model denotes the state of *compliance* by *A=*, obtaining the following compliant submissive phenotypes:

- Aggressive (A=)
- Perfectionistic-aggressive (PA=)
- Narcissistic (NA=)
- Narcissistic-perfectionistic (NPA=).

The NPA-non-compliant type above corresponds to active, motivated, non-confrontational individuals whose baseline personality tends toward submissiveness, as described by Horney in her discussion of inverted sadistic behaviour. In the therapeutic setting, these individuals are found over the spectrum of "type A", dependent, and phobic-anxious personality. The NA-type is a non-perfectionistic, active individual exhibiting pronounced narcissistic behaviour. In the therapeutic setting this is a cyclothymic or dependent histrionic personality.

The compliant types NA= and NPA= above correspond to more profoundly submissive individuals, having more pronounced tendencies toward masochistic behaviour. They correspond to Karen Horney's compliant "self-effacing" personality and to her concept of "moving toward people".

## Resignation: Resigned Character Types

In the character state of resignation the trait of aggression is stunted after maturity because of environmental constraints. Unlike submissive types who readily involve themselves in the relative competition of dominance and submission (and sometimes sadomasochism), resigned types remain relatively detached from such activities and only with difficulty can be stressed to a state of active aggression. However, like submissive types, resigned types can be induced into the *aggressive-vindictive rage*. The model denotes the *state of resignation* by-*A*, obtaining the following resigned phenotypes:

- Aggressive (-A)
- Perfectionistic-aggressive (P-A)
- Narcissistic (N-A)
- Narcissistic-perfectionistic (NP-A).

The resigned types having the narcissistic trait correspond to detached individuals, as described by Karen Horney. She considered that "moving away from people" was a maladaptive response that could develop as a growing individual struggled toward maturity. The NP-A type would tend to have strong perfectionistic tendencies, while the N-A type would be more labile.

## Borderline Types and Mental Illness

In the NPA model borderline types possess only one of the traits of ambition (N or A) and it is only partially expressed, while types in which both the traits (N and A) are profoundly suppressed fall into categories of mental illness, in particular schizophrenia.

One aspect of the model focuses on the dominant types N and NP, which lack the trait A. In analogy with partial expression of the trait A, the theory identifies states of incomplete expression of the trait N, denoted as *N-N=,* and-*N*. Examples of *borderline types* would be N-or N-P above. Types falling into the categories of *mental illness* would be N= or N=P, the latter being a perfectionistic, autistic individual.

## Dominance and Submission

In the NPA model *dominant* character types having the trait *A* have the potential of being reduced to a subdued state acutely or to a subjugated state chronically. Similarly, *submissive* types have the potential of being activated to an energetic *A*+ state resembling dominance, usually for short periods of time.

Thus, the model emphasizes the potential lability of trait *A* in social relations, with dominant and submissive types continually altering their behaviour in competitive interactions with other individuals and in the context of mating. In the extreme, some of these relationships fall into the category of sadomasochism. *Resigned* types, in their detachment from social interactions, usually avoid dominance-submission relationships and, in particular, hierarchal structures where "pecking orders" predominate.

## Mendelian Transmission of NPA Traits

On the basis of archetypal examples, the model assumes that in their full expression the NPA traits are transmitted by autosomal genes, with traits A and N being recessive and trait P being transmitted in the dominant mode. The alleles corresponding to full expression and total suppression of the trait A are denoted by a and a~, respectively, and the corresponding alleles for the trait N are denoted by n and n~.

For the trait P two alleles p and p~ are posited, corresponding to full expression or total absence of the trait P, on the assumption that the trait is always transmitted with complete penetrance. This scheme of inheritance is consistent with the notion that the alleles a~ and n~ control the production of inhibitors of the traits A and N at the level of the central nervous system, with alleles a~ and n~ being dominant with respect to a and n.

The table shows:

- N and A individuals need not have N or A parents. Such individuals can arise *de novo* so long as at least one of the parents is an NP and PA individual, respectively.
- PA individuals must have at least one parent who is of either the PA or A type.
- NP individuals must have at least one parent who is of either the NP or N type.
- NA individuals can arise *de novo* from any combination of phenotypes.

- The mating of two NA types can yield progeny of only NA types.
- The mating of an NPA type with an NA type can yield progeny of only NPA or NA types.
- Certain combinations of parental genotypes may lead to zygotes having only the P trait (P phenotype) or lacking all three traits (null phenotype, denoted by 0). According to NPA theory, zygotes of P or null phenotype would be non-viable. Thus, the model predicts partial or complete infertility in some combinations of parental phenotypes, these being N×A, N×PA, NP×A and NP×PA.

## IMPLICATIONS OF A TRAIT THEORY BASED ON GENETICS

### Evolutionary Origins of NPA Traits

The assumption of a genetic basis to the traits *N, P* and *A* implies that their origins reside in the evolution of humans from precursor species, and in particular, that the traits are likely to be found in primates other than *homo sapiens*. As examples, the model leads to proposed character types as follows:

- The omnivorous, hierarchal, unsmiling baboon, known for its lengthy grooming rituals, would be a likely perfectionist-aggressive *PA* type.
- The herbivorous, aloof, phlegmatic orangutan and gorilla, capable of gingival smiles, would be likely *NP* types.
- Akin to humans, the omnivorous, promiscuous chimpanzee, also capable of the gingival smile, would likely have a heterogeneous distribution of types, with *NA* and *NPA* types predominating.

### Population Genetics

A trait theory based on genetics would imply that the personality structure of a population could be expressed in definitive mathematical terms. The NPA model is amenable to the Hardy-Weinberg approach to quantify the distribution of NPA character types in a given sub-population. With the usual assumptions of gene frequencies *n, p* and *a* and random mating, expressions for the relative incidences of dominant character types are given in the table below. Because of the occurrence of non-viable P and null (0) phenotypes, the assumptions of Hardy-Weinberg equilibrium would not hold, the incidences below representing the phenotypes of the first generation only. The assumption of numerical values for the three gene frequencies *n, p* and *a* generates a hypothetical sub-population, or *habitancy*:

**_Habitancy_**

| *Phenotype* | *Balanced* | *Punctilious* | *Sublime* | *Demonstrative* | *Authoritarian* | *Militant* |
|---|---|---|---|---|---|---|
| N | 7 | 3 | 77 | 2 | 1 | 1 |
| A | 3 | <1 | <1 | 2 | 17 | 34 |
| NP | 22 | 78 | 18 | 7 | 2 | 1 |
| NA | 13 | <1 | 3 | 20 | 6 | 11 |
| PA | 9 | 2 | <1 | 7 | 52 | 35 |
| NPA | 39 | 8 | 1 | 61 | 17 | 12 |
| P | 4 | 8 | <1 | 1 | 4 | 2 |
| null (0) | 1 | <1 | 1 | <1 | 1 | 2 |
| gene *frequencies* | *n* = 0.90 | *n* = 0.90 | *n* = 0.99 | *n* = 0.95 | *n* = 0.50 | *n* = 0.50 |
| | p = 0.50 | p = 0.80 | p = 0.10 | p = 0.50 | p = 0.50 | p = 0.30 |
| | *a* = 0.80 | *a* = 0.30 | *a* = 0.20 | *a* = 0.95 | *a* = 0.95 | *a* = 0.95 |

Frequencies of phenotypes in six habitancies (per 100 zygotes, or pregnancies). The non-viable P and null (0) phenotypes are shown in red. Non-viable types arise when the zygote has neither trait N nor A. The above analysis is confined to *dominant character types* on the assumption of two alleles for each NPA gene.

The table demonstrates that:

- Relatively small changes in gene frequencies could cause large changes in the phenotype frequencies.
- The frequencies of non-viable P and null types are low for these habitancies, on the order of 0 to 8 percent.

Other hypothetical distributions of *dominant NPA character types*, for any combination of gene frequencies, may be calculated here.

## Predictive Aspects of NPA Model

The model would have the potential to be predictive in the following categories:

- The possible genetic character types of children could be deduced from the character types of parents.
- Relations could be defined between genetic character type and susceptibility to certain physical and mental diseases
- Combinations of parental character types prone to infertility problems (miscarriage and stillbirth) could be identified, these combinations being ones which permit the occurrence of a fetus lacking in both traits N and A
- Allele frequencies for the NPA traits, as well as the resultant distributions of NPA character types, in various societies could be analysed on the basis of well-known principles of population genetics.
- Studies with primates could confirm a biological basis for behaviour in the areas of socio-biology and evolutionary psychology.

## Criticism and Controversy

Controversy has always followed past positions taken by the scientific community relating human behaviour to inheritance, as in Arthur Jensen's theories of intelligence, Herrnstein and Murray's "The Bell Curve", or Lewontin and colleagues' "Not in Our Genes"; the NPA personality theory is not exempt. The result of the "nature versus nurture" debate has been that a gauntlet had been thrown to those who espouse genetic underpinnings to behaviour: "show us the relevant genes".

The slow progress of un-ravelling of the genetic basis of personality is the subject of a recent review article by Jang and colleagues. They point out the lack of any genetic framework in the classification of the Diagnostics and Statistical Manual of American psychiatry, and the pressing need to identify "genetically crisp" characteristics – or genetic traits of behaviour that are independent of competing genetic and environmental influences.

The NPA model posits narcissism to be a genetic trait, being related to the parasympathetic branch of the autonomic nervous system, just as aggression is classically related to the sympathetic branch. This concept of narcissism, and the associated narcissistic rage, is not found in any branch of classical medicine or psychiatry and remains a key point requiring validation. Of note is the recent study by Livesley and colleagues with identical and fraternal twins. They found that of a total of eighteen dimensions of personality it was narcissism that clearly had the highest heritability.

The manuscript of the NPA model was copyrighted with the Library of Congress in 1982, being published in book form in 1985 and in a peer-reviewed journal in 1990. Studies are in progress utilizing the *NPA personality test* in obstetric and gynecological patients. The number of subjects taking and submitting the online test, for personal reasons, exceeds ten thousand per year.

Although the NPA model is several decades old, it has not been validated in the sense of withstanding scrutiny by the scientific method – as is true of all other theories of personality as well. Given the recent advances in deciphering the human genome, such scrutiny may soon be possible. The ideas of Karen Horney have been resilient over time, and the validity of her observations that form the basis of the NPA model awaits the relevant studies in the realm of behavioural genetics.

## MEASUREMENT

One would come across many treatises on personality. 'What is Personality', 'Personality Building', 'Magnetic Personality', 'Personality Cult', 'Personality Disorder', are some of the well known captions. They prescribe and recommend many personality aids, improvement recipes and cures and correctives as if personality is a simple and common trait which can be acquired easily; or it is some thing objective which can be everybody's property.

Personality is not such a common and cheap human property. In philosophic sense personality is systematized, integrated and disciplined self. There are three important aspects of human personality namely physical, mental and moral or ethical. A harmonious and conscious development of all the three, is the test of good or balanced personality. Development, dedication and discipline are the three mansions of personal ethics. Development is growth, enfoldment of body, mind and expansion and enrichment of personality to utmost extent. It is positive as the gardener gives manure, sunshine and air to the plants. Dedication consists in the consecration of the disciplined and developed personality to some noble cause. Discipline is a negative quality; and it aims at the control of passions, impulses and appetites as a gardener prunes the plants.

We often hear the phrases, beautiful personality, attractive personality, impressive personality and imposing personality. These epithets refer to the physical aspect of the outward traits of personality. Actually personality is sum-total of various objective and subjective qualities displayed by a person. When all these qualities are assembled in one place, or one is blessed by the virtues like self-confidence, will power, power of concentration, power of discrimination, earnestness, integrity of character, pleasing manners and simple life habits, he has a great personality. No doubt attractive appearance and pleasing out-looks do have external beauty.

As we should not judge a book from its cover, so we must not judge a person from appearances which are often deceptive. It is said that each of us has a personality. A person is handsome if he is a male, beautiful if she is a female. According to dictionary meaning, personality is the integrated organization of all the psychological, intellectual, emotional and physical characteristics of an individual as they are presented to the other people. Ordinarily it stands for individuality, a distinctive or well-marked character. It is man's most precious possession.

A person may be well built, muscular, tall, fair, deep-voiced, short, slim, a talker, or a light upper, a leader, a musician, a painter, an architect, a man of letters and so forth. There is no limit to various divisions, various dissections that a man as a subject of inquiry, can be classified. All these qualities and traits-external, inherent or acquired go to build up his personality or impart individuality.

## Measurement of Personality (Self Description Tests)

Whenever the psychologists talk about instruments of "measuring" personality, they separate out certain aspects or traits from a unified whole person, purely as a matter of convenience. These aspects or traits do not exist as separate entitles. They are only aspects of a ways of looking at the unitary person. However, it is inevitable that we do pick the person to pieces to study and understand him. We cannot look at everything at once. It will be convenient to define the terms to refer to certain segments or respective of personality that we may wish to measure or evaluate. These terms and the meaning attached to them are briefly given below:

Temperament refers to the individual's characteristic mood, activity level, excitability and focus of concern. It includes such dimensions as cheerful-gloomy, energetic-lethargic, excited-calm, introverted-extroverted, and dominant-submissive.

Character relates to those aspects of individual behaviour to which a definite social value has been attached. Honesty, cooperatives, thrift, kindliness, and loyalty are all labels for social virtue.

Adjustment is a term used to indicate how well the individual has been able to make peace with himself and the world around him. In so far as the individual can comfortably accept himself and his world, in so far as his ways of life do not get him in trouble with his social group, he will be considered as well adjusted.

Interests refer to the variety of choices the individual makes with respect to the activities in which he engages he show preference for some, aversion to others.

Attitudes relates to tendencies to accept or reject particular groups of individuals sets of ideas or social Institutions. For the purpose of selection in employment, emphasis is normally given on the measurement of "Temperament" and "Adjustment", though occasionally the "Interest" inventories are also used. Before we describe some of the commonly used personality tests, it is worthwhile to know what a person has to do to answer any such test or inventory adequately.

# 6

# Motivation

Motivation is the driving force which causes us to achieve goals. Motivation is said to be intrinsic or extrinsic. The term is generally used for humans but, theoretically, it can also be used to describe the causes for animal Behaviour as well. This article refers to human motivation. According to various theories, motivation may be rooted in a basic need to minimize physical pain and maximize pleasure, or it may include specific needs such as eating and resting, or a desired object, goal, state of being, ideal, or it may be attributed to less-apparent reasons such as altruism, selfishness, morality, or avoiding mortality. Conceptually, motivation should not be confused with either volition or optimism. Motivation is related to, but distinct from, emotion.

## CONCEPTS OF MOTIVATION

### Intrinsic and Extrinsic Motivation

Intrinsic motivation refers to motivation that is driven by an interest or enjoyment in the task itself, and exists within the individual rather than relying on any external pressure. Intrinsic motivation has been studied by social and educational psychologists since the early 1970s. Research has found that it is usually associated with high educational achievement and enjoyment by students. Explanations of intrinsic motivation have been given in the context of Fritz Heider's attribution theory, Bandura's work on self-efficacy, and Deci and Ryan's cognitive evaluation theory. Students are likely to be intrinsically motivated if they:

- attribute their educational results to internal factors that they can control (e.g. the amount of effort they put in),
- believe they can be effective agents in reaching desired goals (i.e. the results are not determined by luck),
- are interested in mastering a topic, rather than just rote-learning to achieve good grades.

Extrinsic motivation comes from outside of the individual. Common extrinsic motivations are rewards like money and grades, coercion and threat of punishment. Competition is in general extrinsic because it encourages the performer to win and beat others, not to enjoy the intrinsic rewards of the activity. A crowd cheering on the individual and trophies are also extrinsic incentives.

Social psychological research has indicated that extrinsic rewards can lead to overjustification and a subsequent reduction in intrinsic motivation. In one study demonstrating this effect, children who expected to be (and were) rewarded with a ribbon and a gold star for drawing pictures spent less time playing with the drawing materials in subsequent observations than children who were assigned to an unexpected reward condition and to children who received no extrinsic reward.

Self-determination theory proposes that extrinsic motivation can be internalised by the individual if the task fits with their values and beliefs and therefore helps to fulfil their basic psychological needs.

## Self-control

The self-control of motivation is increasingly understood as a subset of emotional intelligence; a person may be highly intelligent according to a more conservative definition (as measured by many intelligence tests), yet unmotivated to dedicate this intelligence to certain tasks. Yale School of Management professor Victor Vroom's "expectancy theory" provides an account of when people will decide whether to exert self control to pursue a particular goal.

Drives and desires can be described as *a deficiency or need that activates Behaviour that is aimed at a goal or an incentive.* These are thought to originate within the individual and may not require external stimuli to encourage the Behaviour. Basic drives could be sparked by deficiencies such as hunger, which motivates a person to seek food; whereas more subtle drives might be the desire for praise and approval, which motivates a person to behave in a manner pleasing to others.

By contrast, the role of extrinsic rewards and stimuli can be seen in the example of training animals by giving them treats when they perform a trick correctly. The treat motivates the animals to perform the trick consistently, even later when the treat is removed from the process.

## THEORIES OF MOTIVATION

### Incentive Theory

A reward, tangible or intangible, is presented after the occurrence of an action (i.e. Behaviour) with the intent to cause the Behaviour to occur again. This is done by associating positive meaning to the Behaviour. Studies show that if the person receives the reward immediately, the effect would be greater, and decreases as duration lengthens. Repetitive action-reward combination can cause the action to become habit. Motivation comes from two sources: oneself, and other people. These two sources are called intrinsic motivation and extrinsic motivation, respectively.

Applying proper motivational techniques can be much harder than it seems. Steven Kerr notes that when creating a reward system, it can be easy to reward A, while hoping for B, and in the process, reap harmful effects that can jeopardize your goals.

A reinforcer is different from reward, in that reinforcement is intended to create a measured increase in the rate of a desirable Behaviour following the addition of something to the environment.

Incentive theory in psychology, treats motivation and Behaviour of the individual, as they are influenced by beliefs, such as engaging in activities that are expected to be profitable. Incentive theory is promoted by behavioural psychologists, such as B.F. Skinner and literalized, by behaviorists, especially by Skinner in his philosophy of Radical behaviorism, to mean that a person's actions always have social ramifications: and if actions are positively received people are more likely to act in this manner, or if negatively received people are less likely to act in this manner. Incentive theorists tend to distinguish between wanting and liking, where *liking* is a passive function evaluating a stimulus, but *wanting* adds an active process "attracting" the person towards the stimulus.

Incentive theory distinguishes itself from other motivation theories, such as drive theory, in the direction of the motivation. In incentive theory, stimuli "attract", to use the term above, a person towards them. As opposed to the body seeking to reestablish homeostasis pushing it towards the stimulus. In terms of behaviorism, *incentive theory* involves positive reinforcement: the stimulus has been conditioned to make the person happier. For instance, a person knows that eating food, drinking water, or gaining social capital will make them happier. As opposed to in *drive theory*, which involves negative reinforcement: a stimulus has been associated with the removal of the punishment— the lack of homeostasis in the body. For example, a person has come to know that if they eat when hungry, it will eliminate that negative feeling of hunger, or if they drink when thirsty, it will eliminate that negative feeling of thirst.

## Drive-reduction theories

There are a number of drive theories. The Drive Reduction Theory grows out of the concept that we have certain biological drives, such as hunger. As time passes the strength of the drive increases if it is not satisfied (in this case by eating). Upon satisfying a drive the drive's strength is reduced. The theory is based on diverse ideas from the theories of Freud to the ideas of feedback control systems, such as a thermostat.

Drive theory has some intuitive or folk validity. For instance when preparing food, the drive model appears to be compatible with sensations of rising hunger as the food is prepared, and, after the food has been consumed, a decrease in subjective hunger. There are several problems, however, that leave the validity of drive reduction open for debate. The first problem is that it does not explain how secondary reinforcers reduce drive. For example, money satisfies no biological or psychological needs, but a pay check appears to reduce drive through second-order conditioning. Secondly, a drive, such as hunger, is viewed as having a "desire" to eat, making the drive a homuncular being—a feature criticized as simply moving the fundamental problem behind this "small man" and his desires.

In addition, it is clear that drive reduction theory cannot be a complete theory of Behaviour, or a hungry human could not prepare a meal without eating the food before he finished cooking it. The ability of drive theory to cope with all kinds of Behaviour, from not satisfying a drive (by adding on other traits such as restraint), or adding additional drives for "tasty" food, which combine with drives for "food" in order to explain cooking render it hard to test.

## Cognitive Dissonance Theory

Suggested by Leon Festinger, this occurs when an individual experiences some degree of discomfort resulting from an incompatibility between two cognitions. For example, a consumer may seek to reassure himself regarding a purchase, feeling, in retrospect, that another decision may have been preferable. Another example of cognitive dissonance is when a belief and a Behaviour are in conflict. A person may wish to be healthy, believes smoking is bad for one's health, and yet continues to smoke.

# NEED THEORIES

## Need Hierarchy Theory

Abraham Maslow's theory is one of the most widely discussed theories of motivation.

The theory can be summarized as follows:

- Human beings have wants and desires which influence their Behaviour. Only unsatisfied needs influence Behaviour, satisfied needs do not.
- Since needs are many, they are arranged in order of importance, from the basic to the complex.
- The person advances to the next level of needs only after the lower level need is at least minimally satisfied.
- The further the progress up the hierarchy, the more individuality, humanness and psychological health a person will show.

The needs, listed from basic (lowest-earliest) to most complex (highest-latest) are as follows:

- Physiology (hunger, thirst, sleep, etc.)
- Safety/Security/Shelter/Health
- Belongingness/Love/Friendship
- Self-esteem/Recognition/Achievement
- Self actualization

## Herzberg's Two-factor Theory

Frederick Herzberg's two-factor theory, a.k.a. intrinsic/ extrinsic motivation, concludes that certain factors in the workplace result in job satisfaction, but if absent, they don't lead to dissatisfaction but no satisfaction.

The factors that motivate people can change over their lifetime, but "respect for me as a person" is one of the top motivating factors at any stage of life.

He distinguished between:

- Motivators; (e.g. challenging work, recognition, responsibility) which give positive satisfaction, *and*
- Hygiene factors; (e.g. status, job security, salary and fringe benefits) that do not motivate if present, but, if absent, result in demotivation.

The name Hygiene factors is used because, like hygiene, the presence will not make you healthier, but absence can cause health deterioration. The theory is sometimes called the "Motivator-Hygiene Theory" and/or "The Dual Structure Theory." Herzberg's theory has found application in such occupational fields as information systems and in studies of user satisfaction.

## Alderfer's ERG Theory

Alderfer, expanding on Maslow's hierarchy of needs, created the *ERG theory*. This theory posits that there are three groups of core needs — existence, relatedness, and growth, hence the label: ERG theory. The existence group is concerned with providing our basic material existence requirements. They include the items that Maslow considered to be physiological and safety needs. The second group of needs are those of relatedness-the desire we have for maintaining important interpersonal relationships. These social and status desires require interaction with others if they are to be satisfied, and they align with Maslow's social need and the external component of Maslow's esteem classification. Finally, Alderfer isolates growth needs' an intrinsic desire for personal development. These include the intrinsic component from Maslow's esteem category and the characteristics included under self-actualization.

## Self-determination Theory

Self-determination theory, developed by Edward Deci and Richard Ryan, focuses on the importance of intrinsic motivation in driving human Behaviour. Like Maslow's hierarchical theory and others that built on it, SDT posits a natural tendency toward growth and development. Unlike these other theories, however, SDT does not include any sort of "autopilot" for achievement, but instead requires active encouragement from the environment. The primary factors that encourage motivation and development are autonomy, competence feedback, and relatedness.

## Broad Theories

The latest approach in developing a broad, integrative theory of motivation is Temporal Motivation Theory, developed by Piers Steel and Cornelius Konig. Introduced in their 2007 *Academy of Management Review* article, it synthesizes into a single formulation the primary aspects of all other major motivational theories, including Incentive Theory, Drive Theory, Need Theory, Self-Efficacy and Goal Setting. Notably, it simplifies the field of motivation considerably and allows findings from one theory to be translated into terms of another.

Also, Achievement Motivation is an integrative perspective as outlined in the "Onion-Ring-Model of Achievement Motivation" by Heinz Schuler, George C. Thornton III, Andreas Frintrup and Rose Mueller-Hanson. It is based on the premise that performance motivation results from the way broad components of personality are directed towards performance. As a result, it includes a range of dimensions that are relevant to success at work but which are not conventionally regarded as being part of performance motivation. Especially it integrates formerly separated approaches as Need for Achievement with e.g. social motives like dominance. The Achievement Motivation Inventory (AMI) (Schuler, Thornton, Frintrup & Mueller-Hanson, 2003) is based on this theory and assesses three factors (17 separated scales) relevant to vocational and professional success.

## COGNITIVE THEORIES

### Goal-setting Theory

Goal-setting theory is based on the notion that individuals sometimes have a drive to reach a clearly defined end state. Often, this end state is a reward in itself. A goal's efficiency is affected by three features: proximity, difficulty and specificity. An ideal goal should present a situation where the time between the initiation of Behaviour and the end state is close. This explains why some children are more motivated to learn how to ride a bike than to master algebra. A goal should be moderate, not too hard or too easy to complete. In both cases, most people are not optimally motivated, as many want a challenge (which assumes some kind of insecurity of success). At the same time people want to feel that there is a substantial probability that they will succeed. Specificity concerns the description of the goal in their class. The goal should be objectively defined and intelligible for the individual. A classic example of a poorly specified goal is to get the highest possible grade. Most children have no idea how much effort they need to reach that goal.

### Models of Behaviour Change

Social-cognitive models of Behaviour change include the constructs of motivation and volition. Motivation is seen as a process that leads to the forming of behavioural intentions. Volition is seen as a process that leads from intention to actual Behaviour. In other words, motivation and volition refer to goal setting and goal pursuit, respectively. Both processes require self-regulatory efforts. Several self-regulatory constructs are needed to operate in orchestration to attain goals. An example of such a motivational and volitional construct is perceived self-efficacy. Self-efficacy is supposed to facilitate the forming of behavioural intentions, the development of action plans, and the initiation of action. It can support the translation of intentions into action.

## Unconscious Motivation

Some psychologists believe that a significant portion of human Behaviour is energized and directed by unconscious motives. According to Maslow, "Psychoanalysis has often demonstrated that the relationship between a conscious desire and the ultimate unconscious aim that underlies it need not be at all direct."

## Intrinsic Motivation and the 16 basic Desires Theory

Starting from studies involving more than 6,000 people, Professor Steven Reiss has proposed a theory that find 16 basic desires that guide nearly all human Behaviour. The desires are:

- Acceptance, the need for approval
- Curiosity, the need to learn
- Eating, the need for food
- Family, the need to raise children
- Honour, the need to be loyal to the traditional values of one's clan/ethnic group
- Idealism, the need for social justice
- Independence, the need for individuality
- Order, the need for organized, stable, predictable environments
- Physical activity, the need for exercise
- Power, the need for influence of will
- Romance, the need for sex
- Saving, the need to collect
- Social contact, the need for friends (peer relationships)
- Status, the need for social standing/importance
- Tranquility, the need to be safe
- Vengeance, the need to strike back/to win

In this model, people differ in these basic desires. These basic desires represent intrinsic desires that directly motivate a person's Behaviour, and not aimed at indirectly satisfying other desires. People may also be motivated by non-basic desires, but in this case this does not relate to deep motivation, or only as a means to achieve other basic desires.

## OTHER THEORIES OF MOTIVATION

### Controlling Motivation

The control of motivation is only understood to a limited extent. There are many different approaches of *motivation training*, but many of these are considered pseudoscientific by critics. To understand how to control motivation it is first necessary to understand why many people lack motivation.

### Employee Motivation

Workers in any organization need something to keep them working. Most times the salary of the employee is enough to keep him or her working for an organization. However, sometimes just working for salary is not enough for employees to stay at an organization. An employee must be motivated to work for a company or organization. If no motivation is present in an employee, then that employee's quality of work or all work in general will deteriorate. When motivating an audience, you can use general motivational strategies or specific motivational appeals. General motivational strategies include soft sell versus hard sell and personality type. Soft sell strategies have logical appeals, emotional appeals, advice and praise. Hard sell strategies have barter, outnumbering, pressure and rank. Also, you can consider basing your strategy on your audience personality. Specific motivational appeals focus on provable facts, feelings, right and wrong, audience rewards and audience threats.

### Drugs

Some authors, especially in the transhumanist movement, have suggested the use of "smart drugs", also known as nootropics, as "motivation-enhancers". The effects of many of these drugs on the brain are emphatically not well understood, and their legal status often makes open experimentation difficult.

## APPLICATIONS OF EDUCATION

Motivation is of particular interest to educational psychologists because of the crucial role it plays in student learning. However, the specific kind of motivation that is studied in the specialized setting of education differs qualitatively from the more general forms of motivation studied by psychologists in other fields.

Motivation in education can have several effects on how students learn and how they behave towards subject matter. It can:

1. Direct Behaviour toward particular goals
2. Lead to increased effort and energy
3. Increase initiation of, and persistence in, activities
4. Enhance cognitive processing
5. Determine what consequences are reinforcing
6. Lead to improved performance.

Because students are not always internally motivated, they sometimes need *situated motivation*, which is found in environmental conditions that the teacher creates.

The majority of new student orientation leaders at colleges and universities recognize that distinctive needs of students should be considered in regard to orientation information provided at the beginning of the higher education experience. Research done by Whyte in 1986 raised the awareness of counsellors and educators in this regard.

In 2007, the National Orientation Directors Association reprinted Cassandra B. Whyte's research report allowing readers to ascertain improvements made in addressing specific needs of students over a quarter of a century later to help with academic success.

There are two kinds of motivation:

- Intrinsic motivation occurs when people are internally motivated to do something because it either brings them pleasure, they think it is important, or they feel that what they are learning is significant. It has been shown that intrinsic motivation for education drops from grades 3-9 though the exact cause cannot be ascertained. Also, in younger students it has been shown that contextualizing material that would otherwise be presented in an abstract manner increases the intrinsic motivation of these students.

- Extrinsic motivation comes into play when a student is compelled to do something or act a certain way because of factors external to him or her (like money or good grades).

Whyte researched and reported about the importance of locus of control and academic achievement. Students tending toward a more internal locus of control are more academically successful, thus encouraging curriculum and activity development with consideration of motivation theories.

Motivation has been found to be an important element in the concept of Andragogy (what motivates the adult learner), and in treating Autism Spectrum Disorders, as in Pivotal Response Therapy.

## Sudbury Model Schools' Approach to Motivation

Sudbury Model schools adduce that the cure to the problem of procrastination, of learning in general, and particularly of scientific illiteracy is to remove once and for all what they call the underlying disease: compulsion in schools. They contend that human nature in a free society recoils from every attempt to force it into a mold; that the more requirements we pile onto children at school, the surer we are to drive them away from the material we are trying to force down their throats; that after all the drive and motivation of infants to master the world around them is legendary. They assert that schools must keep that drive alive by doing what some of them do: nurturing it on the freedom it needs to thrive.

Sudbury Model schools do not perform and do not offer evaluations, assessments, transcripts, or recommendations, asserting that they do not rate people, and that school is not a judge; comparing students to each other, or to some standard that has been set is for them a violation of the student's right to privacy and to self-determination. Students decide for themselves how to measure their progress as self-starting learners as a process of self-evaluation: real life-long learning and the proper educational evaluation for the 21st century, they adduce. According to Sudbury Model schools, this policy does not cause harm to their students as they move on to life outside the school. However, they admit it makes the process more difficult, but that such hardship is part of the students learning to make their own way, set their own standards and meet their own goals. The no-grading and no-rating policy helps to create an atmosphere free of competition among students or battles for adult approval, and encourages a positive cooperative environment amongst the student body.

## Business

At lower levels of Maslow's hierarchy of needs, such as physiological needs, money is a motivator, however it tends to have a motivating effect on staff that lasts only for a short period (in accordance with Herzberg's two-factor model of motivation). At higher levels of the hierarchy, praise, respect, recognition, empowerment and a sense of belonging are far more powerful motivators than money, as both Abraham Maslow's theory of motivation and Douglas McGregor's theory X and theory Y (pertaining to the theory of leadership) demonstrate.

Maslow has money at the lowest level of the hierarchy and shows other needs are better motivators to staff. McGregor places money in his Theory X category and feels it is a poor motivator. Praise and recognition are placed in the Theory Y category and are considered stronger motivators than money.

- Motivated employees always look for better ways to do a job.
- Motivated employees are more quality oriented.
- Motivated workers are more productive.

The average workplace is about midway between the extremes of high threat and high opportunity. Motivation by threat is a dead-end strategy, and naturally staff are more attracted to the opportunity side of the motivation curve than the threat side. Motivation is a powerful tool in the work environment that can lead to employees working at their most efficient levels of production.

Nonetheless, Steinmetz also discusses three common character types of subordinates: ascendant, indifferent, and ambivalent who all react and interact uniquely, and must be treated, managed, and motivated accordingly. An effective leader must understand how to manage all characters, and more importantly the manager must utilize avenues that allow room for employees to work, grow, and find answers independently. The assumptions of Maslow and Herzberg were challenged by a classic study at Vauxhall Motors' UK manufacturing plant. This introduced the concept of orientation to work and distinguished three main orientations: instrumental (where work is a means to an end), bureaucratic (where work is a source of status, security and immediate reward) and solidaristic (which prioritises group loyalty).

Other theories which expanded and extended those of Maslow and Herzberg included Kurt Lewin's Force Field Theory, Edwin Locke's Goal Theory and Victor Vroom's Expectancy theory. These tend to stress cultural differences and the fact that individuals tend to be motivated by different factors at different times.

According to the system of scientific management developed by Frederick Winslow Taylor, a worker's motivation is solely determined by pay, and therefore management need not consider psychological or social aspects of work. In essence, scientific management bases human motivation wholly on extrinsic rewards and discards the idea of intrinsic rewards.

In contrast, David McClelland believed that workers could not be motivated by the mere need for money—in fact, extrinsic motivation (e.g., money) could extinguish intrinsic motivation such as achievement motivation, though money could be used as an indicator of success for various motives, e.g., keeping score. In keeping with this view, his consulting firm, McBer & Company, had as its first motto "To make everyone productive, happy, and free." For McClelland, satisfaction lay in aligning a person's life with their fundamental motivations.

Elton Mayo found that the social contacts a worker has at the workplace are very important and that boredom and repetitiveness of tasks lead to reduced motivation. Mayo believed that workers could be motivated by acknowledging their social needs and making them feel important. As a result, employees were given freedom to make decisions on the job and greater attention was paid to informal work groups. Mayo named the model the Hawthorne effect. His model has been judged as placing undue reliance on social contacts at work situations for motivating employees.

In *Essentials of Organizational Behaviour*, Robbins and Judge examine recognition programs as motivators, and identify five principles that contribute to the success of an employee incentive program:

- Recognition of employees' individual differences, and clear identification of Behaviour deemed worthy of recognition
- Allowing employees to participate
- Linking rewards to performance
- Rewarding of nominators
- Visibility of the recognition process

## Online communities

Motivation to participate and contribute represents one of the most important element in the success of online communities (and virtual communities).

## NEED-BASED THEORIES OF MOTIVATION

The earliest answer to motivation involved understanding individual needs. Specifically, early researchers thought that employees try hard and demonstrate goal-driven Behaviour to satisfy needs. For example, an employee who is always walking around the office talking to people may have a need for companionship and his Behaviour may be a way of satisfying this need. There are four major theories in the need-based category: Maslow's hierarchy of needs, ERG theory, Herzberg's dual factor theory, and McClelland's acquired needs theory.

## Maslow's Hierarchy of Needs

Abraham Maslow is among the most prominent psychologists of the 20th century and the hierarchy of needs, accompanied by the pyramid representing how human needs are ranked, is an image familiar to most business students and managers. Maslow's theory is based on a simple premise: Human beings have needs that are hierarchically ranked. There are some needs that are basic to all human beings, and in their absence, nothing else matters. As we satisfy these basic needs, we start looking to satisfy higher-order needs. Once a lower-level need is satisfied, it no longer serves as a motivator.

The most basic of Maslow's needs are physiological needsphysiological needsThe need for air, food, and water.. Physiological needs refer to the need for air, food, and water. Imagine being very hungry. At that point, all your Behaviour may be directed at finding food. Once you eat, though, the search for food ceases and the promise of food no longer serves as a motivator. Once physiological needs are satisfied, people tend to become concerned about safetysafety needs. The need to be safe from danger, pain, or an uncertain future.. Are they safe from danger, pain, or an uncertain future? One level up, social needssocial needs. The need to bond with other human beings, to be loved, and to form lasting attachments with them refer to the need to bond with other human beings, to be loved, and to form lasting attachments. In fact, having no attachments can negatively affect health and well-being. The satisfaction of social needs makes esteem needsesteem needs. The desire to be respected by one's peers, feeling important, and being appreciated more salient. Esteem needs refer to the desire to be respected by one's peers, feeling important, and being appreciated. Finally, at the highest level of the hierarchy, the need for self-actualization. The quality of "becoming all you are capable of becoming." refers to "becoming all you are capable of becoming." This need manifests itself by acquiring new skills, taking on new challenges, and behaving in a way that will lead to the satisfaction of one's life goals.

Maslow's hierarchy is a systematic way of thinking about the different needs employees may have at any given point and explains different reactions they may have to similar treatment. An employee who is trying to satisfy her esteem needs may feel gratified when her supervisor praises her. However, another employee who is trying to satisfy his social needs may resent being praised by upper management in front of peers if the praise sets him apart from the rest of the group.

So, how can organizations satisfy their employees' various needs? By leveraging the various facets of the planning-organizing-leading-controlling (P-O-L-C) functions. In the long run, physiological needs may be satisfied by the person's paycheck, but it is important to remember that pay may satisfy other needs such as safety and esteem as well. Providing generous benefits, including health insurance and company-sponsored retirement plans, as well as offering a measure of job security, will help satisfy safety needs. Social needs may be satisfied by having a friendly environment, providing a workplace conducive to collaboration and communication with others. Company picnics and other social get-togethers may also be helpful if the majority of employees are motivated primarily by social needs (but may cause resentment if they are not and if they have to sacrifice a Sunday afternoon for a company picnic). Providing promotion opportunities at work, recognizing a person's accomplishments verbally or through more formal reward systems, job titles that communicate to the employee that one has achieved high status within the organization are among the ways of satisfying esteem needs. Finally, self-actualization needs may be satisfied by providing development and growth opportunities on or off the job, as well as by assigning interesting and challenging work. By making the effort to satisfy the different needs each employee may have at a given time, organizations may ensure a more highly motivated workforce.

## ERG Theory

ERG theory of Clayton Alderfer is a modification of Maslow's hierarchy of needs. Instead of the five needs that are hierarchically organized, Alderfer proposed that basic human needs may be grouped under three categories, namely, Existenceexistence, this need corresponds to Maslow's physiological and safety needs., Relatednessrelatedness, This need corresponds to social needs., and Growthgrowth. This need refers to Maslow's esteem and self-actualization. Existence need corresponds to Maslow's physiological and safety needs, relatedness corresponds to social needs, and growth need refers to Maslow's esteem and self actualization.

ERG theory's main contribution to the literature is its relaxation of Maslow's assumptions. For example, ERG theory does not rank needs in any particular order and explicitly recognizes that more than one need may operate at a given time. Moreover, the theory has a "frustration-regression" hypothesis, suggesting that individuals who are frustrated in their attempts to satisfy one need may regress to another one. For example, someone who is frustrated by the lack of growth opportunities in his job and slow progress toward career goals may regress to relatedness needs and start spending more time socializing with one's coworkers. The implication of this theory is that we need to recognize the multiple needs that may be driving an individual at a given point to understand his Behaviour and to motivate him.

## Two-Factor Theory

Frederick Herzberg approached the question of motivation in a different way. By asking individuals what satisfies them on the job and what dissatisfies them, Herzberg came to the conclusion that aspects of the work environment that satisfy employees are very different from aspects that dissatisfy them. Herzberg labelled factors causing dissatisfaction of workers as "hygiene" factors because these factors were part of the context in which the job was performed, as opposed to the job itself. Hygiene factorshygiene factors. The factors that include company policies, supervision, working conditions, salary, safety, and security on the job included company policies, supervision, working conditions, salary, safety, and security on the job. To illustrate, imagine that you are working in an unpleasant work environment. Your office is too hot in the summer and too cold in the winter. You are being harassed and mistreated. You would certainly be miserable in such a work environment. However, if these problems were solved (your office temperature is just right and you are not harassed at all), would you be motivated? Most likely, you would take the situation for granted. In fact, many factors in our work environment are things that we miss when they are absent, but take for granted if they are present.

In contrast, motivators, the factors that are intrinsic to the job, such as achievement, recognition, interesting work, increased responsibilities, advancement, and growth opportunities are factors that are intrinsic to the job, such as achievement, recognition, interesting work, increased responsibilities, advancement, and growth opportunities. According to Herzberg's research, motivators are the conditions that truly encourage employees to try harder.

Herzberg's research, which is summarized in the figure above, has received its share of criticism. One criticism relates to the classification of the factors as hygiene or motivator. For example, pay is viewed as a hygiene factor. However, pay is not necessarily a contextual factor and may have symbolic value by showing employees that they are being recognized for their contributions as well as communicating to them that they are advancing within the company. Similarly, quality of supervision or relationships employees form with their supervisors may determine whether they are assigned interesting work, whether they are recognized for their potential, and whether they take on more responsibilities. Despite its limitations, the two-factor theory can be a valuable aid to managers because it points out that improving the environment in which the job is performed goes only so far in motivating employees.

Plaques and other recognition awards may motivate employees if these awards fit with the company culture and if they reflect a sincere appreciation of employee accomplishments.

## FACTORS OF MOTIVATION

Factors within a human being or animal that arouse and direct goal-oriented behaviour. Motivation has long been a central subject of study in psychology. Early researchers, influenced by Charles Darwin, ascribed much of animal and human behaviour to instinct. Sigmund Freud believed that much of human behaviour was also based on irrational instinctive urges or unconscious motives. Walter B. Cannon proposed that basic human drives served homeostatic functions by directing energies toward the reduction of physiological tensions. Behavioural psychologists, in contrast, stress the importance of external goals in prompting action, while humanistic psychologists examine the role of felt needs. Cognitive psychologists have found that a motive sensitizes a person to information relating to that motive: a hungry subject, for example, will perceive food stimuli as larger than other stimuli.

The intentions, desires, goals, and needs that determine human and animal Behaviour. An inquiry is made into a person's motives in order to explain that person's actions. Different roles have been assigned to motivational factors in the causation of Behaviour. Some have defined motivation as a nonspecific energizing of all Behaviour. Others define it as recruiting and directing Behaviour, selecting which of many possible actions the organism will perform. The likely answer is that both aspects exist. More specific determinants of action may be superimposed on a dimension of activation or arousal that affects a variety of actions nonselectively. The situation determines what the animal does; arousal level affects the vigour, promptness, or persistence with which the animal does it.

Early drive theorists saw motivated Behaviour as adjunct to physiological mechanisms of homeostasis, that is, the mechanisms by which the body regulates internal variables such as temperature, blood sugar level, and the volume and concentration of body fluids. Thus, motivated Behaviour forms part of a negative-feedback loop, an arrangement characteristic of regulatory systems.

However, the homeostatic model faces difficulties. First, not all "basic biological drives" work this way. Second, motivated Behaviour can be influenced by external as well as internal factors. Since these external influences are not coupled with the animal's internal state, they can lead to Behaviour that does not promote homeostasis and may even threaten it. To add to the complexity, internal and external factors are not independent and additive; rather they interact with each other. In such cases, internal influences affect Behaviour by setting the animal's responsiveness to certain external signals. The interaction occurs in the opposite direction as well: external signals can affect internal state. Third, especially in humans, vigorous and persistent goal-directed Behaviour can occur in the absence of any physiological need.

Even relatively simple motives can be influenced by much more than the existing internal and external situation. They respond to potential or expected factors, as registered by cognitive apparatus. Even relatively simple motives such as hunger and thirst are responsive to cognitive factors.

To a hungry rat, food becomes a goal. The rat will make various responses, including arbitrary learned ones or operants, that lead to contact with food. A rat can be trained to do whatever else is necessary (within its capabilities) to attain its goal. It is this flexibility of goal-directed Behaviour that justifies the concept of motivation. If an animal will do whatever is necessary to obtain food, it must want food. Internal factors then may act by setting the goal status of environmental commodities: the effect of hunger is to make food a goal.

There is a question as to how Behaviour can be guided by a state or event (goal attainment) that does not yet exist. Modern approaches to this question lean heavily on cognitive concepts. Mammals, birds, and even some insects can represent to themselves a nonexistent state of affairs. They can represent what a goal object is (search images): a chimpanzee may show behavioural signs of surprise if a different food is substituted for the usual one. They can represent where it is (cognitive maps): a digger wasp remembers the location of its nest relative to arbitrary landmarks, and will fly to the wrong place if the landmarks are moved.

If this idea is generalized, motivated Behaviour can be thought of as guided by a feedback control system with a set point. A set point establishes a goal state which the control system seeks to bring about. Behaviour is controlled, not by present external or internal stimuli alone, but by a comparison between the existing state of affairs and a desired state of affairs, that is, the set point or goal, registered or specified within the brain. The animal then acts to reduce the difference between the existing and the desired state of affairs.

This way of looking at motivation helps bridge the gap between simple motives in animals and complex ones in humans. If to be motivated is to do whatever is necessary to bring about an imagined state of affairs, then human motives can literally be as complex, and be projected as far into the future, as human imaginations permit.

Another approach to motivation comes from ethology, which has formed links with cognitive psychology. The broken-wing display of the piping plover provides an example. If a predator approaches a nest with eggs, the parent bird may behave as if injured (hence easy prey) and thus lead the intruder away from the nest. This action pattern is characteristic of the species and unlearned in its gross topography; yet the bird monitors the intruder's Behaviour and modulates the display accordingly. It may approach more closely and intensify the display if the intruder is not at first diverted from its path. Thus a species-typical action pattern can be used in ways suggestive of purpose and goal direction: the bird modifies it as necessary to promote the goal of diverting the intruder.

Motivation and emotion are closely related. Indeed, it has been argued that emotions are the true motivators and that other factors internal, situational, and cognitive take hold of Behaviour by way of the emotions they evoke. In the simplest case, pleasure and displeasure have been recognized for centuries as having motivational force. In more complex cases, the role of cognitive operations, such as how an individual feels about an event, as well as what is done about it, can depend heavily on how an individual thinks about it.

The culture in which an individual is raised has a powerful effect on how the individual behaves. It has been argued that culture teaches its members what to believe are the consequences of a specific action (cognitive), and how the individuals should feel about those consequences or about the actions themselves (emotional/motivational).

# 7

# Significance of Employee Motivation

Employee motivation is the level of energy, commitment, and creativity that a company's workers apply to their jobs. In the increasingly competitive business environment of recent years, finding ways to motivate employees has become a pressing concern for many managers. In fact, a number of different theories and methods of employee motivation have emerged, ranging from monetary incentives to increased involvement and empowerment. Employee motivation can sometimes be particularly problematic for small businesses, where the owner often has spent so many years building a company that he/she finds it difficult to delegate meaningful responsibilities to others. But entrepreneurs should be mindful of such pitfalls, for the effects of low employee motivation on small businesses can be devastating. Some of the problems associated with unmotivated workers include complacency, declining morale, and widespread discouragement. If allowed to continue, these problems can reduce productivity, earnings, and competitiveness in a small business.

On the other hand, small businesses can also provide an ideal atmosphere for fostering employee motivation, because employees are able to see the results of their contributions in a more immediate way than in large firms. Besides increasing productivity and competitiveness, a highly motivated work force can allow a small business owner to relinquish day-today, operational control and instead concentrate on long-term strategies to grow the business. "Workers really do want to be inspired about their work, and when they are, they work better, smarter, and harder," business coach Don Maruska told *Entrepreneur.*

Moreover, a business that institutes effective ways—whether tangible (such as a financial bonus) or intangible (say, a plum assignment for an upcoming project)—of rewarding employees for good work can be an invaluable tool in employee retention. "People enjoy working, and tend to thrive in organizations that create positive work environments," one business researcher told *HR Focus.* "[They thrive in] environments where they can make a difference, and where most people in the organization are competent and pulling together to move the company forward. Appropriately structured reward and recognition programs are important, but not exclusive, components in this mix."

## What Motivates?

One approach to employee motivation has been to view "add-ins" to an individual's job as the primary factors in improving performance. Endless mixes of employee benefits—such as health care, life insurance, profit sharing, employee stock ownership plans, exercise facilities, subsidized meal plans, child care availability, company cars, and more—have been used by companies in their efforts to maintain happy employees in the belief that happy employees are motivated employees.

Many modern theorists, however, propose that the motivation an employee feels toward his or her job has less to do with material rewards than with the design of the job itself. Studies as far back as 1950 have shown that highly segmented and simplified jobs resulted in lower employee morale and output. Other consequences of low employee motivation include absenteeism and high turnover, both of which are very costly for any company. As a result, "job enlargement" initiatives began to crop up in major companies in the 1950s.

On the academic front, Turner and Lawrence suggested that there are three basic characteristics of a "motivating" job:

1. It must allow a worker to feel personally responsible for a meaningful portion of the work accomplished. An employee must feel ownership of and connection with

the work he or she performs. Even in team situations, a successful effort will foster an awareness in an individual that his or her contributions were important in accomplishing the group's tasks.

2. It must provide outcomes which have intrinsic meaning to the individual. Effective work that does not lead a worker to feel that his or her efforts matter will not be maintained. The outcome of an employee's work must have value to himself or herself and to others in the organization.
3. It must provide the employee with feedback about his or her accomplishments. A constructive, believable critique of the work performed is crucial to a worker's motivation to improve.

While terminology changes, the tenets of employee motivation remain relatively unchanged from findings over half a century ago. Today's buzzwords include "empowerment," "quality circles," and "teamwork." All of these terms demonstrate the three characteristics of motivating jobs set forth in the theory of Turner and Lawrence. Empowerment gives autonomy and allows an employee to have ownership of ideas and accomplishments, whether acting alone or in teams. Quality circles and the increasing occurrence of teams in today's work environments give employees opportunities to reinforce the importance of the work accomplished by members as well as receive feedback on the efficacy of that work.

In small businesses, which may lack the resources to enact formal employee motivation programs, managers can nonetheless accomplish the same basic principles. In order to help employees feel like their jobs are meaningful and that their contributions are valuable to the company, the small business owner needs to communicate the company's purpose to employees. This communication should take the form of words as well as actions. In addition, the small business owner should set high standards for employees, but also remain supportive of their efforts when goals cannot be reached. It may also be helpful to allow employees as much autonomy and flexibility as possible in how their jobs are performed. Creativity will be encouraged if honest mistakes are corrected but not punished. Finally, the small business owner should take steps to incorporate the vision of employees for the company with his or her own vision. This will motivate employees to contribute to the small business's goals, as well as help prevent stagnation in its direction and purpose.

## Motivation Methods

There are as many different methods of motivating employees today as there are companies operating in the global business environment. Still, some strategies are prevalent across all organizations striving to improve employee motivation. The best employee motivation efforts will focus on what the employees deem to be important. It may be that employees within the same department of the same organization will have different motivators. Many organizations today find that flexibility in job design and reward systems has resulted in employees' increased longevity with the company, improved productivity, and better morale.

***Empowerment.*** Giving employees more responsibility and decision-making authority increases their realm of control over the tasks for which they are held responsible and better equips them to carry out those tasks. As a result, feelings of frustration arising from being held accountable for something one does not have the resources to carry out are diminished. Energy is diverted from self-preservation to improved task accomplishment.

***Creativity and Innovation.*** At many companies, employees with creative ideas do not express them to management for fear that their input will be ignored or ridiculed. Company approval and toeing the company line have become so ingrained in some working environments that both the employee and the organization suffer. When the power to create in the organization is pushed down from the top to line personnel, employees who know a job, product, or service best are given the opportunity to use their ideas to improve it. The power to create motivates employees and benefits the organization in having a more flexible work force, using more wisely the experience of its employees, and increasing the exchange of ideas and information among employees and departments. These improvements also create an openness to change that can give a company the ability to respond quickly to market changes and sustain a first mover advantage in the marketplace.

***Learning.*** If employees are given the tools and the opportunities to accomplish more, most will take on the challenge. Companies can motivate employees to achieve more by committing to perpetual enhancement of employee skills. Accreditation and licensing programs for employees are an increasingly popular and effective way to bring about growth in employee knowledge and motivation. Often, these programs improve employees' attitudes toward the client and the company, while bolstering self-confidence. Supporting this assertion, an analysis of factors which influence motivation-to-learn found that it is directly related to the extent to which training participants believe that such participation will affect their job or career utility. In other words, if the body of knowledge gained can be applied to the work to be accomplished, then the acquisition of that knowledge will be a worthwhile event for the employee and employer.

***Quality of life.*** The number of hours worked each week by American workers is on the rise, and many families have two adults working those increased hours. Under these circumstances, many workers are left wondering how to meet the demands of their lives beyond the workplace. Often, this concern occurs while at work and may reduce an employee's productivity and morale. Companies that have instituted flexible employee arrangements have gained motivated employees whose productivity has increased. Programs incorporating flextime, condensed workweeks, or job sharing, for example, have been successful in focusing overwhelmed employees toward the work to be done and away from the demands of their private lives.

***Monetary incentive.*** For all the championing of alternative motivators, money still occupies a major place in the mix of motivators. The sharing of a company's profits gives incentive to employees to produce a quality product, perform a quality service, or improve the quality of a process within the company. What benefits the company directly benefits the employee. Monetary and other rewards are being given to employees for generating cost-savings or process-improving ideas, to boost productivity and reduce absenteeism. Money is effective when it is directly tied to an employee's ideas or accomplishments. Nevertheless, if not coupled with other, nonmonetary motivators, its motivating effects are short-lived. Further, monetary incentives can prove counterproductive if not made available to all members of the organization.

***Other incentives.*** Study after study has found that the most effective motivators of workers are nonmonetary. Monetary systems are insufficient motivators, in part because expectations often exceed results and because disparity between salaried individuals may divide rather than unite employees. Proven nonmonetary positive motivators foster team spirit and include recognition, responsibility, and advancement. Managers who recognize the "small wins" of employees, promote participatory environments, and treat employees with fairness and respect will find their employees to be more highly motivated. One company's managers brainstormed to come up with 30 powerful rewards that cost little or nothing to implement. The most effective rewards, such as letters of commendation and time off from work, enhanced personal fulfilment and self-respect. Over the longer term, sincere praise and personal gestures are far more effective and more economical than awards of money alone. In the end, a program that combines monetary reward systems and satisfies intrinsic, self-actualizing needs may be the most potent employee motivator.

## EXPECTANCY THEORY OF EMPLOYEE MOTIVATION

The significance of employee motivation as the panacea of productivity in organizations is illustrated by the volumes of literature on motivation and human productivity. For example, social theorists are of the view that employees are motivated by their needs and they develop through and in relationship with others (Dawson, 1993). The implication of the preceding statement is that when there is synergy between employees' needs and organizational needs, they – employees – will be more acquiescent to productive tendencies than when their needs are not gratified. Invariably, the balancing of employees' labour with their social needs and expectations is necessary in all organizations, and consequently Vaida (2003) states that incentives are used to reward outstanding performance and to sustain efficiency in work processes. Furthermore, Hoy and

Miskel (1991:191) concur that incentives include money, power and idyllic investments as well as general incentives that are non-material. However, an over-emphasis on incentives and monetary gain overlooks the fact that people make decisions about their own behaviour. Boje and Rosile (2004) thus conclude that motivation theories – which accentuate incentives more than other motivators – incorporate the death wish since social control instrumentalities, valences, and need strengths are manipulated by managers to induce employees' productivity. In addition, the "one shoe fits all" approach of giving incentives may not have the desired effect because of the uniqueness of employees' needs, personalities and behaviour.

One of the assumptions of the Expectancy Theory is that people make decisions among alternative plans of behaviour based on their perceptions [expectancies] of the degree to which a given behaviour will lead to desired outcomes. Typically, in employment relations transactions such as payment for services rendered occur between employers [providers of reward and recognition] and employees [service providers] (Dawson, 1993). Other things being equal, Robinson (1992) argues that there is a link between transactional leadership and Stimulus-Response theories because incentives [in the form of a reward, salary, award etcetera] are used to ensure the reproduction and repetition of desired responses and outcomes in organizations. However, it is observed that in most transactional relationships the power and authority of managers are absolute and incontestable to the extent that employees become automatons in the production system. As a result, those who are viewed to be productive get the rewards while those who are identified not to be productive and competitive are pushed out of the system (Hemming, 1980).

There is a subtle link between expectancy, effort, productivity and reward. Werner (2002, p.335) states that a person will exert a high effort if he/she believes there is reasonable probability that the effort will lead to the attainment of an organizational goal, and the attainment of the organizational goal will become an instrument through which that person will attain his/her personal goals. If this is the case with employees, one would thus conclude that organizational goals will be elevated above personal goals, and this may account for the use of incentives and rewards to recognize the effort made by employees. In the same vein, the Beehive Survey found out that whilst over 60% of organizations in South Africa recognized that pay is just one way to motivate employees, less than 40% created long-term incentives across all levels (Sacht *et al*, 2003). One may argue that inadequate monetary benefits may lead to discontentment and disenchantment that are illustrated by shoddy work and a high labour turnover in some organizations. For example, the Salary Moves and Labour Trends Beehive Survey – conducted by Deloitte and Touché in South African organizations in 2003 – indicated that labour turnover [as a result of dissatisfaction with salaries and incentives] was 15% among key specialists and 17% for general monthly paid employees (Brindle, 2003).

From the preceding discussion it can be deduced that there is a relationship between pay and incentives and cognitive dissonance theories which propound that productivity is a result of the perceived difference between what is expected or desired as fair and reasonable reward – individual motivation and what is experienced in the job situation – organizational incentives. The following discussion will provide an in-depth discussion on Expectancy Theory as documented in literature sources.

The literature study entailed a critical perusal of literature sources using the following key words which have a bearing on the topic: motivation; intrinsic motivation; extrinsic motivation; expectancy theory; locus of control; internal locus of control; external locus of control; goals; potential; effort; equity and outcome. The following discussion will focus on the definition of concepts and how they link with expectancy theory, motivation and locus of control.

## DEFINITION OF CONCEPTS

***Motivation:*** According to Passer and Smith (2004) the concept "motivation" refers to a process that influences the direction, persistence and vigour of goal-directed behaviour. In the same vein, Coetsee (2003) states that the term "motivation" refers to the interaction between forces within an individual and his/her environment. Kreitner and Kinicki (2007) are of the view that in the present context motivation represents psychological processes that cause the arousal, direction, and persistence of voluntary action. Similarly, Werner (2002) describes motivation as being intentional [a person makes a choice to act] and directional [indicating the presence of a driving force aimed at attaining a specific goal]. Applied in the work situation, motivation implies the willingness of individuals and teams to exert high levels of effort to attain organizational goals, conditioned by the effort's capability to satisfy individual and team needs (Coetsee, 2003). From the preceding discussion it can be deduced that there is no single and universal definition for the concept "motivation". However, Boje and Rosile (2004) regard motivation as a repressive and puritanical ideology, a way to manipulate performance (and satisfaction), where visions of self-actualisation, (higher) need gratification and true happiness are fulfilled in acts of work. Boje and Rosile's view may seem too negative to ponder, but the rise of capitalism has been propelled by high intensity motivation programmes which at times turned people into production fanatics.

***Locus of control:*** According to Lefcourt (1976), the term "locus of control" is a generalised expectancy for internal as opposed to external control of reinforcements. In the same vein, Coetsee (2003) states that locus of control refers to what one ascribes responsibility or blames for what is happening in one's life. The dichotomy between external and internal loci of control is aptly captured by Rotter (1975) when he states that internality and externality represent two ends of a continuum, not as either/or typology. A locus of control indicates the influence that circumstances/environment or individual characters/traits have on directing people's activities. Research indicates that people perform better when they have a moderate to strong internal locus of control. In addition, Coetsee (2003) contends that managers with an internal locus of control are comfortable with participative management styles while managers with external locus of control are more authoritarian. The position of the locus of control is significant because all things being equal, people will either see themselves as masters of their destiny or victims of circumstances. However, the latter being true, Maltby, Day and Macaskill (2007) are of the opinion that people with an external locus of control tend to be more stressed and prone to clinical depression. Furthermore, external locus of control makes people vulnerable to manipulation and open to abuse since externals would depend largely on the reinforcement by significant others for everything they do. Conversely, internals are more at peace with themselves and they take responsibility for their mistakes and successes. The following discussion on elements of the expectancy theory is linked to locus of control.

## ELEMENTS OF THE EXPECTANCY THEORY

### Goals/expectations

Many people who study trends in performance and motivation in industries tend to agree that goal-setting and explication generates confidence in the workforce. Clarifying the meaning of goals is necessary for forging a shared understanding of what the organization wants to accomplish. It suffices to state that goals assist in focusing the energy of workers towards attainment of organizational visions, and Coetsee (2003) contends that top performing people are goal-directed. It may be concluded that goal-setting ensures focus on common values, raising of expectations about what ought to be achieved and what can be achieved, growing commitment to improving quality, greater confidence of stakeholders in the work of an organization, and capturing the vision of the organization within manageable short-term goals.

Inasmuch as it is evident that goals enable employees to focus on achievement of organizational vision, fundamental aims and strategic objectives, Dawson (1993) argues that goal-setting ensures development of quality assurance indicators for job performance. The assumption here is that when employees know and understand what is expected from them [the goals], when those expectations are to be met [the timeframe], and how those expectations should be met [ *modus operandi*], they will be motivated to achieve those goals within the set timeframes. Evidently, the proliferation of reciprocal determinism implies that unlocking of potential is a prerequisite for employees' productivity.

### Unlocking Potential

The term potential refers to "possible, as opposed to actual; capable of becoming or latent excellence or ability that may or may not be developed". Coetsee (2003) defines potential as being able to achieve something such as goals or to become something. From the preceding definition of the term "potential" it is noteworthy to state that potential is latent [hibernating/hiding/incubated] excellence which need to be developed, unlocked or unfurled. Mabale (2004) aptly states that one of the most important functions in organizations is to ensure appropriate unfolding of potential and its optimum utilisation.

It is assumed that unlocking of potential is linked to empowerment. The term "empowerment" means giving power, authority and influence which lead to the growth process and changes that are never ending and self-initiated. Unfolding potential also implies that work should be allocated with due consideration of employees' skills, aptitude and abilities [horses for courses] in order not to set them up for failure. Coetsee (2003) thus concludes that the levels of unlocking potential are ability to cope; believing in successful outcomes; and commitment to the realization of goals since when people are empowered they have the confidence to attempt anything.

## Effort

According to *Your Dictionary.com* (sv "effort"), the term effort implies the using of energy to get something done, exertion of mental strength, a try, a product or result of working or trying. In the same vein, Coetsee (2003) is of the view that effort leads to achievement of the longings to be fulfilled – goals or expectations – which epitomize performance and the outcomes that generate a feeling of success. Effort is related to the action of trying, exertion of strength or endeavour. In most cases effort is linked to a series of actions that have to be performed as indicated by grouping of tasks and the division of work, allocation of duties, authority and responsibility without abdicating responsibility, relationships between people, collaboration and coordination as well as forged common objective or motive to achieve goals.

## Equity

The direct definition of the term "equity" in Accounting – as a school subject – refers to the extent to which assets have been funded by the owner. While this definition seems far-fetched in Organizational Behaviour, the relevance of the concept should be understood from the perspective of the equity theory which focuses on *fairness and justice*. The Equity theory is based on the view that employees should receive their fair share for input – aggregated as skills and effort – for the attainment of organizational outcomes. Equity focuses on equivalence of [the owner's] input and [the organization's] output. While Vroom used the term valence to refer to positive or negative values people place on outcomes, Porter and Lawler used the term value of reward to indicate that people desire a combination of outcomes and rewards for what they put into their jobs. It is noted that incongruence and imbalances between the input the output provides ground for inequity and de-motivation. In the same vein, Kew *et al.* (2007) contend that feelings of inequity revolve around a person's evaluation of whether he or she receives adequate rewards to compensate for his or contributive inputs. Striking a balance or maintaining a state of equilibrium between input and output is essential for enhancing performance.

## Performance

Commitment and engagement are critical components for performance. According to Coetsee (2003), performance is the realisation of goals and meeting of expectations. On the other hand, Kew *et al.* (2007) define performance management as a continuous cycle of improving job performance with goal-setting, feedback, coaching, rewards and positive reinforcement. The significance of goal-setting for improving employees' performance has been discussed. According to Kew *et al.* (2007), the following points are necessary for feedback in a high-performance institution: focus on performance not personalities; give specific feedback linked to learning goals and performance outcome goals; give feedback as soon as possible; give feedback for improvement, not just results; and pair feedback with clear expectations for improvement.

Performance feedback should be based on accurate and credible data. In this fashion, employees will understand criteria used for performance evaluation and be more prepared to accept recommendations for improvement of performance. Elements of the Peak Performance Model such as capacity to perform, commitment to performance, and motivating climate (Coetsee, 2003) are therefore critical for enhancing performance. Additionally, managers play an important role in sustaining employees' commitment to perform their jobs because alienation to products of production, low morale and lack of commitment which are indicators of job dissatisfaction, may set in if the elements Coetsee alludes to are neglected. The following discussion focuses on the link between forces in an individual and organizational forces in motivation.

## INDIVIDUAL FORCES AND THE ORGANIZATIONAL FORCES

Just as Lawler and Porter focused on value of outcomes in the form of rewards, Charlton (2000) notes that extrinsic and intrinsic rewards have reciprocal motivational effects since they represent effective methods of energising, promoting and maintaining employees' behaviour. Schultz (2004,) also notes that a reward is first and foremost a people issue: it is about motivating them, reshaping and refocusing their behaviours, and inducing them to accept organizational values. Nevertheless, one should be cognisant of the fact that rewards may or may not have a motivating effect on the basis of their attractiveness to the individual. For this reason, Mayo's conclusions in the Hawthorne Experiments on motivation were that employees' are motivated by more than pay and conditions. In some cases, the need for recognition and a sense of belonging may be important motivators which influence employees' groups and teams to perform beyond expectations.

It is essential to note that motivation ensures voluntary unfolding of employees' talents and potential for the benefit of the organization. To this end, Dawson (1993) regards motivation as the extent to which employees acknowledge the legitimacy of and seek to achieve organizational objectives and interests. The significance of this argument is that the expectancy theory predicts that employees will be motivated when they believe that putting in more effort will yield better job performance. In the same vein, better job performance will lead to organizational rewards, such as an increase in salary or benefits, and these predicted organizational rewards are valued by employees.

## Environmental Factors

The external environment represents factors outside organizations that affect personal functioning and it includes technological acceleration, the effect of social and other groups outside the work environment; and individuals constantly compare personal progress with personal achievement in organizations. All things being equal, the job context environment is the task environment within which an individual functions, and employees who interact with their work environments – not only being defined by such environments but also defining such environments – have a higher degree of motivation than those who accept the *status quo* and let the work environment define them. Similarly, Passer and Smith (2004) contend that the likelihood that people will engage in particular behaviours in given situations is influenced by two factors: expectancy and reinforcement value. Passer and Smith's view makes sense for people with an external locus and employees with a strong internal locus of control. In the same vein, Bandura regards reciprocal determinism as a situation where internal determinants and external determinants interact and cohere to enhance employee motivation (Burger, 2004). The view expressed by Bandura's reciprocal determinism addresses questions whether employees define the work environment or the work environment defines the employees. Subsequently, Van Dyk (2002) concludes that just as individuals can only meet their expectations and needs by joining organizations, they translate their expectations into personal goals before they join organizations.

The preceding discussion clearly indicates that people are not victims of their environments [as arguments for external locus always infer], but they are masters, inventors and creators of new vistas for their lives [as it is always stated in arguments for internal locus]. Werner (2002) rightly observes that people strive towards maturity – through unfolding of their potential – in their work since they experience growth in the context of their work. One would therefore expect creation of the following conditions in order to improve employees' motivation:

- Communication: managers explain expectations and the organization's performance standards (Dawson, 1993);

- Listening: managers listen to employees' views regarding expectations on performance standards;
- Encouragement: managers provide encouragement in order to motivate and inspire employees to improve performance and aspire for quality (Chetty, 1997);
- Agreement: managers forge collective agreements on performance standards and operational strategies (Sono, 2002); and
- Reporting: managers provide feedback on successes and levels of performance of employees as a strategy for improving the quality of production (Van der Westhuizen, 2002).

The creation of an environment that is appropriate for personal growth and development provides enough motivation for working in an organization. When conditions in the organization do not satisfy an employees' physiological, safety and security, acceptance, love and self actualisation needs employees tend to become demotivated, lethargic, unproductive and grumpy.

## Expectations

Employers and employees have expectations when they come into an employment relationship. Kotter (1976) contends that the first group of expectations represents what an individual expects to receive from an organization and what the organization expects to give the individual while the second group of expectations includes what an individual expects to offer the organization and what the organization expects to receive from the individual. The two types of expectations defined above indicate a give-and take relationship which is intended to create a win-win situation for employees and organizations. According to Van Dyk (2002), expectations are contained in psychological contracts which Porter *et al.* (1975) regard as the "dynamics of organization-individual interactions", and cooperative contracts. Similarly, Kreitner and Kinicki (2007) define a psychological contract as an individual's perception about the terms and conditions of a reciprocal exchange with another party. Schein (1980) aptly summarizes the value of expectations when he states:

*... it is my central hypothesis that whether a person generates commitment loyalty, and enthusiasm for the organization and its goals... depends to a large measure on two conditions: (1) the degree to which his own expectations of what the organization will provide him with what he owes organization match with what the organization's are of what it will give and get; (2) assuming there is agreement on expectations what actually is to be exchanged...*

It can be construed that it is necessary for employers and employees to communicate their expectations.

## Esteem

According to Robinson (1992), people want to be secured, to be in control, to seek meaning in the work they do, and to be in winning teams rather than losing teams. The points raised by Robinson are essentials for employees' esteem needs. In addition, employees are more likely to identify with the organization when they have worked there for a long time; the organization is well-known in public [accessibility]; they know who their competitors are and how their organization is distinct from these competitors [comparative fit]; and when the employees are at work discussing issues related to their work place [normative fit] (Turner, 1999). The satisfaction of esteem needs builds congruence between the employee's self-concept and self-esteem. An employee whose esteem needs are assuaged is confident in his or her work, and he or she can operate at higher levels of motivation even if valences and contingencies for motivation are minimal. Similarly, Dawson (1993) notes that every employee needs to be accepted as a valued member of a social grouping in order to build his/her confidence within a community of peers.

# CRITERIA FOR MOTIVATION

## Effective Leadership

The term "leadership" has different interpretations, and only a few will be provided. The *World Book Dictionary* (1989, sv 'leadership') defines the concept "leadership" as "control; being in charge". According to *Webster's New World Encyclopaedia* (1990, sv 'leadership') the concept "leadership" refers to "a process or technique of managing, organising and operating a business." According to Prinsloo (1991), the concept "leadership" implies "inducing stakeholders to act for certain goals that represent values and motivations as well as aspirations and expectations of school managers and stakeholders." Moorhead and Griffin (1989) define the concept "leadership" as:

*... The use of non-coercive influence to direct and co-ordinate activities of group members towards goal accomplishment. Leadership is the set of characteristics attributed to those who are perceived to employ such an influence effectively...*

A few essential points can be lifted from the preceding definitions such as inducing, control, being in charge etcetera. However, the definition that carries more weight is the one provided by Moorhead and Griffin, "non-coercive influence". Leadership implies making people do what the leader wants, but this is not done in an aggressive manner.

Managers are value-directed, and they understand where the organization wants to go [vision], and they point out the direction to their followers. Invariably, machines, materials, methods, markets, and money (five m's) do not provide leadership, even though they are important for the growth and development of an organization (Mabale, 2004), and without effective leadership the factors such as money, equipment, people, and machinery are sterile and useless (Kroon, 1990). It is in this context that Robinson (1992) states:

*... A leader is not appointed because he knows everything and can make every decision. He is appointed to bring together the knowledge that is available and then to create the prerequisites for the work to be done. He creates systems that enable him to delegate responsibility for day-to-day operations...*

Through the astute leadership that is provided in an organization, employees may develop a positive work ethic. In such organizations, employees are willing to achieve organizational objectives and targets because they know what is expected of them. One may conclude that effective leaders do not only blaze the trail and clear stumbling blocks that could hamper productivity; they also set high standards for job performance.

## Goal-setting and Attainment of Objectives

Organizational goals direct the actions of both the employers and employees. As a result, the setting of simple and specific goals which have measurable outcomes assists employees to know clearly what they are supposed to do. In addition, organizations should set attainable and realistic goals for employees and not set employees up for failure with unrealistic expectations. There is therefore sense in what Pascale and Athos (1981) in *The Art of Japanese Management*, as cited in Mwosa (1987), noted when they wrote:

*... Managerial reality is not an absolute; rather, it is socially and culturally determined across all cultures and in all societies. Human beings coming together to perform certain collective acts encounter certain problems that are related to establishing, directing, co-coordinating and motivating. Culture affects how these problems are perceived and how they are resolved. Social learning also establishes horizons of perception...*

Managers are expected to set goals which are within the employees' performance range, and that is why the potential, aptitude, abilities, skills, knowledge and values of employees should be considered before one is engaged to do the work. For example, employing a traditional and conservative Catholic in an abortion clinic may not be advisable – on moral and value-consideration – even if that person is a highly skilled surgeon. It is also necessary to bear in mind that goal-setting should also anticipate the outcomes to be attained. Commitment to the tasks at hand becomes easier when one has a mental construct of what the end of the product of the whole undertaking will be. Coetsee (2003) states that aligned commitment is the extent to which employees understand and live the shared vision of the organization.

## Unlocking/Unfolding of Potential and Effort

Mathibe (1998) notes that in line with industrial needs for productivity and competitiveness, competencies and skills acquisition are the *sine qua non* for task performance in present-day production systems. The words of Frederick Taylor of getting "the right man for the right job" are relevant here because organizations that want to gain competitive advantage over competitors need skilled and well-trained employees.

Additionally, employees that are skilled and trained for the jobs do not feel threatened, either by the changes, the job itself or new entrants – who happen to be well-trained and skilled in the jobs – into the job market. Skill obsolescence in the face of globalization and technological advancements also increases the need for unfolding of potential and development diverse skills in employees. Multi-skilling is the buzz-word in many organizations since it is assumed that it generates a highly developed form of work intensification, flexibility, interchangeability and mobility in the workforce (Tomaney, 1990).

Organizations need workplace practices that unlock potential in order to enable them to be productive. One may argue that job performance [effort] requires interaction, synergy and symmetry between the intellect [the head], emotions [the heart] and skills [the hand].

## Equity, Valences and Incentives

The Expectancy Theory is based on the assumption that people are motivated to behave in ways that produce desired and valued outcomes. This view is closely linked to Skinner's Operant Conditioning because on both occasions an individual or operant is responsible for the outcome or reinforcement which leads to the repetition of desired Behaviours. Mwamwenda (1995) explains that reinforcement follows the repetition of a desired Behaviour [outcome] after a stimulus [input] has been provided. The link with Pavlov's dog which salivated also indicates that stimuli may be generalized just as in the case of employees getting promotion or bonuses at particular intervals for the work they did well. Robinson (1992) contends that effective motivation depends on a concern for ethical values and when duties, responsibilities and formal relationships are appropriately planned, organized and controlled. It suffices to state that ambivalence about the conditions in an organization may generate despondency and lack of motivation (Heystek, 2002), even if an organization has attractive incentive schemes and salary structures. One has to caution though, while dependence on incentives schemes to enhance employees' motivation may ensure efficiency in the short-term, in the long-term one may proof to be an ineffective mechanism for sustainability in the business. For example, in organizations that set production targets as in mining – employees work long hours [over-time] – which may compromise safety standards – just to reach the target and to get the bonuses. Fatalities – in the mines – have been recorded due to this practice, and such mines were forced to close for some time in order to upgrade their safety.

## RESEARCH METHODOLOGY

An empirical study on the relevance of the expectancy theory for employee motivation was conducted at Rustenburg Section of Anglo Platinum. Due to time constraints, the researchers used quantitative research methods for data collection and they distributed questionnaires to 50 contractor facilitators in Part-Time ABET. The questionnaire has two sections: Section dealing with biographical data, and Section B dealing with questions arranged in the 4 point Linkert Scale.

## Discussion

There is a link between facilitators' motivation and the leadership that is provided in ABET. It is interesting to notice that respondents rated item 4 at number 1 with the mean at 4.65 and the standard deviation at 0.56. According to the respondents, employees are exposed to an appraisal system in order to identify and close gaps in performance. From the preceding discussion it can also be concluded that through placement tests, unbundling of unit standards and the integrated learning and assessment programme [ILAP] gaps in performance are identified and closed. However, options rated eight: item 10 "the organization has a well-developed incentive programme for recognition of performance", item 2 "management has a high expectation for employees' performance" and item 6 'employees" training and development programmes are linked to the needs of employees and the organization" indicate sources of de-motivation. In relation to item 10, one may argue that the money paid to facilitators is comparable with the best in the market. However, when one considers the fact that these facilitators are contractors with no extra benefits there is room for discontentment since none of them has job security. Similarly, item 2 suggests that the respondents are of the opinion that management does not have high expectations for their performance. As some of the facilitators explained, the company does not value their services and that is why they are not given long-term contracts and full-time employment hence their response with the mean at 3.99 and the standard deviation of 0.15

## Findings

Managers understand where the organization wants to go [vision], and they point out the direction to their followers. As a result, managers develop communication networks and channels for dissemination of organizational vision, values, mandates and goals to as a strategy for mobilization of employees' energy and enthusiasm. In addition, the empirical investigation indicated that management provides strong leadership to employees. Strong leadership implies that aligning diverse views towards a common vision and programme of action. Just as organizational goals direct the actions of both the employers and employees, the role of management is to communicate organizational goals and procedures, to strengthen group cohesion and organizational effectiveness. On the other hand, respondents indicated that all employees understand the vision, values and mission statement of the organization.

Employees that are skilled and trained for the jobs do not feel threatened, either by the changes, the job itself or new entrants – who happen to be well-trained and skilled in the jobs – into the job market. Similarly, lack of motivation from respondents may be ascribed to the Company's lack of planning for employees' capacity building and empowerment. Incentives and extrinsic rewards enhance motivation are important since employment relations are based on transactions such as payment for services rendered which occur between employers [providers of employment and reward] and employees [service providers]. In the same vein respondents indicated their lack of motivation and poor response to the lack of the lack of a well-developed incentive programme for recognition of performance.

## Recommendations

Managers should explain the vision, values and missions/ goals of the organizations to their subordinates in order to win their confidence and commitment to organizational goals. Such explanations should also cover issues such as incentive schemes the organization provides, developmental opportunities as well as performance standards that are expected. One should also stress the importance of communication in leadership since it dispels all fears and misunderstandings that may develop between management and employees. Organizational goals should be explained to all employees as strategy for getting their buy-in. When employees know the goals of the organization they serve, they can then be expected to work towards the realization of such goals. In this respect, employees should be able to walk the talk and not just end at the rhetoric of "talking about the walk". SMART goals should thus be developed; work shopped and implemented in order to inspire the employees and to indicate to them what management's expectations are.

There is a need for intensive and expansive programmes aimed at unfolding employees' potential. Skilled and empowered people are always confident workers. As such, people development is very important in most organizations that regard themselves as learning organizations. A learning organization recognizes that it exists in the midst of a developing and changing world, and as a result investment in the unfolding of employees' potential is regarded as a not-negotiable necessity. Unfolding of potential is not only undertaken for improved work performance, it is also undertaken as a strategy for countering skill obsolescence that typifies technological development and advancement. In spite of the negative hype against extrinsic rewards, they still remain one source of motivation that people with an external locus relate to. A case in point, there are indications that external rewards Google gives to its employees may be ascribed for its status throughout the world as the best employer. One may therefore argue that there is a need for organizations to provide schedules of reinforcement in order to sustain employees' levels of motivation.

# 8

# Workplace of Employee Counselling

The latest trend catching up in the corporate HR across the world is 'Employee Counselling at Workplace'. In the world of ever increasing complexity and the stress in the lives, especially the workplaces of the employees, employee counselling has emerged as the latest HR tool to attract and retain its best employees and also to increase the quality of the workforce.

In today's fast-paced corporate world, there is virtually no organisation free of stress or stress-free employees. The employees can be stressed, depressed, suffering from too much anxiety arising out of various workplace related issues like managing deadlines, meeting targets, lack of time to fulfil personal and family commitments, or bereaved and disturbed due to some personal problem etc. Organisations have realized the importance of having a stress-free yet motivated and capable workforce. Therefore, many companies have integrated the counselling services in their organisations and making it a part of their culture. Organisations are offering the service of employee counselling to its employees.

## What is Employee Counselling?

Employee counselling can be explained as providing help and support to the employees to face and sail through the difficult times in life. At many points of time in life or career people come across some problems either in their work or personal life when it starts influencing and affecting their performance and, increasing the stress levels of the individual.

Counselling is guiding, consoling, advising and sharing and helping to resolve their problems whenever the need arises. Technically, Psychological Counselling, a form of counselling is used by the experts to analyze the work related performance and behaviour of the employees to help them cope with it, resolve the conflicts and tribulations and re-enforce the desired results.

## Ingredients of Counselling:

Counselling of staff is becoming an essential function of the managers. The organisation can either take the help of experienced employees or expert, professional counsellor to take up the counselling activities. Increasing complexities in the lives of the employees need to address various aspects like:

- Performance counselling: Ideally, the need for employee counselling arises when the employee shows signs of declining performance, being stressed in office-hours, bad decision-making etc. In such situations, counselling is one of the best ways to deal with them. It should cover all the aspects related to the employee performance like the targets, employee's responsibilities, problems faced, employee aspirations, inter-personal relationships at the workplace, et al.
- Personal and Family Wellbeing: Families and friends are an important and inseparable part of the employee's life. Many a times, employees carry the baggage of personal problems to their workplaces, which in turn affects their performance adversely. Therefore, the counsellor needs to strike a comfort level with the employees and, counselling sessions involving their families can help to resolve their problems and getting them back to work-all fresh and enthusiastic.
- Other Problems : Other problems can range from work-life balance to health problems. Counselling helps to identify the problem and help him/her to deal with the situation in a better way.

## Need of Counselling at Workplace

Apart from their personal problems, there are various reasons which can create stress for the employees at the workplace like unrealistic targets or work-load, constant pressure to meet the deadlines, career problems, responsibility and accountability, conflicts or bad inter-personal relations with superiors and subordinates, problems in adjusting to the organizational culture. Counselling helps the employee to share and look at his problems from a new perspective, help himself and to face and deal with the problems in a better way. Counselling at workplace is a way of the organisation to care about its employees.

## HURDLES FACED FOR COUNSELLING AT WORKPLACE

The biggest bottleneck in employee counselling at the workplace is the lack of trust on the employee's part to believe in the organisation or his superior to share and understand his problems. Also, the confidentiality that the counsellor won't disclose his personal problems or issues to others in the organisation. Time, effort and resources required on the part of the organisation are a constraint.

### Benefits of Counselling

- Helping the individual to understand and help himself
- Understand the situations and look at them with a new perspective and positive outlook
- Helping in better decision making
- Alternate solutions to problems
- Coping with the situation and the stress.

### Basic Requisites of Employee Counselling

- Employee Counselling needs to be tackled carefully, both on the part of the organisation and the counsellor. The counselling can turn into a sensitive series of events for the employee and the organisation; therefore, the counsellor should be either a professional or an experienced, mature employee.
- The counsellor should be flexible in his approach and a patient listener. He should have the warmth required to win the trust of the employee so that he can share his thoughts and problems with him without any inhibitions.

- Active and effective listening is one of the most important aspects of the employee counselling.
- Time should not be a constraint in the process.
- The counsellor should be able to identify the problem and offer concrete advice.
- The counsellor should be able to help the employee to boost the morale and spirit of the employee, create a positive outlook and help him take decisions to deal with the problem.

Counselling can go a long way in helping the employees to have better control over their lives, take their decisions wisely and better charge of their responsibilities, reduce the level of stress and anxiety. Counselling of employees can have desirable consequences for the organisation. It helps the organisation when the employees know that the organization cares for them, and build a sense of commitment with it. It can prove to be of significant help to modify the behaviour of the employees and more so to re-enforce the desired behaviour and improve and increase the employee productivity.

## EMPLOYEE COUNSELLING – ARE WE READY FOR IT?

Many firms today realize the importance of attracting and retaining highly skilled, quality employees as a necessary component of their competitive advantage. One of the reasons that a quality workforce along with innovative tools for attracting and retaining has become so important is because previous sources of competitive advantage have become less important overtime.

For example, previously, a firm's success was attributed to an emphasis on product and process technology, access to financial markets, developing economies of scale & learning curves, patents, protected and regulated markets & individual attractiveness. Recently, however, some scholars have noted that these traditional sources of success are less important than in the past and emphasize that the selection and management of a quality workforce has become an increasingly critical factor to organizational success. Today, HR practitioners are busy developing new and innovative tools to attract and retain quality workforce.

One such tool that soon is likely to gain popularity in the corporate world is Employee Counselling. Employee Counselling is a service offered by companies to their employees. Organizations that care for their employees are perceived as more meaningful and purposeful. Every organization has economic and social goals. Here, it is worthwhile to note some observations made by the Chairman of Infosys in this regard. He states, "The task of leadership is to make people believe in themselves, the organization, in the aggressive targets the organization sets. Belief comes from trust: the trust that this organization isn't about making one set of stakeholders better off; it is about making every one of us better off...."

A firm may gain competitive advantages from Employee Counselling activities especially if its reputation and image is valuable, rare and not easily imitated. Employee Counselling therefore is a very powerful tool in the hands of companies in attracting and retaining quality workforce.

Although Counselling is known by many names like 'therapy' or 'helping' it is by and large, an attempt to encourage change. The counselle's problems could be so complex that it might be difficult to see any system of help as an elegant solution. But, Counselling has shown some effectiveness over the years, as a process of helping people come through with their troubles.

Counselling is a process of helping people to learn how to solve certain interpersonal, emotional and decision problems. Counsellors help their counselles to 'learn'. The criterion for success in any Counselling is real changes in behaviour on the part of the counselle. Counsellors are concerned that their counselles become independent problem solvers. Continued dependence on the counsellor as well as others is discouraged. Counsellors are concerned with habit changes that increase peoples' satisfaction with themselves. It could be anything from helping people choose a career option, becoming appropriately assertive or communicating more harmoniously with team members. Largely, Counselling has been a 'remedial approach'. But recently there has been a slight change in emphasis, from remedial to 'preventive'.

No human being is perfect and we all constantly fight our own inadequacies in our own ways. Working in any organization requires an individual to be geared up to face the challenges of work-life. This does not mean he/she can escape the duties and responsibilities of family life, whether married or unmarried. Not every individual is competent enough to take and manage the stress of a hectic life style. Thus, we cannot deny the fact that every individual has intra and inter-personal problems whether at work or at home. The HR function of any organization has the most important challenging job of "making the most" of their Human Resource. An employee can give his best to the organization only if he is in a positive "frame of mind". A mentally preoccupied or troubled individual will be in a position to give very little to his company.

No successful organization will ever be free from stress among its employees. Organization should be able to deal with stress on individuals at all levels. Here the role of Counselling comes in, where people can talk and attempt to solve their personal and work related worries. Need for employee counselling arises due to various causes in addition to stress. These causes include: to deal effectively with one's own emotions, interpersonal problems and lack of team spirit at workplace, inability to meet job demands, over work-load, confrontation with authority, responsibility and accountability, conflicts with superiors, subordinates and management and various family problems, health problems, career problems, etc. Counselling is a process of helping an individual to help himself.

Counselling, basically aims at helping individuals take charge of their lives. For this, individuals need two types of skills: ability to make decisions wisely and altering one's own behaviour to yield desirable consequences. A counsellor's job, then, becomes one of arranging appropriate learning experiences so that people develop these skills. Counsellors avoid giving speeches about what should be done, but ideas for action are developed with the active co-operation of the counselle. The Counsellor does not try to talk the client into feeling that the situation is hopeless. Instead, he/she encourages the client to begin taking action, the successful consequences of which would encourage the client to continue. According to Eisenberg & Delaney, the aims of counselling are as follows:

1. Understanding self

2. Making impersonal decisions
3. Setting achievable goals which enhance growth
4. Planning in the present to bring about desired future
5. Effective solutions to personal and interpersonal problems.
6. Coping with difficult situations
7. Controlling self defeating emotions
8. Acquiring effective transaction skills.
9. Acquiring 'positive self-regard' and a sense of optimism about one's own ability to satisfy one's basic needs.

Counselling is discussion of an employee's problem that usually has an emotional content to it, in order to help the employee cope with the situation better. Counselling seeks to improve employee's mental health. People feel comfortable about themselves and about other people and are able to meet the demands of life when they are in good mental health.

Counselling and 'Psychological Counselling' are different from each other. Counselling in the form of advising, consoling and sharing happens in all spheres of life and does not need a specialized counsellor. Even in organizations, this kind of Counselling usually happens at all levels. This is informal or friendly form of Counselling. Psychological Counselling is a process that emphasizes a formal relationship between the counselle and the counsellor. The focus of the relationship is achieving specific goals, that is, solving the problems as disclosed by the clients. The help is confined to specific times and days and the relationship ends when the objectives are achieved. The counsellor has specialized training and applies the principles of psychology to help clients. There are several institutes, which provide courses in counselling. These courses train postgraduate students of psychology in the specialized field of Counselling. These professionally trained counsellors are well equipped to help individuals needing assistance. They are trained to maintain confidentiality, to maintain objectivity and minimize biases or prejudices.

In order to establish a helpful relationship, the counsellor may acquire certain attitudes and certain skills. The set of attitudes required for an efficient counsellor are:

- Respect i.e. High esteem for human dignity, recognition of a person's freedom & rights and faith in human potential to grow.
- Sincerity, authenticity.
- Understanding
- Non-judgemental approach towards the counselle.

The set of skills required for an efficient counsellor are:

- Decency skills i.e. social etiquettes, warm manners
- Excellent communication skills which also include non-verbal communication and listening skills
- Objectivity
- Maintaining confidentiality
- Empathy.

Through these attitudes and skills the counsellor creates a positive feeling in the counselle, and a hope that the counsellor will be of some help. The establishment of this rapport marks the start of treatment.

There are seven core techniques given by Rogers, Carkheff and Patterson, which assist the counsellor to apply appropriate core counselling conditions. They are as follows:

- Structuring
- Active Listening
- Silence
- Responding
- Reflection
- Questioning
- Interpretation.

Models for human development like mentoring, coaching and counselling are no longer confined to the non-corporate world. These systems are today a part of Human Resource Management of the corporate sector. Inspite of counselling being an upcoming HR system like coaching and mentoring, few companies recognize the significance of Counselling and that their employees will benefit from such a service but may not employ a full time counsellor. Awareness need to be created not only at the individual employee level but also at the industry level about Employee Counselling. This is clearly brought out by the primary research conducted by the author herself.

A primary research was carried out in the year 2002 at a manufacturing company based in Mumbai, India. This public limited company has five manufacturing sites across the country and four sales divisions. This research aimed at investigating the (felt) need for employee counselling in the organization. The design of this research study was exploratory in nature. The primary source of data collection was structured interviews, the sample being one hundred and ten (110) employees which is 20 % of the employee strength – five hundred and fifty three (553) of the corporate office of the company. The interview schedule comprised of both closed and open ended questions. A random sampling technique was used. The employee sample was 20 % of each of the divisions operating from the corporate office and was a perfect mix of managerial level employees, staff level employees and worker level employees. Some important conclusions that were derived from the research study are:

- Majority of the employees of the company (61% of the sample) were unaware of the concept of Employee Counselling. Those employees who had a partially correct idea (25 % of the sample) about employee counselling knew that it was related to helping an employee in distress, advising, creating self-awareness and personality development. The remaining 14 % had an incorrect understanding about the concept.
- After the researcher had explained what employee counselling was all about, 69 % of the sample agreed that there was a (perceived) need for employee counselling in the company. The reasons were many, most common ones being to assist employees solve their personal and/or work related problems and to improve the employee relationships and overall culture of the workplace. Among the 31 % who were of the viewpoint that employee counselling as an institutionalized process was not needed in the company, 57 % of this group felt that the company had a family culture and the informal relationships between the employees could be leveraged upon.

- Only 22 % of the sample disagreed on the importance of employee counselling as a part of HR –systems while 78 % of the employees felt that counselling is an important HR function.
- 83 % of the employees were unaware of the companies practicing Employee Counselling in India (this could also be because the sample was a mix of managerial employees, staff level and workers)

The research results indicate that majority of the sample under study responded positively to the hypothesis i.e. a need for Employee Counselling was felt and that it would benefit the organization. However, the awareness about the concept of counselling and employee counselling, particularly so was found to be exceptionally low.

Psychological counselling is of various types. Rational Emotive Behaviour Therapy by Dr. Albert Ellis popularly known as REBT is most widely applied.

REBT is a practical, action-oriented approach to coping with problems and enhancing personal growth. REBT places a good deal of its focus on the present: on currently-held attitudes, painful emotions and maladaptive Behaviours that can sabotage a fuller experience of life. REBT then provides a variety of methods to help people reformulate their dysfunctional beliefs into more sensible, realistic and helpful ones by employing the powerful REBT technique called "disputing." Ultimately, REBT helps people to develop a philosophy and approach to living that can increase their effectiveness and happiness at work, in living successfully with others, in parenting and educational settings, in making our community and environment healthier, and in enhancing their own health and personal welfare.

REBT is based on a few simple principles having profound implications:

1. You are responsible for your own emotions and actions,
2. Your harmful emotions and dysfunctional Behaviours are the product of your irrational thinking,
3. You can learn more realistic views and, with practice, make them a part of you,

4. You'll experience a deeper acceptance of yourself and greater satisfactions in life by developing a reality-based perspective.

REBT distinguishes clearly between two very different types of difficulties: practical problems and emotional problems. Your flawed Behaviour, unfair treatment by others, and undesirable situations, represent practical problems. Regrettably, your human tendency is to upset yourself about these practical problems, thereby unnecessarily creating a second order of problems—emotional suffering.

Some other types of counselling processes are Sigmund Freud's Psychoanalytic Therapy; Carl Roger's Client Centred Therapy; Carkhuff Model of Personal Counselling; Gestalt approach to counselling; Rational Emotive Behaviour Therapy by Albert Ellis. Freud's Psychoanalytic Therapy is based on the power of the unconscious mind. According to Freud, who is the Father of Psychology the human mind is like an iceberg. As only the tip of the iceberg is seen by the naked eye so is only one tenth of the human mind known to us. Psychoanalytic therapy taps this semi and unconscious mind through different techniques like dream analysis, etc. It was Carl Roger who supported a view that counselles should be addressed as 'clients' and unlike Freud's psychoanalytic therapy where a counselle plays a passive role, in Client centred therapy the client plays a more active role as compared to the counsellor. Hence the name Client Centred Therapy". Carkhuff model of personal counselling is an offshoot of Roger's Client Centred Therapy. It focuses on attending, responding, personalizing and initiating action as indispensable counsellor skills. Gestalt approach to counselling focuses on looking at human beings from a 'holistic' perspective. The word 'gestalt' means "a whole being".

Whatever type of therapy the counsellor has expertise in, whether it be Client Centred Therapy or REBT or any other, institutionalizing an employee counselling system in an organization is a different ball game all together. Right from getting top management approvals and budgetary sanctions to getting trained counsellors on the rolls or on part time basis all are equally challenging. Preparing the employees for counselling is another yet important areas. One of the biggest fears that prevent employees from using the services of a counsellor is the social and professional stigma attached to counselling.

If a system is being introduced in an organization for the first time, it is advisable to do a pilot. For example, the company in which the author has done primary research on employee counselling – an institutionalized set-up for counselling can be initiated at a particular division/location on an experimentation basis. If this process succeeds overtime, the same model can perhaps be replicated throughout the company. However for this, the process should be predictable, repeatable and measurable. Some criteria to gauge the impact of employee counselling are feedbacks, dip-stick surveys, focus groups, indirect or direct effect on absenteeism, employee turnover, work performance and productivity, motivation levels of employee's et al.

For introducing and sustaining any new system, the following four steps prove handy – create awareness, educate the employees, then motivate them and finally all this will lead to (expected or required) actions.

## Creating Awareness

The starting point to introducing any new system in an organization is creating awareness. Infact in the above mentioned research, 75 % of the sample population was not aware about a trained counsellor in the company (please note the counsellor is not officially designated the position of a 'counsellor' but is occupying some other 'post'). Awareness can be created by various means the most common ones being posters and notice boards.

***Education:*** "The roots of education are bitter, but the fruit is sweet" – Aristotle

Educating the employees implies some formal training about the new process to be introduced or leveraging on informal channels. However, a systematic and planned formal approach is usually preferred.

***Motivation:*** After creating awareness and educating the employees, it is imperative to motivate them with the right set of attitudes and values as required for the process. Especially for a process like employee counselling, the mind-set of the employees plays a crucial role in influencing the success or failure.

***Action:*** As is commonly known, actions speak louder than words. If the above three steps are methodically followed, it generally leads to positive results.

Introducing a system is not more challenging than sustaining a newly introduced system. To ensure sustainability of a new system, whether it is employee counselling or any other, the parameters to determine success need to be well defined. For any system to sustain itself, the process should be crystal clear.

The way the corporate sector has opened up to the world economy, it is now high time for organizations to open up for employee-orientated HR processes like counselling, coaching and mentoring. The corporate world is changing and so are the Human Resource Management practices. It is imperative that we adapt the changing styles to manage our people better. It is not just for the benefit of the employees but in the interest of the organization to show that 'we care' about this important segment of our stakeholders.

## EMPLOYEE COUNSELLING AT THE WORKPLACE

A complex and stressful lifestyle compounded with uncertain employment conditions brought about by the recession, has witnessed a sudden spurt in the number of employees needing counselling in the last 18 months. Counselling (professional and personal), in fact, has come into focus with most organizations today considering it as an integral retention tool that can go a long way in bonding an employee to the organization, improve his performance and productivity. Significantly, it is not only an initiative for employee welfare but also organizational well being.

Today stress and anxiety has become a part of everyone's life and there is no such thing as a stress-free employee. Stress is not always work-related, but due to problems like inability to find work-life balance and other personal issues. The only solution is to deal with it positively, and it is for the organization to take the initiative to encourage employees to opt for such counselling sessions. "Organizations have realized the importance of having a stress-free yet motivated and capable workforce. Therefore, many companies have introduced counselling services in their organizations and are making it a part of their culture," stated Vignesh Hebbar, Associate Vice President India, Marlabs Software.

It is also important to understand that the word counselling is different from "psychiatric" help. Anagha Wankar, Group Manager-HR, Fujitsu Consulting India, agrees that earlier, counselling meant a "bad" word—where you went only if you were not "mentally" strong to deal with issues. "Mostly, counselling meant a face to face session with psychiatrists. However, now there is an increasing awareness of the difference between counselling and psychiatric treatment. Face-to-face interactions continue to be the most influential method of counselling; but now there is a trend to opt for online counselling or phone counselling," pointed out Wankar.

## Changing the Paradigm

The work environment has become more volatile as a result of the changes in the economic climate and the uncertainties brought about by the same. Explains Deependra Chumble, Chief People Officer, Hexaware Technologies, "The economy was booming and so were employee salaries which made most of them over extrapolate their expenses. Suddenly everything came crashing down and a never before seen downslide prevailed. This created new financial problems and social pressures which caused stress to many people. Many employees saw their strong relationships getting stret-ched and strained, some making it to the breaking point. The inability of employees to handle such a situation themselves became clearly evident. Some of them couldn't go to their parents, siblings or spouses as most of them were also going through the same and were not coping up too well." All this and much more pressure made it almost necessary for HR to bring in professional counselling at the workplace.

Interestingly, most organizations would not like to see it as an intervention, but an effort to help the employee find the solution to his problem himself. Laveena Bhatia, Senior Manager, Human Resources, CSC in India, concedes that counselling helps employees to manage their own problems, using their own resources. "An organization can earn competitive advantage through workplace counselling as this is a powerful tool for maximizing work performance and attracting and retaining quality workforce," pointed out Bhatia.

## TYPES OF COUNSELLING

The different types of counselling efforts generally initiated by organizations are—face-to-face counselling, telephonic counselling and online counselling.

At Hexaware, the first type of counselling is regular internal counselling, which is done by the immediate supervisor, senior managers or by HR. This is very effective if the problems are more related to internal environment, e.g. peer-superior relationship, career progression, any kind of on-the-job harassment, etc. "HR also goes a step ahead and helps employees by giving them a shoulder for their general life grievances. Then there are certified counsellors whom the organization makes available for the employees, either on the premises or somewhere outside. These can be individual or some special organization which are known for giving professional help while maintaining privacy. We, at Hexaware, have professional counsellors in our centres and employees are encouraged to meet them for any of their personal issues. This is besides HR performing the role of a counsellor," said Deependra Chumble.

The fact that employees often hesitate to approach the counsellor, made Fujitsu Consulting India, start with online counselling and have face to face counselling only once a month. "It requires effort from both HR and the line managers to maintain the support for employees who need counselling. A lot of HR inputs are sent in to counsellors and employees need to experience that their confidentiality is maintained by all those involved," added Wankar.

### Focused Efforts by the Organization

Initiating counselling is in fact the easiest part, to make employees attend the sessions and maintain consistent efforts to continue with the same is the difficult aspect. Organizations encourage employees to volunteer themselves, and sometimes a little nudge is needed from the HR department. For instance, in Kale Consultants posters of 'I Talk' are put up to encourage employees to discuss their problems.

NetApp offers counselling services to not just the employees but their immediate dependent family as well. "This is a very confidential service provided to employees. The company does not force its employees to utilize the services. However, if we come across any signs that an employee would need counselling, we recommend to him/her the service available," stated Manjunath S.R., Senior HR Director, NetApp-India. The process for referral by managers is as follows:

- Recognize signs
- Meet in private
- Determine if referral is required
- When in doubt, consult HR
- Suggest counselling—informal or formal
- Follow-up.

According to Bhatia the challenges faced by any organization while introducing an employee counselling program are:

- To analyze the demographics of their employee base, understand their needs and design the program accordingly
- To ensure effective communication to the employees about the scope and benefits of the program
- To ensure employees' confidence in the program
- To have an effective mechanism in place for data analysis, while maintaining employee confidentiality.

Ramanand Padiyar, Global Head, Human Resources, Kale Consultants, agreed that mindset is the only constraint—employees need to be open to the idea that they need counselling for finding a solution to their problem. "He himself has to realize it. We can only help in finding the solution—it is not prescriptive but descriptive. In fact, 80% of the time the counsellors do the listening and speak only 20%. Our motto is to help the employee to help himself," pointed out Padiyar.

Kale does not engage outside counsellors, it is done by those few HR personnel who have the natural disposition to be great counsellors, in particular, patient listeners.

## BENEFITS FOR THE INDIVIDUAL AND THE ORGANIZATION

It is only an engaged and happy employee who can possess the motivation to make the customer happy. Confidential counselling service at the workplace can guide an employee in meeting all the challenges that he might face in his personal or professional life. Professional counsellors can help an employee in many ways to develop skills to cope with their problems, make important decisions or just explore new avenues for change and growth.

"Counselling service is committed to provide employees total well-being—and believes that their emotional well-being is as critical as their physical well-being. To this end, the company ties up with a counselling service provider to offer an Employee Assistance Program, which is designed to provide help and support when an employee feels the need. This in turn helps the company to increase its productivity and retain its key talent," added Manjunath.

If done right and if sponsored adequately, counselling contributes positively to the EQ of the employee and can yield definite business results. Narayan Krishnaswamy, Co-Founder & CEO, Talking Heads (HR company) believes that for organizations, it really makes a difference in building a great place to work and to help build differentiation in the employer brand given the clamor in the marketplace.

"Today, it is the knowledge possessed by employees that represents a key source of sustainable competitive advantage for organizations. Retaining and building that knowledge is one of the major contributions that we can make as human resource professionals," added Krishnaswamy.

Hebbar asserted that counselling programs should begin with an objective and it should end up achieving those objectives, failing which the entire program can become a futile exercise. Clear communication to the employees on the benefits of the program, identifying an experienced and a professional counsellor are the keys for success. It is also very important to make sure that organizations measure the effectiveness of the program by conducting frequent reviews. Counselling programs should be an ongoing process that can contribute to the learning curve of both employees and organizations. Employee counselling services, in fact, should be considered as a business initiative that is integral to improve employee productivity and benefit the organization.

## INTRODUCTION TO EMPLOYEE COUNSELLING

Human resource management was not a very popular discipline in the earlier part of the last century. Managers at that time viewed labour force as a commodity to be bought or sold like any other commodity. This type of management was probably effective at its time. But it proved to be short lived, which is evident from the ever-increasing importance of what, is now called Human Resource Management. Human Resource Management is the part of the organization that is concerned with the people dimension, consisting of staff support and function in the organization.

Every organization is comprised of people (Hoque, 2000:17) and deals with acquiring their services, developing their skills, motivating them to high levels of performance. Getting and keeping good people is critical to the success of every organization. One important aspect of human resource management is to continuously monitor and maintain employee performance. Improving employee performance is important both to the employee themselves and to the organization. It makes sense to have a healthy high performing work force as not only does it create happier individuals who provide quality service but also their contribution to drive and achieve set organizational objectives

Workplace Counselling may focus on work performance but its emphasis is more on a problem solving approach, which is concerned with the discussion and analysis of problems and issues that affect an employees work performance in an attempt to find solutions. There seems to be an ever-increasing importance could it be because mangers have suddenly woken up to the fact that it helps to retain valuable employees, or because people are more prone to problems than ever before. The correct answer would be a combination of both. In the face of increasing employee turnover and escalating recruitment/ training costs, many managers find counselling a better alternative to retain troubled employees by helping them resolve problems. Counselling is also used for other potential problem areas in an organization such as career planning and development or to help employees prepare for implementing changes such as retirement, changes caused by health, stress, conflict etc.

Work and careers are important aspects of society and we live in a society where rate of change appears to be accelerating. Career counselling helps people of all ages to make appropriate and realistic career choices. Job seekers who are having trouble deciding what they want in a career and needing direction whether it is about their current job activities or deciding on a course of study can receive assistance through career counselling. A counsellors approach is based on measurement, through testing, of the employees aptitudes and interests followed by a recommendation made by the counsellor on occupation, which provide a match in terms of the aptitudes and interests required..

Career counselling is directed towards helping employees first to acquire greater freedom of choice in their occupational lives, secondly to develop their capacity to make such choices effectively and finally to manage their occupation relation problems. But as Nathan and Hills point out it is a process, which enables people to recognize and utilize their resources to make career related decisions and manage career related problems. Although this focuses on work related part of an employees life, it also takes into account the interdependence of career and non career considerations.

Career counselling is normally available for those who want it and who pay for it or who may have access to it without paying. Those individuals who may be able to get it without paying would include employees being offered free career counselling by their employers (where the counselling on offer may be provided by line management, the personnel function, an employee counselling service or independent consultants) and trainees on trainee courses. Organizations around the worlds are beginning to establish Employment Assistant Programs (EAPs), which can be cost effective and provide professional, confidential and a broad range of counselling services for supporting employees and their families.

Till the 1960s the main focus was only on alcohol and drug related problems, which was a probable reason of the limited success of the program. However, during the 1960s, 1970s and the 1980s the advent of Employment Assistant programs was aimed at solving a broad range of problems, which could explain its rate of success. Other changes were taking place with the EAPs provision that more closely ally counselling with organization culture, management and performance appraisals. EAPs being the most visible form of counselling provision were set up as either internal or external services portrayed by Hoskinson (1994:10). Today companies who utilize counselling provision whether external or internal tend to combine counselling with a broad range of other helpful facilities and see it as a helpful mode of organizational change and not just an aid to individuals within the organization. Employers offer career help to their staff for example career development workshops for women, helping with job-hunting for people who are being made redundant, retirement planning services and career counselling sessions with a personnel officer.

However there are difficulties involved in providing help, which is independent, and client centred rather than organization centred. On the other hand there are independent services staffed by specialist career counsellors, occupational psychologists and counselling psychologists, for people with career related dissatisfactions. Staff could go to the on site career counsellor and let rip about anything, from how they hate their job to how they could take the bosss place. Employers are convinced it is a small price to pay to ensure that staff give their best. If employees dont show initiative and perform badly the organization will suffer. Counselling is meant to enable people to do as the world changes around them and improves the morale of the workforce because it shows concern for staff. More tangibly it enables employers to gain from their staffs hidden talents and interests.

Golzen and Garner (1990) have surveyed some of the changes in career and work patterns. They note, following Peter Drucker (1969), that what employers are primarily selling to employees is knowledge and skills, and that such knowledge is either relevant to the task in hand, or irrelevant. Traditional expectations of employer employee loyalty no longer match current realities or can be expected to do so. Despite advantages of workplace counselling, criticism have been made leveled at introducing counselling as part of workplace life. Some see it as becoming part of the politics of the organization and used by factors for their own ends. There is no doubt that politics play a large part in workplace life and, given the opportunity, certain individuals and departments would make capital out of owing or not owing the counselling service.

Some organizations predetermine the approach such as length of time employees can be seen (for eg four to six sessions), or by insisting that assessments are first made by psychologist before referral to the counsellor. This again may be a point out of lack of clarity about the precise aims and objectives of workplace counselling. This could be viewed as a strength rather than a weakness as it allows for flexibility for counsellors, particularly adaptation to an organization and a multiplicity of approaches that widens than restricts choices. Another criticism of counselling is its way of managing emotions where it could be viewed as a method of organizational social control dictating to individuals employees which emotions are permissible and which are not within the organization. In some organizations there is a great deal of anxiety that going for counselling will be seen as a weakness that will take its toll on career and promotion. However, counselling helps employees deal with emotions that ought to be more appropriately directed outwards towards career progress.

Organizations are changing rapidly, that staff must be more flexible in what they do for example in moving from retail to marketing and is also an opportunity for the organization to tell the employee how they need to adapt to changes such as new technology. The employer can identify the skills needed and work out whether they can be developed in house or whether they should be brought in. However, that as a result employees cannot expect to move automatically to more senior positions as there is more opportunity for development, but less for promotion. Some of the technology giants have used career counselling to help employees to adapt to change (Pamelia, 2001) Conclusion While counsellors are concerned with human tasks of listening to and address individual struggles, managers struggle to get things done and do so efficiently. Employers are turning to counselling as one way of helping to manage the mammoth changes taking place in organizations. Change is never easy: it disrupts, disorientates, causes grievances and takes time.

Support is needed for employees and teams as transition in organizations are managed. Employees do not leave their problems aside as they turn to face their working day. Eventually the organization will face financial costs of psychological and social problems. Counselling helps employees to deal with a variety of problems and if left unattended may and do affect performance in the working environment, a variety of which may lead to employee termination. If they successfully practice it they can cut down on costs associated with recruitment and training.

## COUNSELLING THE JOB-INSECURE CLIENT

In today's workplace, employees are faced with the potential of corporate downsizing, mergers and acquisitions, and job restructuring and relocation. These trends create a sense of job insecurity for the individual. Job insecurity affects the individual's life in a variety of ways, including emotional and psychological consequences, marital and family consequences, and organizational consequences. This article presents an overview of the effects of job insecurity and strategies that counsellors can use in working with the job-insecure client.

The landscape of today's workplace is marred by the threat of corporate downsizing, mergers and acquisitions, and changing work roles. In addition to the proliferation of corporate restructuring, the core of U.S. industrial structure has shifted from a manufacturing base to a service and technological base that has altered the focus of work duties in the twenty-first century. The decrease of union representation has resulted in a lack of information and involvement in the decisions made by corporate entities. As a result, workers are more vulnerable than ever "to the effects of unilateral decisions from which they have little recourse". The consequence of these workplace trends is the growth of job insecurity among workers. Dekker and Schaufelt (1995) found that the experience of job insecurity had more detrimental effects on the individual than actual termination.

The purpose of this article is to present an overview of the literature on the consequences of job insecurity. On the basis of a review of the literature, job insecurity has been found to affect not only the individual worker but it can also affect the family and the organization. Counselling interventions can address issues pertaining to job insecurity on a number of systematic levels.

This sense of job insecurity or job stress is not limited to the United States. Studies concerning the presence of job insecurity and its effects in the international workforce have begun to appear. Although the issue of job insecurity has reached an international audience, research in this area has been limited to certain fields. The bulk of literature on the topic is found in journals of management, organizational Behaviour, and organizational psychology. The field of counselling, social work, and psychology has paid little attention to the need for interventions with this population.

The definition of job insecurity has taken many forms and has been extended in recent years to include not only the anxiety of losing one's job but also the change of work roles and job features. Mauno et al. (2001) included the loss of job features, such as a potential for job transfer, in their definition of job insecurity. Greenhalgh and Rosenblatt (1984) defined job insecurity as "perceived powerlessness to maintain desired continuity in a threatened job situation". Ashford, Lee, and Bobko (1989) viewed job insecurity in a comprehensive manner that includes (a) degree of severity of threat to one's job and aspects of the work, (b) importance of the threatened job feature, (c) the negative effect of perceived threats on the entirety of the work situation, (d) the total of the aforementioned, and (e) subjective sense of powerlessness. Lim (1997) identified job insecurity as a work stressor that results in detrimental job attitudes and Behaviours.

The experience of job insecurity generates stress for the individual (Lim, 1997). Lim differentiated between the terms job stressor and job strain in his study of work-based support and job insecurity. Job stressor is defined as "causes of or inputs to job stress" and job strains as "the individual outcomes associated with the stressor" (Lim, 1997). In a longitudinal study of job insecurity in three organizations in Finland over a 3-year period, Mauno et al. (2001) found that job insecurity is a chronic job stressor "that may operate as a stable stress factor at the workplace".

Lazarus (1980) described three types of situations that result in feelings of stress. These include situations that (a) represent harm and loss; (b) are perceived as a threat to one's sense of well-being; and (c) are positive challenges in one's life, such as a new job or a job relocation. The job-insecure client may experience one or more of these situations. As a result, job-insecure clients can be viewed as a vulnerable population. The stress and strain experienced by job-insecure clients permeate a spectrum of the world in which they live. The consequences of job insecurity and its concomitant aspects affect the individual's emotional and psychological health, his or her family, and organizational productivity.

## CONSEQUENCES OF JOB INSECURITY

Workers who experience job insecurity are affected in a number of areas. Research has found that individuals may experience psychological and emotional consequences, marital and family consequences, and organizational consequences.

### Psychological and Emotional Consequences

Researchers have found that job insecurity and its accompanying stress have resulted in increased levels of emotional and physical symptomatology. Individuals experiencing job insecurity have an increased risk for anxiety, depression, substance abuse, and somatic complaints. Studies on the influence of job insecurity and personality characteristics have focused on four areas: powerlessness, locus of control, self-esteem, and positive and negative affectivity.

Greenhalgh and Rosenblatt (1984) believed that a sense of powerlessness can increase the sense of threat experienced by the individual. They pointed to this powerless feeling occurring due to (a) the lack of protection a worker feels; (b) the ambiguity of what type of interventions will guarantee job continuity; (c) the culture of the organization, particularly if it is authoritarian in nature; and (d) the standard operating procedure for dismissal versus the arbitrariness of a reduction in workforce (RIF).

Employees who experience a RIF present with feelings of grief and loss not unlike those individuals experiencing an anticipated death. The construct of locus of control (Rotter, 1966) is an important feature of whether an individual experiences a sense of powerlessness.

According to Greenhalgh and Rosenblatt, individuals whose locus of control is internal will experience a higher degree of powerlessness than those individuals who possess an external locus of control. This finding is in contrast to a study by Orpen (1994), who found that an internal locus of control is a moderating factor in the impact of job insecurity.

Self-esteem is affected by job insecurity, because the individual may lose a sense of himself or herself during this time. The role of work—and its salience in defining the individual—is a critical factor. Hansen (as cited in Zunker, 2002) has described the four roles in a person's life:

(a) the worker role,

(b) the citizen role,

(c) the family role, and

(d) the leisure role.

The threat of job loss or significant job features (e.g., commuting time, travel, benefits, hours, place of business, job responsibilities) can alter an individual's perception of self in regard to the worker role.

In today's workplace, employees are faced with the potential of corporate downsizing, mergers and acquisitions, and job restructuring and relocation. These trends create a sense of job insecurity for the individual. Job insecurity affects the individual's life in a variety of ways, including emotional and psychological consequences, marital and family consequences, and organizational consequences. This article presents an overview of the effects of job insecurity and strategies that counsellors can use in working with the job-insecure client.

The landscape of today's workplace is marred by the threat of corporate downsizing, mergers and acquisitions, and changing work roles. In addition to the proliferation of corporate restructuring, the core of U.S. industrial structure has shifted from a manufacturing base to a service and technological base that has altered the focus of work duties in the twenty-first century.

The decrease of union representation has resulted in a lack of information and involvement in the decisions made by corporate entities. As a result, workers are more vulnerable than ever "to the effects of unilateral decisions from which they have little recourse". The consequence of these workplace trends is the growth of job insecurity among workers. Dekker and Schaufelt (1995) found that the experience of job insecurity had more detrimental effects on the individual than actual termination.

The purpose of this article is to present an overview of the literature on the consequences of job insecurity. On the basis of a review of the literature, job insecurity has been found to affect not only the individual worker but it can also affect the family and the organization. Counselling interventions can address issues pertaining to job insecurity on a number of systematic levels.

This sense of job insecurity or job stress is not limited to the United States. Studies concerning the presence of job insecurity and its effects in the international workforce have begun to appear. Although the issue of job insecurity has reached an international audience, research in this area has been limited to certain fields.

The bulk of literature on the topic is found in journals of management, organizational Behaviour, and organizational psychology. The field of counselling, social work, and psychology has paid little attention to the need for interventions with this population.

The definition of job insecurity has taken many forms and has been extended in recent years to include not only the anxiety of losing one's job but also the change of work roles and job features. Mauno et al. (2001) included the loss of job features, such as a potential for job transfer, in their definition of job insecurity. Greenhalgh and Rosenblatt (1984) defined job insecurity as "perceived powerlessness to maintain desired continuity in a threatened job situation". Ashford, Lee, and

Bobko (1989) viewed job insecurity in a comprehensive manner that includes (a) degree of severity of threat to one's job and aspects of the work, (b) importance of the threatened job feature, (c) the negative effect of perceived threats on the entirety of the work situation, (d) the total of the aforementioned, and (e) subjective sense of powerlessness. Lim (1997) identified job insecurity as a work stressor that results in detrimental job attitudes and Behaviours.

The experience of job insecurity generates stress for the individual (Lim, 1997). Lim differentiated between the terms job stressor and job strain in his study of work-based support and job insecurity. Job stressor is defined as "causes of or inputs to job stress" and job strains as "the individual outcomes associated with the stressor". In a longitudinal study of job insecurity in three organizations in Finland over a 3-year period, Mauno et al. (2001) found that job insecurity is a chronic job stressor "that may operate as a stable stress factor at the workplace".

Lazarus (1980) described three types of situations that result in feelings of stress. These include situations that (a) represent harm and loss; (b) are perceived as a threat to one's sense of well-being; and (c) are positive challenges in one's life, such as a new job or a job relocation.

The job-insecure client may experience one or more of these situations. As a result, job-insecure clients can be viewed as a vulnerable population. The stress and strain experienced by job-insecure clients permeate a spectrum of the world in which they live. The consequences of job insecurity and its concomitant aspects affect the individual's emotional and psychological health, his or her family, and organizational productivity.

## Marital and Family Consequences

Westman et al. (2001) conducted a study on job insecurity among married couples in an organization undergoing downsizing. The focus of the research was to determine the degree of crossover effects of burnout that spouses experienced during this period. Westman et al. found that wives experienced more crossover effects from their husbands' downsizing during this period than did their husbands. In addition, they found that continued feelings of job insecurity and stress lessened for husbands once they found new jobs, whereas wives continued to experience job stress even after their husbands' reemployment. They concluded that wives may act as "shock absorbers taking on the men's stress and protecting them".

Wilson et al. (1993) found that stress levels of spouses whose partners were experiencing a downsizing resulted in increased health and emotional difficulties. Although job insecurity can be identified as a marital stressor, some couples find mutual support during this period and are able to weather negative effects.

Other couples experience an increase in stress and withdrawal. In addition, Wilson et al. found that younger employees and their spouses were more affected by job insecurity and hypothesized that older couples have negotiated ways of dealing with stressful events in their marriage.

The effects of job stress have been studied regarding the roles that affect the individual at home, such as the parent—child role, leisure activities, and home-management role. The spillover of the psychological absorption that an individual has concerning work can affect marriage and parenting concerns. In addition, work stress can lead to physical and psychological exhaustion, which results in depleted energy levels, compromising leisure activities. Job insecurity can affect an individual's ability to function in these roles due to increased focus on the work situation, which affects the degree of physical and psychological energy.

## Organizational Consequences

Employees and their families are not the only injured parties during a corporate restructuring; organizations experience consequences of their actions as well. Researchers have studied the effects of job insecurity within the organization. Job insecurity has been found to affect employee morale, turnover rate, and commitment to the organization. What organizations can do to buffer the deleterious effects of downsizing and restructuring has also been studied.

Social support has been defined as "information that leads a person to believe that he or she is cared for, esteemed, valued and belongs to a network of communication and mutual obligation". Work has been found to be a primary source of social connection, along with family and community (Erera, 1992). The use of an individual's support network during times of job insecurity has yielded some interesting results in terms of the type and source of social support that is needed during this period.

Erera (1992) examined the perception of social support in employees experiencing organizational ambiguity. She looked at the employees' view of the social support defined as (a) emotional; (b) tangible; and (c) approval they received from peers, subordinates, and supervisors. The findings indicated that subordinates were found to be most supportive, providing both emotional and approval support, whereas superiors were found to withhold emotional support and to be inconsistent in their provision of tangible support.

It is interesting that peers were found to withhold emotional support, and colleagues in different departments were seen as competitive and mistrustful. Erera found that "alienation activated such dysfunctional attitudes as blame, anger, suspicion, and mistrust, all of which are plainly counterproductive to social support". As a result of this alienation, employees will often withdraw, and communication channels will be shut down.

Lim (1997) studied the relationship between social support and job insecurity as measured by job dissatisfaction and noncompliant Behaviours. Similar to Erera (1992), Lim found that communication breaks down in times of job insecurity and communication channels between employees and supervisors are diminished. Noncompliant Behaviours increase when social support is absent. Although one would think that, in a period of job insecurity, individuals would focus on their work duties to avert a potential layoff, the opposite occurs. Lim hypothesized that an inequitable employment relationship develops, resulting in withdrawal and reduction in communication among employees and the organization.

Brockner et al. (1990) and Casey et al. (1997) examined information-seeking Behaviours of employees during a period of job insecurity. Given that communication breaks down, job commitment decreases, and turnover increases, what types of information do employees need to address their concerns? Brockner et al. identified five variables that affect employees' work Behaviours and attitudes during a layoff: (a) unusualness of the layoff, (b) avoidability of a layoff, (c) lack of clarity of the decisional basis to keep certain employees and lay off others, (d) unfairness of the decisional basis to keep certain employees and layoff others, and (e) perceived adequacy of organizational caretaking in the event of future layoffs. The degree of clarity provided by management concerning reasons for the layoff buffered negative work Behaviours and attitudes.

The importance of information-seeking Behaviours during a RIF was studied by Casey et al. (1997). Similar to Brockner et al. (1990), Erera (1992), and Lim (1997), Casey et al. found that job insecurity was heightened when communication channels were closed. In an effort to seek out information, employees used a number of different strategies to cope with a RIF. Casey et al. found that regardless of an individual's need for feedback, employees often seek out information through third parties (i.e., peers), as opposed to overtly questioning management about the RIF.

Employees will obtain information through second parties (i.e., supervisors who are not organization decision makers), observation, and indirect sources. As a result, misinformation can occur and exacerbate the sense of job insecurity. This need for management to convey clear messages to employees undergoing job transition has led to the birth of "change management" within an organization. Consultants' provision of change management training and counselling is a growing field in career counselling.

## IMPLICATIONS FOR COUNSELLORS

As the phenomena of corporate downsizing, restructuring, and redefinition of job roles continue to occur, job insecurity will be a common experience felt by employees. This phenomenon of job insecurity provides a fertile ground for counsellors in not only filling a counselling role but also in a collaboration/consultant and advocacy role. Holm and Hovland (1999) addressed ways in which counsellors can be of assistance to the job-insecure employee and the organization. They recommended that counsellors intervene through exploration of grief and loss issues, stress inoculation, vocational support, and reemployment information. In addition, they advised counsellors to help clients in understanding how best to gather the information needed to understand the transitions occurring in their workplace.

Finally, Holm and Hovland recommended that counsellors aid clients in understanding themselves and their needs in the workplace. Known as "the boundaryless career," the protean career, or personal agency person, the shift toward self-management is a trend that requires counsellors to teach clients how to take ownership of their career path (Schein, 1990). Holm and Hovland stated that on the basis of the research addressing the importance of social support, clients should be encouraged to interact with coworkers during periods of job insecurity.

Using Holm and Hovland's (1999) recommendations, it is proposed that counselling interventions for the job-insecure client focus on the following. Given that job insecurity affects a myriad of compartments in an individual's life, the counsellor should be attuned to the symptoms presented (i.e., anxiety, anger, depression, adjustment issues, grief) and explore the presence of any recent job transitions. Exploration about job changes, layoffs, downsizing, and so on should be discussed at the intake phase for clients seeking individual, marital, and family counselling.

Grief and loss work should follow along the stage model identified by Kubler-Ross (1969). Canaff (2000) stated that many clients become mired in the anger stage, resulting in a paralysis that makes the job-hunting process impossible. Some clients get stuck in the denial stage and continue to prepare to go to work each day, without informing their spouses or friends that they have been downsized. Counsellors can educate clients on Kubler-Ross's stages and allow them the opportunity to grieve. According to the findings of Mauno et al. (2001), this sense of grief and loss can continue even after reemployment. Counsellors must be cognizant that the grief process may still be present even if the client has found a new job. Many workers of today have been downsized numerous times and may have unresolved grief issues. Although they may have "landed" a new job, the continuing anxiety of "waiting for the other shoe to drop" may be present.

Job insecurity can affect an individual's marriage and family life. The threat of losing a job, being relocated, or surviving a downsizing disrupts the equilibrium of the family system. Spouses may become anxious, withdraw, or present an act of bravado so as not to upset the other spouse. Communication within the marriage can be thwarted, and financial concerns can increase. From a family systems perspective, the family can become imbalanced, and dysfunction can develop. Because the employee at work may feel withdrawal and alienation, interventions aimed at reducing the sense of alienation and withdrawal within the marriage are recommended. Exploration concerning the types of social support needed by the job-insecure client should be addressed.

Family members, especially children, may experience anxiety about a potential move. Canaff (2000) found that young children (age 9 and younger) often express fears about leaving their friends and their home. Children's financial concerns are limited, because their cognitive level may not perceive that as important. Counsellors should advise clients to explain their job situation in simple, concise ways that are appropriate to the child's developmental level.

Similar to Holm and Hovland (1999), I (first author) encourage counsellors in working with clients to identify appropriate sources of reliable information within their organizations. Companies undergoing the process of downsizing, mergers, acquisitions, and restructuring are fertile ground for the rumor mill. Casey et al. (1997) found that employees relied on third parties for information concerning the workplace in times of transition.

This results in "water cooler" talk that is often inaccurate and anxiety provoking for the employee. Counsellors can assist clients in examining their anxieties, exploring their rational and irrational thoughts, and developing strategies to obtain accurate information. This may entail role modeling with clients around speaking with their managers to understand the reasons behind a downsizing and the decision-making process behind it.

Lewis et al. (2003) proposed a new model of community counselling that includes the need for advocacy, consultation, collaboration, and attention to diversity and multicultural issues. Within the context of job insecurity, counsellors can act as advocates, collaborators, or consultants within organizations undergoing transition. As clients become more culturally diverse, exploration concerning the role of work in an individual's culture is imperative (Canaff, 2001). Many clients come from a culture that is not familiar with corporate downsizing, and confusion, shame, and loss of self-esteem may occur in a job-insecure climate. Counsellors must educate culturally diverse clients about the manner in which organizations operate.

Counsellors working with the job-insecure client should acquaint themselves with counselling interventions that can incorporate the family and the organization. In addition to issues of grief and loss, diversity, family systems, and organizational Behaviour, counsellors can use a number of modalities in treating this population.

On the basis of the presenting problems experienced by the job-insecure client, counsellors need to determine whether individual, family, or group counselling, or a combination of formats, is warranted. Individual counselling is recommended with clients who are experiencing high levels of stress, anxiety, or depression in response to job insecurity. Cognitive-behavioural approaches are beneficial in addressing these symptoms. Counsellors need to assess whether symptoms of depression or anxiety require referral for medication. Family counselling is recommended when marital discord and family dysfunction occur. In my (the first author's) experience, some spouses welcome the opportunity to join in the counselling process, whereas others avoid the issue. Counsellors working with job-insecure clients need to explore family functioning and changes that have occurred during times of job stress. Group counselling is beneficial in providing support and group problem solving. In conducting a group, counsellors need to be aware of the varying levels of anger, grief, loss, or anxiety that members are experiencing. If a group member is experiencing a high level of anger, individual counselling may be more appropriate. Group goals should focus on support, coping, and problem solving. Groups allow the members to see that one is not alone in this situation. Often the job-insecure client has lost social support from neighbors and friends and has become isolated. The group can provide social support and serve as a network of people who understand the emotions that occur in job insecurity. As with all groups, counsellors need to conduct a careful screening of members and their appropriateness for group counselling.

In today's workplace, employees will be faced with the continuing threat of job insecurity, whether this includes job loss, job change, or relocation. The effects of job insecurity affect a variety of areas in an individual's life, and because the effects are widespread, there are a number of areas in which counsellors can be helpful and a wide range of interventions that counsellors can use to help clients, their families, and organizations deal effectively with job insecurity.

# 9

# Organizational Learning and Theory

Organizational learning is an area of knowledge within organizational theory that studies models and theories about the way an organization learns and adapts.

In Organizational development (OD), learning is a characteristic of an *adaptive* organization, i.e., an organization that is able to sense changes in signals from its environment (both internal and external) and adapt accordingly. OD specialists endeavour to assist their clients to learn from experience and incorporate the learning as feedback into the planning process.

## Models

Argyris and Schön were the first to propose models that facilitate organizational learning; others have followed in the tradition of their work:

- Argyris & Schön (1978) distinguished between single-loop and double-loop learning, related to Gregory Bateson's concepts of first and second order learning. In single-loop learning, individuals, groups, or organizations modify their actions according to the difference between expected and obtained outcomes. In double-loop learning, the entities (individuals, groups or organization) question the values, assumptions and policies that led to the actions in the first place; if they are able to view and modify those, then second-order or double-loop learning has taken place. Double loop learning is the learning about single-loop learning.

- Kim (1993), integrates Argyris, March and Olsen and another model by Kofman into a single comprehensive model; further, he analyzes all the possible breakdowns in the information flows in the model, leading to failures in organizational learning; for instance, what happens if an individual action is rejected by the organization for political or other reasons and therefore no organizational action takes place?
- Nonaka & Takeuchi (1995) developed a four stage spiral model of organizational learning. They started by differentiating Polanyi's concept of "tacit knowledge" from "explicit knowledge" and describe a process of alternating between the two. Tacit knowledge is personal, context specific, subjective knowledge, whereas explicit knowledge is codified, systematic, formal, and easy to communicate. The tacit knowledge of key personnel within the organization can be made explicit, codified in manuals, and incorporated into new products and processes. This process they called "externalization". The reverse process (from explicit to implicit) they call "internalization" because it involves employees internalizing an organization's formal rules, procedures, and other forms of explicit knowledge. They also use the term "socialization" to denote the sharing of tacit knowledge, and the term "combination" to denote the dissemination of codified knowledge. According to this model, knowledge creation and organizational learning take a path of socialization, externalization, combination, internalization, socialization, externalization, combination... etc. in an infinite spiral. Recently Nonaka returned to this theme in an attempt to move this model of knowledge conversion forwards (Nonaka & von Krogh 2009)
- Bontis, Crossan & Hulland (2002) empirically tested a model of organizational learning that encompassed both stocks and flows of knowledge across three levels of analysis: individual, team and organization. Results showed a negative and statistically significant

relationship between the misalignment of stocks and flows and organizational performance.

- Flood (1999) discusses the concept of organizational learning from Peter Senge and the origins of the theory from Argyris and Schön. The author aims to "re-think" Senge's *The Fifth Discipline* (Senge 1990) through systems theory. The author develops the concepts by integrating them with key theorists such as Bertalanffy, Churchman, Beer, Checkland and Ackoff. Conceptualizing organizational learning in terms of structure, process, meaning, ideology and knowledge, the author provides insights into Senge within the context of the philosophy of science and the way in which systems theorists were influenced by twentieth-century advances from the classical assumptions of science.
- Imants (2003) provides theory development for organizational learning in schools within the context of teachers' professional communities as learning communities, which is compared and contrasted to teaching communities of practice. Detailed with an analysis of the paradoxes for organizational learning in schools, two mechanisms for professional development and organizational learning, (1) steering information about teaching and learning and (2) encouraging interaction among teachers and workers, are defined as critical for effective organizational learning.
- Common (2004) discusses the concept of organizational learning in a political environment to improve public policy-making. The author details the initial uncontroversial reception of organizational learning in the public sector and the development of the concept with the learning organization. Definitional problems in applying the concept to public policy are addressed, noting research in UK local government that concludes on the obstacles for organizational learning in the public sector: (1) overemphasis of the individual, (2) resistance to change and politics, (3) social learning is self-limiting, i.e. individualism, and (4) political "blame culture." The concepts of *policy learning* and *policy transfer* are then

defined with detail on the conditions for realizing organizational learning in the public sector.

- Bontis & Serenko (2009a), and Bontis & Serenko (2009b) proposed and validated a causal model explicating organizational learning processes to identify antecedents and consequences of effective human capital management practices in both for-profit and non-profit sectors. The results demonstrate that managerial leadership is a key antecedent of organizational learning, highlight the importance of employee sentiment, and emphasize the significance of knowledge management.

## Organizational Knowledge

Some of this knowledge can be termed technical – knowing the meaning of technical words and phrases, being able to read and make sense of data and being able to act on the basis of generalizations. Scientific knowledge is 'propositional'; it takes the form of causal generalizations – whenever A, then B. For example, whenever water reaches the temperature of 100 degrees, it boils; whenever it boils, it turns into steam; steam generates pressure when in an enclosed space; pressure drives engines.

A large part of the knowledge used by managers, however, does not assume this form. The complexities of a manager's task are such that applying A may result in B, C, or Z. A recipe or an idea that solved very well a particular problem, may, in slightly different circumstances backfire and lead to ever more problems. More important than knowing a whole lot of theories, recipes and solutions for a manager is to know which theory, recipe or solution to apply in a specific situation. Sometimes a manager may combine two different recipes or adapt an existing recipe with some important modification to meet a situation at hand.

Managers often use knowledge in the way that a handyman will use his or her skills, the materials and tools that are at hand to meet the demands of a particular situation. Unlike an engineer who will plan carefully and scientifically his or her every action to deliver the desired outcome, such as a steam engine, a handyman is flexible and opportunistic, often using materials in unorthodox or unusual ways, and relies a lot on trial and error. This is what the French call 'bricolage', the resourceful and creative deployment skills and materials to meet each challenge in an original way. Rule of thumb, far from being the enemy of management, is what managers throughout the world have relied upon to inform their action.

In contrast to the scientific knowledge that guides the engineer, the physician or the chemist, managers are often informed by a different type of know-how. This is sometimes referred to a 'narrative knowledge' or 'experiential knowledge', the kind of knowledge that comes from experience and resides in stories and narratives of how real people in the real world dealt with real life problems, successfully or unsuccessfully. Narrative knowledge is what we use in everyday life to deal with awkward situations, as parents, as consumers, as patients and so forth. We seek the stories of people in the same situation as ourselves and try to learn from them. As the Chinese proverb says "A wise man learns from experience; a wiser man learns from the experience of others."

Narrative knowledge usually takes the form of organization stories. These stories enable participants to make sense of the difficulties and challenges they face; by listening to stories, members of organizations learn from each other's experiences, adapt the recipes used by others to address their own difficulties and problems. Narrative knowledge is not only the preserve of managers. Most professionals (including doctors, accountants, lawyers, business consultants and academics) rely on narrative knowledge, in addition to their specialist technical knowledge, when dealing with concrete situations as part of their work. More generally, narrative knowledge represents an endlessly mutating reservoir of ideas, recipes and stories that are traded mostly by word or mouth on the internet. They are often apocryphal and may be inaccurate or untrue-yet, they have the power to influence people's sense making and actions.

## Individual Learning

Learning by individuals in an organizational context is the traditional domain of human resources, including activities such as: training, increasing skills, work experience, and formal education. Given that the success of any organization is founded on the knowledge of the people who work for it, these activities will and, indeed, must continue. However, individual learning is only a prerequisite to organizational learning.

Others take it farther with continuous learning. The world is orders of magnitude more dynamic than that of our parents, or even when we were young. Waves of change are crashing on us virtually one on top of another. Change has become the norm rather than the exception. Continuous learning throughout one's career has become essential to remain relevant in the workplace. Again, necessary but not sufficient to describe organizational learning. What does it mean to say that an organization learns? Simply summing individual learning is inadequate to model organizational learning. The following definition outlines the essential difference between the two: A learning organization actively creates, captures, transfers, and mobilizes knowledge to enable it to adapt to a changing environment. Thus, the key aspect of organizational learning is the interaction that takes place among individuals.

A learning organization does not rely on passive or ad hoc process in the hope that organizational learning will take place through serendipity or as a by-product of normal work. A learning organization actively promotes, facilitates, and rewards collective learning. Creating (or acquiring) knowledge can be an individual or group activity. However, this is normally a small-scale, isolated activity steeped in the jargon and methods of knowledge workers. As first stated by Lucilius in the 1st century BC, "Knowledge is not knowledge until someone else knows that one knows."

Capturing individual learning is the first step to making it useful to an organization. There are many methods for capturing knowledge and experience, such as publications, activity reports, lessons learned, interviews, and presentations. Capturing includes organizing knowledge in ways that people can find it; multiple structures facilitate searches regardless of the user's perspective (e.g., who, what, when, where, why,and how). Capturing also includes storage in repositories, databases, or libraries to ensure that the knowledge will be available when and as needed. Transferring knowledge requires that it be accessible to as needed. In a digital world, this involves browser-activated search engines to find what one is looking for. A way to retrieve content is also needed, which requires a communication and network infrastructure. Tacit knowledge may be shared through communities of practice or consulting experts. Knowledge needs to be presented in a way that users can understand it, and it must suit the needs of the user to be accepted and internalized.

Mobilizing knowledge involves integrating and using relevant knowledge from many, often diverse, sources to solve a problem or address an issue. Integration requires interoperability standards among various repositories. Using knowledge may be through simple reuse of existing solutions that have worked previously. It may also come through adapting old solutions to new problems. Conversely, a learning organization learns from mistakes or recognizes when old solutions no longer apply. Use may also be through synthesis; that is creating a broader meaning or a deeper level of understanding. Clearly, the more rapidly knowledge can be mobilized and used, the more competitive an organization. An organization must learn so that it can adapt to a changing environment. Historically, the life-cycle of organizations typically spanned stable environments between major socioeconomic changes. Blacksmiths who didn't become mechanics simply fell by the wayside. More recently, many Fortune 500 companies of two decades ago no longer exist. Given the ever-accelerating rate of global-scale change, the more critical learning and adaptation become to organization relevance, success, and ultimate survival.

Organizational learning is a social process, involving interactions among many individuals leading to well-informed decision making. Thus, a culture that learns and adapts as part of everyday working practices is essential. Reuse must equal or exceed reinvent as a desirable Behaviour. Adapting an idea must be rewarded along with its initial creation. Sharing to empower the organization must supersede controlling to empower an individual. Clearly, shifting from individual to organizational learning involves a non-linear transformation. Once someone learns something, it is available for their immediate use. In contrast, organizations need to create, capture, transfer, and mobilize knowledge before it can be used. Although technology supports the latter, these are primarily social processes within a cultural environment, and cultural change, however necessary, is a particularly challenging undertaking.

## Learning Organization

The work in Organizational Learning can be distinguished from the work on a related concept, the learning organization. This later body of work, in general, uses the theoretical findings of organizational learning (and other research in organizational development, system theory, and cognitive science) in order to prescribe specific recommendations about how to create organizations that continuously and effectively learn. This practical approach was championed by Peter Senge in his book *The Fifth Discipline*.

## Diffusion of Innovations

Diffusion of innovations theory explores how and why people adopt new ideas, practices and products. It may be seen as a subset of the anthropological concept of diffusion and can help too explain how ideas are spread by individuals, social networks and organizations.

# SOCIAL LEARNING THEORY

Social learning theory has its roots in the behaviorist notion of human Behaviour as being determined by learning, particularly as shaped by reinforcement in the form of rewards or punishment. Early research in behaviorism conducted by Ivan Pavlov, John Watson, and B. F. Skinner used animals in a laboratory. Subsequently, researchers became dissatisfied with the capacity of their findings to fully account for the complexities of human personality. Criticism centred particularly on the fact that behaviorism's focus on observable Behaviours left out the role played by cognition.

The first major theory of social learning, that of Julian B. Rotter, argued that cognition, in the form of expectations, is a crucial factor in social learning. In his influential 1954 book, Social Learning and Clinical Psychology, Rotter claimed that Behaviour is determined by two major types of "expectancy": the expected outcome of a Behaviour and the value a person places on that outcome. In Applications of a Social Learning Theory of Personality (1972), Rotter, in collaboration with June Chance and Jerry Phares, described a general theory of personality with variables based on the ways that different individuals habitually think about their experiences. One of the major variables was I-E, which distinguished "internals," who think of themselves as controlling events, from "externals," who view events as largely outside their control. Correlations have since been found between I-E orientations and a variety of Behaviours, ranging from job performance to attitudes toward one's health.

The social learning theories of Albert Bandura emphasize the reciprocal relationship among cognition, Behaviour, and environment, for which Bandura coined the term reciprocal determinism. Hostile thoughts can result in hostile Behaviour, for example, which can effect our environment by making others hostile and evoking additional hostile thoughts. Thus, not only does our environment influence our thoughts and Behaviour-our thoughts and Behaviour also play a role in determining our environment. Bandura is especially well known for his research on the importance of imitation and reinforcement in learning. His work on modeling has been influential in the development of new therapeutic approaches, especially the methods used in cognitive-Behaviour therapy. Bandura also expanded on Rotter's notion of expectancy by arguing that our expectations about the outcome of situations are heavily influenced by whether or not we think we will succeed at the things we attempt. Bandura introduced the term self-efficacy for this concept, arguing that it has a high degree of influence not only on our expectations but also on our performance itself.

Most recently, Walter Mischel, building on the work of both Rotter and Bandura, has framed the determinants of human Behaviour in particular situations in terms of "person variables." These include competencies (those things we know we can do); perceptions (how we perceive our environment); expectations (what we expect will be the outcome of our Behaviour); subject values (our goals and ideals); and self-regulation and plans (our standards for ourselves and plans for reaching our goals).

## SOCIAL PERCEPTION

Social perception is the process of forming impressions of individuals. The resulting impressions that we form are based off of information available in the environment, our previous attitudes about relevant stimuli, and our current mood. Humans tend to operate under certain biases when forming impression of other individuals. For example, we are more like to perceive a beautiful person as being good (i.e. possessing desirable personality traits such as kindness, sociability, intelligence) than less attractive people. This particular bias is often called the halo effect. Social perception is, in psychology and other cognitive sciences, that part of perception that allows us to understand the individuals and groups of our social world, and thus an element of social cognition.

It allows us to determine how people will affect our personal lives. While social perceptions can be flawed, they help people to form impressions of others by making the necessary information available to assess what people are like. Missing informations are filled in by using an implicit personality theory: If a person is observed to have one particular trait, we assume that he or/she has other traits related to this observed one. These assumptions help us to "categorize" people and then infer additional facts and predict Behaviour.

Social perceptions are also interlinked with self-perceptions. Both are influenced by self-motives. Society has the desire to achieve beneficial outcomes for the self and to maintain a positive self-image, both for personal psychic benefits and because we know that others are perceiving us as well. Just as you prejudge the people you come across in society, you are being judged by them. It is human nature to want to put off a good impression on people, almost as if your self-perceptions are other's social perceptions.

## Structural and Functional Factors

David Krech and Richard S. Crutchfield believe there to be two major determinants of perception, structural factors and functional factors. By structural factors we mean those factors driving solely from the nature of the physical stimuli and the natural effects they evoke in the nervous system of the individual. Thus, for the Gestalt psychologist, perceptual organizations are determined primarily by the psychological events occurring in the nervous system of the individual in direct reaction to the stimulation by the physical objects. Sensory factors are independent of the perceiving individual's needs and personality.

## Functional Factors

The functional factors of perceptual organization are those, which derive primarily from the needs, moods, past experience and memory of the individual. All functional factors in perception are social in the usual sense of the term. In one experiment, for example, Levine, Chein and Murphy presented a series of ambiguous drawings to hungry college students and found a marked tendency for such drawings to be perceived as food objects such as sandwiches, salads, roasts etc.

There was no such effect when the same drawings were shown to students who had just finished eating. The different perceptions of the hungry and not-hungry students could not be due to "structural" factors, since the same pictures were presented to both groups, but could be due only to the differences in need or motivation of the members of the two groups.

While quantitative laws of how these functional factors actually operate in perception are lacking, a great deal of experimental work is available that demonstrates their pervasive influence in perception.

## Interrelationship between Structural and Functional Factors

The interaction that is true for most psychological processes is also characteristic of the operation of structural and functional factors in perception. Neither set operates alone and every perception involves both kinds of factors. Although we can experiment with structural factors alone in perception or with functional factors alone, we must realize that this is done only for experimental convenience. It means that whatever perception is being observed is a function of both sets of factors.

It is important to recognize the relationship between these two sets of factors because it is at this point that a reconciliation can be made between the behavioural psychologists who tend to break Behaviour down into its component parts and the gestalt psychologists who seek to understand man as an indivisible entity.

## WHAT IS SOCIAL PSYCHOLOGY?

Social psychology focuses on social Behaviour, including group Behaviour. Learn more in this overview of social psychology. According to psychologist Gordon Allport, social psychology is a discipline that uses scientific methods "to understand and explain how the thought, feeling and Behaviour of individuals are influenced by the actual, imagined or implied presence of other human beings" (1985). Social psychology looks at a wide range of social topics, including group Behaviour, social perception, leadership, nonverbal Behaviour, conformity, aggression and prejudice. It is important to note that social psychology is not just about looking at social influences. Social perception and social interaction are also vital to understanding social Behaviour.

### Brief History of Social Psychology

While Plato referred to the idea of the "crowd mind" and concepts such as social loafing and social facilitation were introduced in the late-1800s, it wasn't until after World War II that research on social psychology would begin in earnest. The horrors of the Holocaust led researchers to study the effects of social influence, conformity, and obedience. The U.S. government also became interested in applying social psychological concepts to influencing citizens. Social psychology has continued to grow throughout the twentieth century, inspiring research that has contributed to our understanding of social experience and Behaviour.

# 10

# Attitude of Social Psychology

Attitude is a mental position relative to a way of thinking, behaving or leaning toward that which you believe. It is the way a person thinks about somebody or something and the way she behaves toward someone. It is her personal view or opinion of something. It also describes her general emotional approach to any person or situation. From a personal development standpoint, attitude is broader than this popular usage. A positive attitude implies a way of thinking that is predominantly positive and optimistic. The opposite inclination, a negative attitude is predominantly pessimistic.

## COMPONENTS OF ATTITUDE

Attitude has three components, namely:

### Emotional

The emotional component represents a person's feelings towards an object. In other words, it is the disposition towards something. For example, a sales representative behaves in a positive manner with his clients. He feels that the client can do good to him by making a purchase, therefore he has a positive emotional component.

### Informational

The informational component consists of the information, idea or beliefs that a person has about the object. For example, if someone feels that his partner can not play cricket very well, he would not let him take charge if needed. Therefore, the belief plays the role of determining the informational component.

## Behavioural

The behavioural component represents how a person actually behaves. It consists of cognitive and affective (values & beliefs) parts. Our beliefs and values are combined with our cognitive component; thus, two components (affective and cognitive) give us our long range or persistent measurements for dealing with the world.

While a person may have the competency to perform a task, that does not mean he or she will have the desire (attitude) to do so correctly. In other words, competencies give us the ability to perform, while attitudes give us the desire to perform. Attitudes change with various events in a person's life. These emotional changes also vary in length of time.

## POSITIVE AND NEGATIVE AFFECTIVITY

### Positive Affectivity (PA)

It may be defined as a sense of well being, pleasantly involved in life and having positive attitudes. Positive attitude, positive thinking, and optimism are now known to be a root cause of many positive life benefits-the good life and well being. You'll live longer and be healthier and happier with a positive attitude toward life. In addition, you're more likely to be successful if you learn to use the power of thinking positive, adopting positive attitudes, and affirmations to gain important life benefits.

A positive attitude and optimistic thinking early in life predict health and well being in later years. Analysis of 99 Harvard graduates found a strong correlation between their optimistic thinking as college students and good health at age 40 and above. In his ground-breaking book, A Primer in Positive Psychology, Christopher Petersen, PhD, says, "...optimism has demonstrable benefits, and pessimism has drawbacks." He goes on to say, "...optimism...has been linked to positive mood and good morale; to perseverance and effective problem solving; to academic, athletic, military, occupational, and political success; to popularity; to good health; and even to long life and freedom from trauma." Even if a person has been a pessimistic, negative thinker for many years, it is never too late to change the way of thinking and reap the benefits of a positive attitude. Optimists believe they are accountable for good things and that good things will generally come their way. If something bad comes instead, optimists tend to write it off as an isolated incident, an anomaly, or something out of their control; optimists believe things will be better in the future.

## Negative Affectivity (NA)

It is the state of being nervous, tense, worried, distressed and pessimistic. Negative affectivity (NA) has been defined as reflecting individual differences in negative emotion and self concept (Watson & Clark, 1984). It has been argued that NA may affect perceived levels of stress by influencing perceptions of the self or environment. Accordingly, individuals found to be high in NA tend to report higher levels of dissatisfaction and perceived stress, when compared with individuals who have lower levels of NA. Although there is strong empirical evidence linking NA to psychological well-being outcomes some authors have suggested that this relationship originates out of a tendency of those individuals high in NA to respond to self report methodologies with an overall negative perception.

Moyle (1995), in a comprehensive analysis of the effects of NA on a number of outcome measures, found that negative affectivity did not universally affect all outcomes in a similar manner. Instead she found that NA functioned in a number of different ways to influence outcomes. Moyle noted that NA was not simply a generic nuisance variable but rather it played a complex and substantive role within the stress process.

# FUNCTIONS OF ATTITUDE

## Adjustment Function

Attitudes help employees in organizations to adjust to the organizational environment. For example, if an employee finds his job satisfying and develops a positive attitude towards it, he or she is more likely to adjust with the organizational environment as compared to the one who has developed a negative attitude towards the job or the organization.

## Ego Defence Function

Attitude defines and defends self image. A person may make a poor decision and stick to it despite warnings and in the process, develop a negative attitude towards the one who had warned him, considering him inexperienced and irreverent. Hence, later this attitude would protect the ego of the person when he shall refuse to listen to the warnings.

## Value Expressive Function

Attitudes towards certain things help in expressing the values possessed. A person, who has a strong negative attitude towards a liar, has his values of not telling a lie represented by this attitude.

## Knowledge Function

Attitude helps to understand and explain the world. A person may have negative attitude towards a group and therefore consider everything said or done by that group to be wrong or threatening. He has developed a frame of reference to assay the group which is a function of his attitude.

## Changing Attitudes

Changing attitudes in organizations and in general is a difficult task; however, modification of existing attitudes is much easier. The first step in trying to change or modify attitudes is to identify the barriers in it and demolish them. The common barriers are as follows:

## Prior Commitment

Prior commitment of people prevents attitudinal change in them. It is actually disposition towards certain beliefs. For example, a graduate from a foreign university would often be considered suitable for a number of jobs irrespective of his interest and aptitude, based on the belief that he or she is a foreign qualified person. This belief may be harmful for the organization. It is actually a prior commitment of the hiring people.

## Insufficient Information

Another barrier to bringing about attitudinal change is insufficiency of information. People do not find sufficient reasons for changing their attitude which may become a hindrance in changing attitudes.

## HOW TO CHANGE ATTITUDES

Probably most overlooked is this strategy. Most often we forget that one of the reasons people don't change their attitude is that they have made a conscious or subconscious prior commitment. Uncovering those hidden agendas usually results in an opportunity to change one's attitude about previous commitments. Even stability can be a prior commitment and until I understand that this new change, method or system is going to produce stability–I am not willing to let go of what is stable.

### Provide New/different Information

Often, people don't see or feel the need to change. Providing information to support change or the need to change can often open previously closed doors. Communicating change initiatives prior to implementation is often scary but almost always better than not doing it until the implementation begins.

### Use Fear/punishment

Fear can be positive if we take the time to frame it correctly. Fear of some sort, often creates the urgency needed for change to take place and for change gaps to be bridged, but the key to using fear is to show how the present path is not the best one. You don't just threaten people by stating if they don't do it they will suffer the consequences. You use a combination of tactics to show with information how the present direction will lead to lower levels of benefits and more sacrifice than changing directions–personally or organizationally.

### Influence friends/family

One of the major reasons–in my view–for using 360 degree assessment is so that someone can get hit over the head by people whose opinions often matter–saving leadership from doing it. While this may be the crass side of 360, it does work because of the influence of friends and peers. 360s certainly have weaknesses and used solely for the purpose of changing attitudes is probably more harmful than helpful in the "long term." However, a structured ongoing program of development that includes regular 360 assessments and training can be effective in changing attitudes.

## Psychotherapy

Psychotherapy is actually the treatment of mental and emotional disorders using psychological methods. Psychotherapy, thus, does not include physiological interventions, such as drug therapy or electroconvulsive therapy, although it may be used in combination with such methods. Behaviour therapy aims to help the patient eliminate undesirable habits or irrational fears through conditioning. Humanistic therapy tends to be more optimistic, basing its treatment on the theory that individuals have a natural inclination to strive toward self-fulfilment. Therapists such as Carl Rogers and Abraham Maslow used a highly interactive client-therapist relationship, compelling clients to realize exactly what they are saying or how they are behaving, in order to foster a sense of self-awareness. Cognitive therapies try to show the client that certain, usually negative, thoughts are irrational, with the goal of restructuring such thoughts into positive, constructive ideas. Such methods include Albert Ellis's rational-emotive therapy, where the therapist argues with the client about his negative ideas.

Psychotherapy may be brief, lasting just a few sessions, or it may extend over many years. More than one client may be involved, as in marriage or family counselling, or a number of individuals, as in group psychotherapy.

## Cooperate, Involve in Decision Making

Giving people–whose attitude is deviant from the norm–leadership opportunity can often lead to positive change for the person and the organization. Some say resistance is energy and this resistant energy occurs often in the form of challenging attitudes and opposition–disagreeableness. Yet, often this energy can be harnessed to propel the organization forward while leading to attitudinal change in the opposition.

## Seek First to Understand

An age old maxim made popular by Stephen Covey's 7 habits, empathy like compassion forces us to take the view of the opposing force and to attempt to understand the reasons for the resistance. Much has been written about this "soft" skill but by far, the caring sense that someone expresses authentically towards another person removes barriers to changes in attitudes. Empathy creates openings for new information and influence to reach through previously locked doors.

### Resolve Cognitive Dissonance

Most often, each of us has a dialectic taking place inside ourselves about our attitudes and about the results of our Behaviours. To resolve this dissonance or conflict can often lead to positive changes in attitudes for us personally as well as in organizations. People are certain that their Behaviour always works, yet must often protect that faulty Behaviour with an attitude. Helping them to understand the conflict between their attitude and the Behaviour can lead to positive change.

## PSYCHOLOGICAL ATTITUDE

An attitude is a hypothetical construct that represents an individual's degree of like or dislike for an item. Attitudes are generally positive or negative views of a person, place, thing, or event—this is often referred to as the attitude object. People can also be conflicted or ambivalent toward an object, meaning that they simultaneously possess both positive and negative attitudes toward the item in question.

Attitudes are judgments. They develop on the ABC model (affect, Behaviour, and cognition) Template:Van den Berg et al., 2006; Eagly & Chaiken, 1998. The *affective* response is an emotional response that expresses an individual's degree of preference for an entity. The *behavioural* intention is a verbal indication or typical behavioural tendency of an individual. The *cognitive* response is a cognitive evaluation of the entity that constitutes an individual's beliefs about the object. Most attitudes are the result of either direct experience or observational learning from the environment.

### Attitude Formation

Unlike personality, attitudes are expected to change as a function of experience. Tesser (1993) has argued that hereditary variables may affect attitudes-but believes that they may do so indirectly. For example, consistency theories, which imply that we must be consistent in our beliefs and values. The most famous example of such a theory is Dissonance-reduction theory, associated with Leon Festinger, although there are others, such as the balance theory.

## Attitude Change

Attitudes can be changed through persuasion and we should understand attitude change as a response to communication. Experimental research into the factors that can affect the persuasiveness of a message include:

1. Target Characteristics: These are characteristics that refer to the person who receives and processes a message. One such trait is intelligence-it seems that more intelligent people are less easily persuaded by one-sided messages. Another variable that has been studied in this category is self-esteem. Although it is sometimes thought that those higher in self-esteem are less easily persuaded, there is some evidence that the relationship between self-esteem and persuasibility is actually curvilinear, with people of moderate self-esteem being more easily persuaded than both those of high and low self-esteem levels (Rhodes & Woods, 1992). The mind frame and mood of the target also plays a role in this process.
2. Source Characteristics: The major source characteristics are expertise, trustworthiness and interpersonal attraction or attractiveness. The credibility of a perceived message has been found to be a key variable here; if one reads a report about health and believes it came from a professional medical journal, one may be more easily persuaded than if one believes it is from a popular newspaper. Some psychologists have debated whether this is a long-lasting effect and Hovland and Weiss (1951) found the effect of telling people that a message came from a credible source disappeared after several weeks (the so-called "sleeper effect"). Whether there is a sleeper effect is controversial. Perceived wisdom is that if people are informed of the source of a message before hearing it, there is less likelihood of a sleeper effect than if they are told a message and then told its source.

3. Message Characteristics: The nature of the message plays a role in persuasion. Sometimes presenting both sides of a story is useful to help change attitudes.

Cognitive Routes: A message can appeal to an individual's cognitive evaluation to help change an attitude. In the *central route* to persuasion the individual is presented with the data and motivated to evaluate the data and arrive at an attitude changing conclusion. In the *peripheral route* to attitude change, the individual is encouraged to not look at the content but at the source. This is commonly seen in modern advertisements that feature celebrities. In some cases, physician, doctors or experts are used. In other cases film stars are used for their attractiveness.

## EMOTION AND ATTITUDE CHANGE

Emotion is a common component in persuasion, social influence, and attitude change. Much of attitude research emphasized the importance of affective or emotion components. Emotion works hand-in-hand with the cognitive process, or the way we think, about an issue or situation. Emotional appeals are commonly found in advertising, health campaigns and political messages. Recent examples include no-smoking health campaigns and political campaign advertising emphasizing the fear of terrorism. Attitudes and attitude objects are functions of cognitive, affective and conative components. Attitudes are part of the brain's associative networks, the spider-like structures residing in long term memory that consist of affective and cognitive nodes.

By activating an affective or emotion node, attitude change may be possible, though affective and cognitive components tend to be intertwined. In primarily affective networks, it is more difficult to produce cognitive counterarguments in the resistance to persuasion and attitude change.

Affective forecasting, otherwise known as intuition or the prediction of emotion, also impacts attitude change. Research suggests that predicting emotions is an important component of decision making, in addition to the cognitive processes. How we feel about an outcome may override purely cognitive rationales.

In terms of research methodology, the challenge for researchers is measuring emotion and subsequent impacts on attitude. Since we cannot see into the brain, various models and measurement tools have been constructed to obtain emotion and attitude information. Measures may include the use of physiological cues like facial expressions, vocal changes, and other body rate measures. For instance, fear is associated with raised eyebrows, increased heart rate and increase body tension (Dillard, 1994). Other methods include concept or network mapping, and using primes or word cues.

## Components of Emotion Appeals

Any discrete emotion can be used in a persuasive appeal; this may include jealousy, disgust, indignation, fear, blue, disturbed, haunted,and anger. Fear is one of the most studied emotional appeals in communication and social influence research.

Important consequences of fear appeals and other emotion appeals include the possibility of reactance which may lead to either message rejections or source rejection and the absence of attitude change. As the EPPM suggests, there is an optimal emotion level in motivating attitude change. If there is not enough motivation, an attitude will not change; if the emotional appeal is overdone, the motivation can be paralyzed thereby preventing attitude change.

Emotions perceived as negative or containing threat are often studied more than perceived positive emotions like humour. Though the inner-workings of humour are not agreed upon, humour appeals may work by creating incongruities in the mind. Recent research has looked at the impact of humour on the processing of political messages. While evidence is inconclusive, there appears to be potential for targeted attitude change is receivers with low political message involvement.

Important factors that influence the impact of emotion appeals include self efficacy, attitude accessibility, issue involvement, and message/source features. Self efficacy is a perception of one's own human agency; in other words, it is the perception of our own ability to deal with a situation. It is an important variable in emotion appeal messages because it dictates a person's ability to deal with both the emotion and the situation. For example, if a person is not self-efficacious about their ability to impact the global environment, they are not likely to change their attitude or Behaviour about global warming. Dillard (1994) suggests that message features such as source non-verbal communication, message content, and receiver differences can impact the emotion impact of fear appeals. The characteristics of a message are important because one message can elicit different levels of emotion for different people. Thus, in terms of emotion appeals messages, one size does not fit all. Attitude accessibility refers to the activation of an attitude from memory in other words, how readily available is an attitude about an object, issue, or situation. Issue involvement is the relevance and salience of an issue or situation to an individual. Issue involvement has been correlated with both attitude access and attitude strength. Past studies conclude accessible attitudes are more resistant to change

## IMPLICIT AND EXPLICIT ATTITUDES

There is also considerable research on implicit attitudes, which are generally unacknowledged or outside of awareness, but have effects that are measurable through sophisticated methods using people's response times to stimuli. Implicit and explicit attitudes seem to affect people's Behaviour, though in different ways. They tend not to be strongly associated with each other, although in some cases they are. The relationship between them is poorly understood.

### Jung's Definition

Attitude is one of Jung's 57 definitions in Chapter XI of *Psychological Types*. Jung's definition of attitude is a "readiness of the psyche to act or react in a certain way". Attitudes very often come in pairs, one conscious and the other unconscious. Within this broad definition Jung defines several attitudes. The main (but not only) attitude dualities that Jung defines are the following.

- Consciousness and the unconscious. The "presence of two attitudes is extremely frequent, one conscious and the other unconscious. This means that consciousness has a constellation of contents different from that of the unconscious, a duality particularly evident in neurosis".

- Extraversion and introversion. This pair is so elementary to Jung's theory of types that he labelled them the "attitude-types".
- Rational and irrational attitudes. "I conceive reason as an attitude".
- The rational attitude subdivides into the thinking and feeling psychological functions, each with its attitude.
- The irrational attitude subdivides into the sensing and intuition psychological functions, each with its attitude. "There is thus a typical thinking, feeling, sensation, and intuitive attitude".
- Individual and social attitudes. Many of the latter are "isms".

In addition, Jung discusses the abstract attitude. "When I take an abstract attitude...". Abstraction is contrasted with concretism. "CONCRETISM. By this I mean a peculiarity of thinking and feeling which is the antithesis of abstraction". For example "i hate his attitude for being Sarcastic.

## MBTI Definition

The MBTI write-ups limit the use of "attitude" to the extraversion-introversion (EI) and judging-perceiving (JP) indexes.

The JP index is sometimes referred to as an orientation to the outer world and sometimes JP is classified as an "attitude." In Jungian terminology the term *attitude* is restricted to EI. In MBTI terminology *attitude* can include EI and also JP..

The above MBTI Manual statement, is restricted to EI," is directly contradicted by Jung's statement above that there is "a typical thinking, feeling, sensation, and intuitive attitude" and by his other uses of the term "attitude". Regardless of whether the MBTI simplification (or oversimplification) of Jung can be attributed to Myers, *Gifts Differing* refers only to the "EI preference", consistently avoiding the label "attitude". Regarding the JP index, in *Gifts Differing* Myers does use the terms "the *perceptive* attitude and the *judging* attitude". The JP index corresponds to the irrational and rational attitudes Jung describes, except that the MBTI focuses on the preferred orientation in the outer world in order to identify the function hierarchy. To be consistent with Jung, it can be noted that a rational extraverted preference is accompanied by an irrational introverted preference.

## SOCIAL PSYCHOLOGY

Social psychology is the scientific study of how people's thoughts, feelings, and Behaviours are influenced by the actual, imagined, or implied presence of others. By this definition, *scientific* refers to the empirical method of investigation. The terms *thoughts*, *feelings*, and *Behaviours* include all of the psychological variables that are measurable in a human being. The statement that others may be *imagined* or *implied* suggests that we are prone to social influence even when no other people are present, such as when watching television, or following internalized cultural norms.

Social psychologists typically explain human Behaviour as a result of the interaction of mental states and immediate social situations. In Kurt Lewin's famous heuristic formula, Behaviour can be viewed as a function of the person and the environment, $B = f(P, E)$. In general, social psychologists have a preference for laboratory based, empirical findings. Social psychology theories tend to be specific and focused, rather than global and general.

Social psychology is an interdisciplinary domain that bridges the gap between psychology and sociology. During the years immediately following World War II, there was frequent collaboration between psychologists and sociologists. However, the two disciplines have become increasingly specialized and isolated from each other in recent years, with sociologists focusing on "macro variables" (e.g. social structure) to a much greater extent. Nevertheless, sociological approaches to social psychology remain an important counterpart to psychological research in this area.

In addition to the split between psychology and sociology, there has been a somewhat less pronounced difference in emphasis between American social psychologists and European social psychologists. As a broad generalization, American researchers traditionally have focused more on the individual, whereas Europeans have paid more attention to group level phenomena.

## History

The discipline of social psychology began in the United States at the dawn of the 20th century. The first published study in this area was an experiment in 1898 by Norman Triplett on the phenomenon of social facilitation. During the 1930s, many Gestalt psychologists, most notably Kurt Lewin, fled to the United States from Nazi Germany. They were instrumental in developing the field as something separate from the behavioural and psychoanalytic schools that were dominant during that time, and social psychology has always maintained the legacy of their interests in perception and cognition. Attitudes and small group phenomena were the most commonly studied topics in this era.

During WWII, social psychologists studied persuasion and propaganda for the U.S. military. After the war, researchers became interested in a variety of social problems, including gender issues and racial prejudice. In the sixties, there was growing interest in new topics, such as cognitive dissonance, bystander intervention, and aggression. By the 1970s, however, social psychology in America had reached a crisis. There was heated debate over the ethics of laboratory experimentation, whether or not attitudes really predicted Behaviour, and how much science could be done in a cultural context. This was also the time when a radical situationist approach challenged the relevance of self and personality in psychology.

Social psychology reached maturity in both theory and method during the 1980s and 1990s. Careful ethical standards now regulate research, and greater pluralism and multiculturalism perspectives have emerged. Modern researchers are interested in a many phenomena, but attribution, social cognition, and the self-concept are perhaps the greatest areas of growth in recent years. Social psychologists have also maintained their applied interests with contributions in health and environmental psychology, as well as the psychology of the legal system.

## INTRAPERSONAL PHENOMENA

In social psychology, attitudes are defined as learned, global evaluations of a person, object, place, or issue that influence thought and action. Put more simply, attitudes are basic expressions of approval or disapproval, favorability or unfavorability, or as Bem put it, likes and dislikes. Examples would include liking chocolate ice cream, being against abortion, or endorsing the values of a particular political party.

Social psychologists have studied attitude formation, the structure of attitudes, attitude change, the function of attitudes, and the relationship between attitudes and Behaviour. Because people are influenced by the situation, general attitudes are not always good predictors of specific Behaviour. For a variety of reasons, a person may value the environment and not recycle a can on a particular day. Attitudes that are well remembered and central to our self-concept, however, are more likely to lead to Behaviour, and measures of general attitudes do predict patterns of Behaviour over time. Large amount of recent research on attitudes is on the distinction between traditional, self-report attitude measures and "implicit" or unconscious attitudes. For example, experiments using the Implicit Association Test have found that people often demonstrate bias against other races, even when their questionnaire responses reveal equal mindedness. One study found that explicit attitudes correlate with verbal Behaviour in interracial interactions, whereas implicit attitudes correlate with nonverbal Behaviour. Attitudes are also involved in several other areas of the discipline, such as the following;conformity, interpersonal attraction, social perception, and prejudice.

## Persuasion

The topic of persuasion has received a great deal of attention in recent years. Persuasion is an active method of influence that attempts to guide people toward the adoption of an attitude, idea, or Behaviour by rational or emotive means. Persuasion relies on "appeals" rather than strong pressure or coercion. Numerous variables have been found to influence the persuasion process, and these are normally presented in five major categories: *who* said *what* to *whom* and *how*.

1. The Communicator, including credibility, expertise, trustworthiness, and attractiveness.
2. The Message, including varying degrees of reason, emotion (such as fear), one-sided or two sided arguments, and other types of informational content.

3. The Audience, including a variety of demographics, personality traits, and preferences.
4. The Channel, including the printed word, radio, television, the internet, or face-to-face interactions.
5. The Context, including the environment, group dynamics, pre-amble to the message

Dual process theories of persuasion (such as the elaboration likelihood model) maintain that the persuasive process is mediated by two separate routes. Persuasion can be accomplished by either superficial aspects of the communication or the internal logic and evidence of the message. Whether someone is persuaded by a popular celebrity or factual arguments is largely determined by the ability and motivation of the audience.

Persuasion attempts that rely on the mass media frequently result in failure. This is because people's attitudes and Behaviours are often established habits that tend to be resistant to change. Communication campaigns are most likely to succeed when they use entertaining characters and messages, tailor the message to fit the audience, and repeat messages across relevant media channels. An example of a highly effective mass media campaign is the Got Milk campaign.

## Social Cognition

Social cognition is a growing area of social psychology that studies how people perceive, think about, and remember information about others. Person perception is the study of how people form impressions of others. The study of how people form beliefs about each other while interacting is known as interpersonal perception.

A major research topic in social cognition is attribution. Attributions are the explanations we make for people's Behaviour, either our own Behaviour or the Behaviour of others. We can ascribe the locus of a Behaviour to either internal or external factors. An *internal*, or dispositional, locus of causality involves factors within the person, such as ability or personality. An *external*, or situational, locus involves outside factors, such as the weather. A second element of attribution ascribes the cause of Behaviour to either stable or unstable factors. Finally, we also attribute causes of Behaviour to either controllable or uncontrollable factors.

Numerous biases in the attribution process have been discovered. The fundamental attribution error is the tendency to make dispositional attributions for Behaviour. The actor-observer effect is a refinement of this bias, the tendency to make dispositional attributions for other people's Behaviour and situational attributions for our own. The just-world phenomenon is the tendency to blame victims (a dispositional attribution) for their suffering. This is believed to be motivated by people's anxiety that good people, including themselves, could be victimized in an unjust world. Finally, the self-serving bias is the tendency to take credit for successes, and blame others for failure. Researchers have found that depressed individuals often lack this bias and actually have more realistic perceptions of reality.

Heuristics are cognitive short cuts. Instead of weighing all the evidence when making a decision, people rely on heuristics to save time and energy. The availability heuristic occurs when people estimate the probability of an outcome based on how easy that outcome is to imagine. As such, vivid or highly memorable possibilities will be perceived as more likely than those that are harder to picture or are difficult to understand, resulting in a corresponding cognitive bias. Numerous other biases have been found by social cognition researchers. The hindsight bias is a false memory of having predicted events, or an exaggeration of actual predictions, after becoming aware of the outcome. The confirmation bias is a type of bias leading to the tendency to search for, or interpret information in a way that confirms one's preconceptions.

Another key concept in social cognition is the assumption that reality is too complex to easily discern. As a result, we tend to see the world according to simplified schemas or images of reality. Schemas are generalized mental representations that organize knowledge and guide information processing. Schemas often operate automatically and unintentionally, and can lead to biases in perception and memory. Expectations from schemas may lead us to see something that is not there. One experiment found that people are more likely to misperceive a weapon in the hands of a black man than a white man. This type of schema is actually a stereotype, a generalized set of beliefs about a particular group of people. Stereotypes are often related to negative or preferential attitudes (prejudice) and Behaviour (discrimination). Schemas for types of events (e.g. going to McDonalds, doing laundry) are known as *scripts*.

## Self-concept

The fields of social psychology and personality have merged over the years, and social psychologists have developed an interest in self-related phenomena. In contrast with traditional personality theory, however, social psychologists place a greater emphasis on cognitions than on traits. Much research focuses on the self-concept, which is a person's understanding of his or her self. The self-concept is often divided into a cognitive component, known as the *self-schema*, and an evaluative component, the *self-esteem*. The need to maintain a healthy self-esteem is recognized as a central human motivation in the field of social psychology.

Self-efficacy beliefs are cognitions that are associated with the self-schema. These are expectations that performance on some task will be effective and successful. Social psychologists also study such self-related processes as self-control and self-presentation.

People develop their self-concepts by varied means, including introspection, feedback from others, self-perception, and social comparison. By comparison to relevant others, people gain information about themselves, and they make inferences that are relevant to self-esteem. Social comparisons can be either "upward" or "downward," that is, comparisons to people who are either higher in status or ability, or lower in status or ability. Downward comparisons are often made in order to elevate self-esteem.

Self-perception is a specialized form of attribution that involves making inferences about oneself after observing one's own Behaviour. Psychologists have found that too many extrinsic rewards (e.g. money) tend to reduce intrinsic motivation through the self-perception process, a phenomenon known as overjustification. People's attention is directed to the reward and they lose interest in the task when the reward is no longer offered. This is an important exception to reinforcement theory.

## Cognitive Dissonance

Cognitive dissonance is a feeling of unpleasant arousal caused by noticing an inconsistency among one's cognition. These contradictory cognitions may be attitudes, beliefs, or ones awareness of his or her Behaviour. The theory of cognitive dissonance proposes that people have a motivational drive to reduce dissonance by changing their attitudes, beliefs, and Behaviours, or by justifying or rationalizing their attitudes, beliefs, and Behaviours. Cognitive dissonance theory is one of the most influential and extensively studied theories in social psychology.

Cognitive dissonance theory was originally developed as a theory of attitude change, but it is now considered to be a theory of the self-concept by many social psychologists. Dissonance is strongest when a discrepancy has been noticed between one's self-concept and one's Behaviour, e.g. doing something that makes one ashamed. This can result in self-justification as the individual attempts to deal with the threat. Cognitive dissonance typically leads to a change in attitude, a change in Behaviour, a self-affirmation, or a rationalization of the Behaviour.

An example of cognitive dissonance is smoking. Smoking cigarettes increases the risk of cancer, which is threatening to the self-concept of the individual who smokes. Most of us believe ourselves to be intelligent and rational, and the idea of doing something foolish and self-destructive causes dissonance. To reduce this uncomfortable tension, smokers tend to make excuses for themselves, such as "I'm going to die anyway, so it doesn't matter."

# INTERPERSONAL PHENOMENA

## Social Influence

Social influence refers to the way people affect the thoughts, feelings, and Behaviours of others. Like the study of attitudes, it is a traditional, core topic in social psychology. In fact, research on social influence overlaps considerably with research on attitudes and persuasion. Social influence is also closely related to the study of group dynamics, as most of the principles of influence are strongest when they take place in social groups.

Conformity is the most common and pervasive form of social influence. It is generally defined as the tendency to act or think like other members of a group. Group size, unanimity, cohesion, status, and prior commitment all help to determine the level of conformity in an individual. Conformity is usually viewed as a negative tendency in American culture, but a certain amount of conformity is not only necessary and normal, but probably essential for a community to function.

The two major motives in conformity are *normative* influence, the tendency to conform in order to gain social acceptance, and avoid social rejection or conflict, as in peer pressure; and *informational* influence, which is based on the desire to obtain useful information through conformity, and thereby achieve a correct or appropriate result. Minority influence is the degree to which a smaller faction within the group influences the group during decision making. Note that this refers to a minority position on some issue, not an ethnic minority. Their influence is primarily informational and depends on consistent adherence to a position, degree of defection from the majority, and the status and self-confidence of the minority members. Reactance is a tendency to assert oneself by doing the opposite of what is expected. This phenomenon is also known as *anticonformity* and it appears to be more common in men than in women.

There are two other major areas of social influence research. Compliance refers to any change in Behaviour that is due to a request or suggestion from another person. The Foot-in-the-door technique is a compliance method in which the persuader requests a small favor and then follows up with a larger favor, e.g. asking for the time, and then asking for ten dollars. A related trick is the Bait and switch. The third major form of social influence is obedience. This is a change in Behaviour that is the result of a direct order or command from another person.

A different kind of social influence is the self-fulfilling prophecy. This is a prediction that, in being made, actually causes itself to become true. For example, in the stock market, if it is widely believed that a crash is imminent, investors may lose confidence, sell most of their stock, and actually cause the crash. Likewise, people may expect hostility in others and actually induce this hostility by their own Behaviour.

## Group Dynamics

A group can be defined as two or more individuals that are connected to each another by social relationships. Groups tend to interact, influence each other, and share a common identity. They have a number of emergent qualities that distinguish them from aggregates:

- Norms-implicit rules and expectations for group members to follow, e.g. saying thank you, shaking hands.
- Roles-implicit rules and expectations for specific members within the group, e.g. the oldest sibling, who may have additional responsibilities in the family.
- Relations-patterns of liking within the group, and also differences in prestige or status, e.g. leaders, popular people.

Temporary groups and aggregates share few or none of these features, and do not qualify as true social groups. People waiting in line to get on a bus, for example, do not constitute a group.

Groups are important not only because they offer social support, resources, and a feeling of belonging, but because they supplement an individual's self-concept. To a large extent, humans define themselves by the group memberships which form their social identity. The shared social identity of individuals within a group influences intergroup Behaviour, the way in which groups behave towards and perceive each other. These perceptions and Behaviours in turn define the social identity of individuals within the interacting groups. The tendency to define oneself by membership of a group leads to intergroup discrimination, which involves favourable perceptions and Behaviours directed towards the in-group, but negative perceptions and Behaviours directed towards the out-group. Intergroup discrimination leads to prejudice and stereotyping, while the processes of social facilitation and group polarization encourage extreme Behaviours towards the out-group.

Groups often moderate and improve decision making, and are frequently relied upon for these benefits, such as committees and juries. A number of group biases, however, can interfere with effective decision making. For example, group polarization, formerly known as the "risky shift," occurs when people polarize their views in a more extreme direction after group discussion. More problematic is the phenomenon of groupthink. This is a collective thinking defect that is characterized by a premature consensus or an incorrect assumption of consensus, caused by members of a group failing to promote views which are not consistent with the views of other members. Groupthink occurs in a variety of situations, including isolation of a group and the presence of a highly directive leader. Janis offered the 1961 Bay of Pigs Invasion as a historical case of groupthink.

Groups also affect performance and productivity. Social facilitation, for example, is a tendency to work harder and faster in the presence of others. Social facilitation increases the likelihood of the *dominant response*, which tends to improve performance on simple tasks and reduce it on complex tasks. In contrast, social loafing is the tendency of individuals to slack when working in a group. Social loafing is common when the task is considered unimportant and individual contributions are not easy to see.

Social psychologists study group-related (collective) phenomena such as the Behaviour of crowds. An important concept in this area is deindividuation, a reduced state of self-awareness that can be caused by feelings of anonymity. Deindividuation is associated with uninhibited and sometimes dangerous Behaviour. It is common in crowds and mobs, but it can also be caused by a disguise, a uniform, alcohol, dark environments, or online anonymity.

## Relations with Others

Social psychologists are interested in the question of why people sometimes act in a prosocial way (helping, liking, or loving others), but at other times act in an antisocial way (hostility, aggression, or prejudice against others).

Aggression can be defined as any Behaviour that is intended to harm another human being. *Hostile* aggression is accompanied by strong emotions, particularly anger. Harming the other person is the goal. *Instrumental* aggression is only a means to an end. Harming the person is used to obtain some other goal, such as money. Research indicates that there are many causes of aggression, including biological factors like testosterone and environmental factors, such as social learning. Immediate situational factors such as frustration are also important in triggering an aggressive response.

Although violence is a fact of life, people are also capable of helping each other, even complete strangers in emergencies. Research indicates that altruism occurs when a person feels empathy for another individual, even in the absence of other motives. However, according to the bystander effect, the probability of receiving help in an emergency situation drops as the number of bystanders increases. This is due to both conformity and diffusion of responsibility, the tendency for people to feel less personally responsible when other people are around.

## Interpersonal Attraction

A major area in the study of people's relations to each other is interpersonal attraction. This refers to all of the forces that lead people to like each other, establish relationships, and in some cases, fall in love. Several general principles of attraction have been discovered by social psychologists. For example, physical proximity tends to increases attraction, whereas long distances make relationships difficult to form and maintain. Even very small differences in distance—such as the case of a next door neighbour versus someone who lives down the block—can make a significant difference in friendship patterns. Familiarity, or "mere exposure," also increases attraction, influencing people even if the familiarity is not consciously noticed. One of the most important factors in interpersonal attraction is similarity: the more similar two people are in attitudes, background, and other traits, the more probable it is that they will like each other. Contrary to popular opinion, opposites do not usually attract.

Physical attractiveness is an important element of romantic relationships, particularly in the early stages characterized by high levels of passion. Later on, similarity and other compatibility factors become more important, and the type of love people experience shifts from *passionate* to *companionate*. Robert Sternberg has suggested that there are actually three components of love: intimacy, passion, and commitment. When two people experience all three, they are said to be in a state of consummate love; this condition is relatively rare and difficult to maintain for a long period of time.

According to social exchange theory, relationships are based on rational choice and cost-benefit analysis. If one partner's costs begin to outweigh his or her benefits, that person may leave the relationship, especially if there are good alternatives available. This theory is similar to the minimax principle proposed by mathematicians and economists. With time, long term relationships tend to become communal rather than simply based on exchange.

## Research Methods of Social Psychology

Social psychology is an empirical science that attempts to answer questions about human Behaviour by testing hypotheses, both in the laboratory and in the field. Careful attention to sampling, research design, and statistical analysis is important, and results are published in peer reviewed journals such as the Journal of Experimental Social Psychology, Personality and Social Psychology Bulletin and the Journal of Personality and Social Psychology. Social psychology studies also appear in general science journals such as Psychological Science and Science.

Experimental methods involve the researcher altering a variable in the environment and measuring the effect on another variable. An example would be allowing two groups of children to play violent or nonviolent videogames, and then observing their subsequent level of aggression during free-play period. A valid experiment is controlled and uses random assignment.

Correlational methods examine the statistical association between two naturally occurring variables. For example, one could correlate the amount of violent television children watch at home with the number of violent incidents the children participate in at school. Note that this study would *not* prove that violent TV causes aggression in children. It's quite possible that aggressive children choose to watch more violent TV.

Observational methods are purely descriptive and include naturalistic observation, "contrived" observation, participant observation, and archival analysis. These are less common in social psychology but are sometimes used when first investigating a phenomenon. An example would be to unobtrusively observe children on a playground (with a videocamera, perhaps) and record the number and types of aggressive actions displayed.

Whenever possible, social psychologists rely on controlled experimentation. Controlled experiments require the manipulation of one or more independent variables in order to examine the effect on a dependent variable. Experiments are useful in social psychology because they are high in internal validity, meaning that they are free from the influence of confounding or extraneous variables, and so are more likely to accurately indicate a causal relationship. However, the small samples used in controlled experiments are typically low in external validity, or the degree to which the results can be generalized the larger population. There is usually a trade-off between experimental control (internal validity) and being able to generalize to the population (external validity).

Because it is usually impossible to test everyone, research tends to be conducted on a sample of persons from the wider population. Social psychologists frequently use survey research when they are interested in results that are high in external validity. Surveys use various forms of random sampling to obtain a sample of respondents that are representative of a population. This type of research is usually descriptive or correlational because there is no experimental control over variables. However, new statistical methods like structural equation modeling are being used to test for potential causal relationships in this type of data. Regardless of which method is used, it is important to evaluate the research hypothesis in light of the results, either confirming or rejecting the original prediction. Social psychologists use statistics and probability testing to judge their results, which define a significant finding as less than 5% likely to be due to chance. Replications are important, to ensure that the result is valid and not due to chance, or some feature of a particular sample.

## Ethics

The goal of social psychology is to understand cognition and Behaviour as they naturally occur in a social context, but the very act of observing people can influence and alter their Behaviour. For this reason, many social psychology experiments utilize deception to conceal or distort certain aspects of the study. Deception may include false cover stories, false participants (known as confederates or stooges), false feedback given to the participants, and so on.

The practice of deception has been challenged by some psychologists who maintain that deception under any circumstances is unethical, and that other research strategies (e.g. roleplaying) should be used instead. Unfortunately, research has shown that role-playing studies do not produce the same results as deception studies and this has cast doubt on their validity. In addition to deception, experimenters have at times put people into potentially uncomfortable or embarrassing situations (e.g. the Milgram experiment, Stanford prison experiment), and this has also been criticized for ethical reasons.

To protect the rights and well-being of research participants, and at the same time discover meaningful results and insights into human Behaviour, virtually all social psychology research must pass an ethical review process. At most colleges and universities, this is conducted by an ethics committee or Institutional Review Board. This group examines the proposed research to make sure that no harm is done to the participants, and that the benefits of the study outweigh any possible risks or discomforts to people taking part in the study.

Furthermore, a process of informed consent is often used to make sure that volunteers know what will happen in the experiment and understand that they are allowed to quit the experiment at any time. A debriefing is typically done at the conclusion of the experiment in order to reveal any deceptions used and generally make sure that the participants are unharmed by the procedures. Today, most research in social psychology involves no more risk of harm than can be expected from routine psychological testing or normal daily activities.

## Famous Experiments

The Asch conformity experiments demonstrated the power of conformity in small groups with a line estimation task that was designed to be extremely easy. On over a third of the trials, participants conformed to the majority, even though the majority judgment was clearly wrong. Seventy-five percent of the participants conformed at least once during the experiment.

Muzafer Sherif's Robbers' Cave Experiment divided boys into two competing groups to explore how much hostility and aggression would emerge. Sherif's explanation of the results became known as realistic group conflict theory, because the intergroup conflict was induced through competition over resources. Inducing cooperation and [superordinate goals] later reversed this effect.

In Leon Festinger's cognitive dissonance experiment, participants were asked to perform a boring task. They were divided into 2 groups and given two different pay scales. At the end of the study, some participants were paid $1 to say that they enjoyed the task and another group of participants was paid $20 to say the same lie. The first group ($1) later reported liking the task better than the second group ($20). Festinger's explanation was that people justified their lies by changing their previously unfavorable attitudes about the task.

One of the most infamous experiments in social psychology was the Milgram experiment, which studied how far people would go to obey an authority figure. Following the events of The Holocaust in World War II, the experiment showed that normal American citizens were capable of following orders from an authority even when they believed they were causing an innocent person to suffer.

Albert Bandura's Bobo doll experiment demonstrated how aggression is learned by imitation. This was one of the first studies in a long line of research showing how exposure to media violence leads to aggressive Behaviour in the observers.

In the Stanford prison experiment, by Philip Zimbardo, a simulated exercise between student prisoners and guards showed how far people would follow an adopted role. In just a few days, the "guards" became brutal and cruel, and the prisoners became miserable and compliant. This was an important demonstration of the power of the immediate social situation, and its capacity to overwhelm normal personality traits.

## RESEARCH AREAS IN SOCIAL PSYCHOLOGY

Social psychology research topics including social influence, social perception, social interaction and group Behaviour.

Now that you have a better understanding of what social psychology is, we are going to look at some of the major topics that social psychologists investigate in their research. Many of these topics are related to social influence, social perception and social interaction. The following are just a few of the areas of interest within social psychology.

### Social Cognition

Social cognition is concerned with the processing, storage and application of social information. This research area is closely related to the field of cognitive psychology, this research area focuses largely on the concept of schemas. Schemas are our general ideas about the world, how things are and how things work. These mental shortcuts allow us to function without constantly stopping to interpret everything around us. We also develop associations between related schemas, which plays an important role in the thought process and social Behaviour.

### Attitudes and Attitude Change

Another major research area in social psychology involves the study of attitudes. Social psychologists are interested in the components of attitudes, how attitudes develop and how attitudes change. Researchers have described three core components of attitude: an affective component, a behavioural component and a cognitive component. Often referred to as the "ABC's of attitude," these elements describe how we feel, behave and understand.

### Violence and Aggression

What causes violence and aggression? Social psychologists are interested in how and why people engage in violence or act aggressively. Research in this area looks at numerous factors that may cause aggression including social variables and media influences. Researchers often look at the role social learning plays in producing aggressive Behaviours and actions.

## Prosocial Behaviour

Prosocial Behaviour is another major research area in social psychology. What is prosocial Behaviour? Prosocial Behaviours are those that involve helping and cooperating. Researchers often look at why people help others, as well as why they sometimes refuse to help or cooperate.

Much of the research in this area was prompted by the murder of a young woman named Kitty Genovese. This case captured national attention when reports revealed that neighbors had witnessed her attack and murder, but failed to call the police for help. Research inspired by the case produced a great deal of information on prosocial Behaviour and how and why people choose-or sometimes refuse-to help others.

## Prejudice and Discrimination

Prejudice, discrimination and stereotypes exist in any social group. Social psychologists are interested in the origins, causes and effects of these types of attitudes and social categorizations. How does prejudice develop? Why are stereotypes maintained in the face of contrary evidence? These are just a few of the questions social psychologists seek to answer.

## Self and Social Identity

Our perceptions of social identities and ourselves are another important research area in social psychology. How do people come to know and understand themselves? How do these self-perceptions affect our social interactions? Social psychologists are interested in learning more about how this inner life influences our outer lives and social world. Self-awareness, self-esteem and self-expression are just a few of the factors that influence our social experience.

## Group Behaviour

The Behaviour of groups is one of the largest research areas in social psychology. Most people realize that groups tend to behave differently than individuals. These group Behaviours are sometimes beneficial and positive, but they can also be detrimental and negative. Social psychologists often look at topics such as group dynamics, leadership, group decision-making, conflicts, cooperation and group influence.

## Social Influence

Social psychologists are also interested in the role that social influence has on Behaviour and decision-making. Topics such as the psychology of persuasion, peer pressure, conformity and obedience are just a few of those studied in this area of social psychology. Research has helped reveal the power of social influence and has uncovered ways to help people resist influence.

## PERSUASION TECHNIQUES

## Interpersonal Relationships

Social relationships play a major role in shaping Behaviour, attitudes, feelings and thoughts. Social psychologists study how these interpersonal relationships affect people by looking at attachment, liking, love and attraction. How do close relationships affect individuals? How important are these interpersonal relationships? These are just a few of the questions social psychologists seek to explain.

# 11

# Organizational Psychology in Human Resource Management

Organizational Psychology is a subject which applies the principles of psychology into one of the most important areas of people's life-work. Specifically, we work with the human aspects of the workplace and aim at improving people's efficiency, and hence organizational effectiveness, through our knowledge about human functioning.

There exist a group of professionals who share a similar aim and are working closely with us, the human resource professionals. Despite the close relationship with HR professionals, Organizational Psychologists are distinctive professionals. Unfortunately, there is always some confusion among the general public that people just cannot tell who is who. More importantly, even some HR professionals do not know what we are doing and what can we offer them.

When we tell them we are Psychologists, a frequent reply is "but we don't have any mental problems"!

As Organizational Psychologists, we work with a wide range of domains that are related to people's everyday work life. We design work activities, schedules and workplaces; we design reward principles that are based on human motivation theories; we develop training principles and train the trainers; we develop selection procedures and tools; we formulate performance appraisal systems; and we advise on organizational development issues as well as career development decisions. As you may recognise, our work reaches every working individual on the planet and our working field is very closely related with the work of HR professionals.

Although there are quite a few overlapping areas between Organizational Psychology and Human Resource Management (HRM), there are fundamental differences between us.

The first and perhaps the most obvious difference between us is the knowledge foundation. As psychologists, we base our work heavily on science. All work has to be backed up by scientific evidence and statistics is always in our toolbox.

In contrast, HRM is essentially a business study which emphasizes more on the practical side, with less focus on the scientific side. Moreover, in addition to working on overlapping areas, we work on different levels. Organizational Psychologists focus more on the design and development of procedures, tools and principles while HR professionals work more on the operational level, such as implementation of selection systems and applying training principles in real training scenarios.

## ORGANIZATIONAL PSYCHOLOGISTS AND HR PROFESSIONALS

The discrepancy between the knowledgebase of Organizational Psychologists and HR professionals has been documented in academic journals.

For example Sally Carless and colleagues pointed out that although there are important advancements in HR-related research, the everyday HR practice have benefited from it to a minimum level. They found that this is due to the lack of knowledge among HR professionals, especially when the training of the HR professionals emphasizes on general skill and knowledge in favour of science.

In contrast, the training of Organizational Psychologists is built upon the scientist-practitioner model which emphasizes on both research and practical skills and stipulates that practice must be supported by scientific evidence.

Another reason may lie in the Continuous Professional Development (CPD) requirement. As Organizational Psychologists, CPD is a statutory condition for registration and this helps them to keep updated with the latest developments in the field. However there is no such requirement for HR professionals. Carless's study confirmed that Organizational Psychologists are experts in the field, especially in the area of selection and the authors articulated that "scientific integrity is a key differentiating feature of I/O (Organizational) psychologists."

Having closely related working areas, our work is actually complementary to each other. Without Organizational Psychologists in the design and development work of various HR processes and tools, the HR professional would not be enjoying these scientific and highly effective products.

On the other hand, without the help of HR professionals we could never apply our work to such a broad range of people. Moreover, our relationship is much more complex and interactive than one might be aware of. Besides the above mentioned supplier-user relationship, HR professionals are also partners, advisors and sometimes suppliers for Organizational Psychologists.

HR professionals are our partners in projects where we provide them with the technical skills and knowledge while they take care of the operational part. Furthermore, HR professionals are experts of their company; therefore we work side by side during consulting jobs where we need them to assist us with internal matters as well as providing us with an insider view.

More importantly, as HR professionals are frequent users of our services and products, we rely a lot on their opinions and requests in developing our products and services. They are also providers of valuable data and participants for us to carry out scientific studies (e.g. validation of assessment tools). All in all, we are inter-dependent parties with entwined relationships rather than independent parties or competitors.

Being Organizational Psychologists, what can we offer to HR professionals? A lot. With the expertise in assessing human characteristics and knowledge about human performance, we are experts in selection.

Based on the understanding about the requirements of the job as well as the characteristics needed for any particular position, we can come up with an ideal person profile that the organization is looking for. Then we can design, or choose among proper tools that accurately measure the required characteristics, knowledge and skills.

According to research these procedures enable us to create the best selection system which predicts future performance of the employed staff. One should not be surprised that the best selection tools like psychometric tests, assessment centres, and structured interviews as well as standardized selection procedures are all designed and developed by Organizational Psychologists.

## Organizational Psychology Profession and HR Field

Another contribution of the organizational psychology profession to the HR field is in training. A brief look at the training market reveals that it is flooded with many training courses and providers.

Obviously their quality varies and some of them do not even know what they are talking about! Our own company has undertaken work for clients who have come to us after being dissatisfied with trainers who appear to have simply taken some information from the internet to put together a training session without any real understanding of the subject matter!

As Organizational Psychologists we are working hard to turn around this situation. We are experts in training design; some understand how people learn and how people learn the best! In designing and delivering training courses, scientific human learning theories and training principles are followed, but not just by gut feelings or experience only. Factors like transfer of learning, specific needs of the organization and maintenance of learning are all fully considered.

Besides selection and training, Organizational Psychologists also offer various consultancy and advisory services to HR professionals. The range of work can be as small as reviewing a performance appraisal check list or an assessment centre exercise to as big as designing a tailored selection system.

On top of that, we can also go into the organization to diagnose the roots of problems and solve them accordingly, using our scientific approach and advanced knowledge about mechanisms and dynamics within the workplace. However, as mentioned at the beginning of this article, one big obstacle we face is the lack of knowledge about our profession within the HR profession (particularly in Asia), as well as the public in general.

The implication is that we often face questions like "what is organizational psychology?", "what is the difference between Organizational Psychologists and HR consultants?" and even "why do I need to employ scientific tools and procedures?" It can be hard work explaining all this to prospective clients! Another related problem is people always think we are very expensive!

But the fact is all the products and services we offer are based on scientific research which means they have undergone lengthy and sophisticated processes of development and the cost of all these are huge. By employing our scientific tools and principles the benefit is long lasting and continuously contributing to the performance of the organization, and these are all documented in the scientific literature.

Another hidden obstacle for us in Asia is caused by the organizational hierarchy. Very often, the first contact point between our clients and ourselves are assistants of HR professionals who have minimal understanding of what we are talking about. When they do not understand they just cannot relay our message precisely to their manager.

The result is obviously that the management level does not receive our message and the name of Organizational Psychology just remains unheard no matter how hard we try!

As Organizational Psychologists, we see a real need to educate the public, and more importantly, HR professionals about the subject of Organizational Psychology so that the fruit of science can be returned to them.

There are major overlapping work areas between Organizational Psychologists and HR professionals such as selection, training, career development and performance management, but we work on different levels and perspectives thus our relationship is actually collaborative rather than competitive.

Organizational Psychologists can offer help to HR professionals in various areas such as training design, development of selection systems, supervising performance management processes and many more. Nevertheless Organizational Psychologists in Asia face obstacles as the subject is relatively unheard of among HR professionals and communication is often blocked by organizational hierarchy.

Therefore one very important task for us as Organizational Psychologist is to promote this subject so that people know what we can offer and make use of our expertise! We are sure that with the growing popularity of the subject, HR professionals, and other related professionals like career counsellors and coaches, will benefit highly from Organizational Psychology.

## EMERGING ISSUES IN HUMAN RESOURCE MANAGEMENT

Some critical issues have clearly emerged-planning, acquisition and development of human resources, responding to the demands of the work place and, above all, evolving a strategy of dealing with industrial conflict. As a management practice, it covers all the conventional areas of personnel management and industrial relations, as well as the relatively new areas such as communication, counselling, training and development, and job enrichment. An attempt has been made in this paper to point out the experiences on the emerging issues in managing human resources.

## THE CHANGING NATURE OF HRM FUNCTION

Today, competitive advantage is based on the successful application of knowledge. Managing people, as an HRM function, has broadened, to include managing organizational capabilities, relationships, learning and knowledge. These functions include four generic areas, i.e., (i) Roles, (ii) Relationships, (iii) Strategic focus, (iv) Learning focus. These areas are different from each of the economy functions, like traditional, transitional and knowledge.

Innovate HRM

- Crafting creative business strategies
- Organizational restructuring
- Creating social networks

- Invoking new challenges
- Shifting approach
- Enabling companies to go global
- Leading to superior performance
- Creating knowledge work force

## Human Resource Information System (HRIS) for Effective HRM

In today's competitive business environment, the cutting edge for any organization is given by the speed with which it takes decisions to respond to changes in the environment, internal or external. A well-designed computerized HRIS alone can provide the information and analysis within the shortest possible time. Now-a-days, many organizations are using the computerized HRIS. They keep records in a compact manner, enabling access and retrieval, in a flexible way.

## Benefits of HRIS

- Simplified data entry
- Less paperwork
- Fast and accurate
- Better use of feedback
- Increased efficiency
- Improved tools for data analysis.

HRIS has great significance in every sector and it can play a vital role. It helps to have a better communication process in the organization and we can offer better service with less effort at reduced cost. Most importantly, organizations can hire and retain top performers, improve productivity and enhance job satisfaction of the employees.

## Aspects of HRM

- Human Resource Planning
- Recruitment
- Selection
- Placement
- Inductions
- Transfer & Planning

- Job Analysis
- Performance Appraisal
- HR Audit
- Total Quality Management
- Quality of Working Environment
- Quality Cycle.

HRM in the Present Scenario:

- Low motivation or mounting frustration
- Promotions are consolations for transfers
- Cadre conflict
- Reward and punishment system
- Development of strong training system.

## HR, HRM & HRD

Human Relations is called HR also known as Human Resources. Managing HR is called Human Resources Management (HRM). Developing HR is called HRD. HRM is a philosophy, while HRD includes the activities and processes undertaken to promote the intellectual, moral, psychological, cultural, social and economic development of the individuals in an organization, in order to help them to achieve higher human potential as a resource for the community. It is a continuous process by which the employees are assisted in a planned way to develop capabilities.

## Trends in HRM

An organization's labour force comes from its external labour market-individuals who are actively seeking employment. HRM helps organizations find and keep the best possible fit between their social system and technical system. Organizations need employees with broad skills and strong motivation. Recruiting and selection decisions are especially important for organizations that rely on knowledge workers. Employees' responsibility and authority are given to make decisions regarding all aspects of product development or customer service. HR professionals can support organizational strategies for quality growth and efficiency. Organizations with international operations hire employees in foreign countries, where they operate, as they need knowledge of differences in culture and business practices.

Now-a-days, information system has become a tool for more HR professionals, and often, these systems are provided through the Internet. The widespread usage of the Internet also includes HRM applications. Organizations search for talents, and screening candidates online. Employees may receive training online. The employment relationship takes the form of a psychological contract that describes what employers and employees expect from the employment relationship. The employees are looking for flexible work schedules, comfortable working conditions and greater autonomy, opportunities for training and development, and performance-related financial incentives. For HRM, the changes require planning for flexible staffing levels. Organizations seek flexibility in staffing levels through alternatives to the employment relationship. They may use outsourcing as well as temporary and contract workers.

## Strategic HRM

It is that set of managerial decisions and actions that determine the long term performance of a corporation. It includes environmental scanning, strategy formulation, implementation, evaluation and control. The biggest benefit that strategic HRM offers is competitive advantage by building critical capabilities of HR in an organization. Strategic HRM facilitates in strategy formulation by making an organization's SWOT analysis, and also in policy implementation by providing competent human resources and competitive intelligence.

## HRM in LPG (Liberalization, Privatization & Globalization) Era

We can divide HRM into seven sections, i.e., HRM-Environment and Strategies, HRM-Acquisition and Absorption, Development, Maintenance and Retention, Control, Miscellaneous, HRM Practices.

*HRM Environment and Strategies* includes objectives, scope and functions, evolution and development of HRM. *Acquisition and Absorption includes* HR planning, job analysis and design, recruitment, selection, placement, induction and socialisation. *Development section includes* career planning and development, employee training, executive development, organization development and internal mobility and separation.

*Maintenance and Retention section includes* job evaluation, wage and salary administration, incentives and benefits, motivation, employee empowerment, workers participation in management, employee health and safety, social security, employee discipline, employee grievance, industrial relations, industrial disputes, trade unions, collective bargaining, performance & potential appraisal.

*Control section includes* personnel research and audit, human resource audit and human resource information system. *Miscellaneous section includes* HRM in a changing environment, IHRM, HRM in virtual organizations. *The final section is HRM Practices* in various organization levels.

## CORPORATE STRATEGY IN HUMAN RESOURCE MANAGEMENT

Today, there is an urgent need to link human resource management, inextricable, to the business of the organization, at both the strategic and practical levels. The HR manager has the task of being on a constant look-out for the right choice of employees, fine-tuning the job mix and compensation package to benefit the individual and the organization, devising a flat organization structure and organizing training programmes for continuing the education at different levels in the organization.

### Best Practices in HRM

A best practice in HRM has invoked a great deal of interest among HR professionals. Companies that are currently under-performing in the HR area can learn and adopt some of the best practices from organizations that have acquired some mastery over the good practices in HR.

In the era of liberalization, the competitive scenario in the business environment has changed a lot. Consequently, HR practices have also changed phenomenally. The performance of the employees determines the failure or the success of an organization. There are four stages of integration between HR functions and the strategic management functions:-

- Administrative Linkage
- One-way Linkage

- Two-way Linkage
- Integrative Linkage.

HR experts are having the opinion that, though "best practices in HRM" cannot be uniformly applied to all the organizations, they have a kind of uniform applicability in some functional areas, where psychological factors play an important role. Such areas are broadly classified as follows:-

- Process of selecting and recruiting the best talent.
- Allotment of work and responsibility, as would be appropriate to the employees natural talent and skill.
- System of initial training for new employees and specialized training for the experienced and skilled employees.
- Inculcation of a sense of team spirit.
- System of healthy and transparent communication, intra and extra company.
- System of periodic appraisal of the performance of employees.
- Suitable policy for career advancement of employees.
- Suitable policy for placement and transfer of employees.
- Suitable policy of recognizing and rewarding merit.
- Provision of security in service, to the deserving employees.

## HRM in Cross-Cultural Context

Multi-cultural workforce congregations have become today's workplace realities. The cross-border market terrorism spared by MNCs evoked counter-insurgency and strategic warfare from domestic businesses. Partnering people in this race is vital for success in the market place. Workplaces have increasingly symbolized multi-cultural villages, resulting in a growing need for cross-cultural intelligence. The future competitiveness of corporations will depend on their ability to attract and manage diverse talents effectively. Cross-cultural training will give managers on international assignments the cultural understanding essential to accomplish their tasks. Cross-cultural differences are the cause of failed negotiations and interactions, resulting in losses to the firms. The strategic role of HRM in strengthening and sustaining corporate growth has assumed paramount significance, the world over.

## Employee Engagement

Products and process alone can't help organizations to sustain loyal customers. They also need highly-motivated, dedicated and involved employees who are very passionate about their work and their organization; in short, they need "engaged employees". But, nurturing engaged employees requires a lot of effort and skill on the part of HR managers and calls for a different HR philosophy in the organization.

We need employee engagement to serve as a core competency of an organization that would provide sustainable competitive advantage. We know employee engagement towards their work, throw few test "symptoms", i.e., feeling of creating value, having a direction to follow, an air of trust, creating engaged employees through top management endorsement, a work environment to cherish, innovative leadership and clear growth trajectories, 'one step up from commitment'. Employee engagement is the new buzzword. A successful business is directly linked to the commitment of its employees. Employee engagement ensures the successful execution of any business strategy.

# HR FUNCTION & PERFORMANCE MANAGEMENT

The challenge before human resource professionals today is to create an enabling organizational climate for the employees, For this, they need to examine relevant issues such as training and development, performance appraisal and career planning in the organization. Selection and recruitment of personnel is an important responsibility of the human resource department. The recruitment policy provides competitive remuneration as per industry norms, maintains high standards for selection of recruits, and encourages lateral induction to infuse fresh ideas and new skills in the organization.

## Trends in Recruitment

Recruitment is increasingly becoming a two-way process, as a result of both employers and employees having higher expectations from one another. The first trend is using the resume database for recruitment; the other trend gaining prominence is the recruitment of key personnel from competitors, which is called "poaching".

## Training

After successful selection and recruitment of manpower, it is essential that all employees undergo specific training programmes that help in maximizing their potential. Today's need is to place training and development at the heart of a business strategy. Training should be a continuous process keeping in view the changing market demands, the environment and the organizations' own culture. The role of a trainer, on the other hand, should be that of a mentor, facilitator and change agent. Action Plan for Initiating Training & Development:

- Assess the training needs of individuals who will be undergoing training, to avoid a mismatch with training programme.
- Provide a questionnaire to help the participants analyze their own capabilities. This includes their knowledge, skill, aptitude and attitude.
- Bring out the latent potential in people and channelize it towards the common goal of the organization.
- Design training programmes.
- Ensure that the programme covers behavioural and cognitive leaning, focuses on upgradation of skills and encourages group participation.
- Include the real world programmes to solve the real life problems.

## Role of HR Manager in Employee Training

- To serve as an internal consultant.
- To identify programmes for individuals in tune with their individual skills.
- To plan a judicious mix of internal and external training programmes.
- To follow up activities to ensure that new skills learned, are applied in the organization.
- To monitor the performance appraisal of employees, to ascertain the impact of the training programmes and identify the future training needs.

## ESSENTIALS OF PERFORMANCE APPRAISAL

### Alignment, Standards, Commitment

Performance appraisal is a process of assessing the capabilities, both known and hidden, of employees, so that their strengths and weaknesses can be determined for increasing the organizational effectiveness. The appraisal is for identifying, whether the employee is: (i) Due for a promotion or reward or an increase in salary. (ii) Capable of handling additional responsibilities or needs future training and development to upgrade their skills. (iii) Incapable of meeting the requirement and is, thus, dispensable.

360° feedback appraisal system is the formal performance appraisal system. In this system, the employee receives feedback from his manager, supervisor, peers and others, that he comes in contact with. It helps in increasing employee participation, makes the person feel more committed, increases his sense of ownership for company policies, and allows alignment of personal expectations with organizational goals. It helps in assessing the employee strengths and weaknesses.

### Action Plan for an Effective Performance Appraisal

- The HR manager should explain the basic purpose of the exercise.
- Formal communication workshops should be organized.
- HR department should keep the confidentiality of the appraisal report; two-way feed-back should be created, the exercise should be presented as a forum.
- HR department should make a time-table for the appraisal process and review discussion in forums.
- HR department should work out the methods, incentives and department-wise ratings.

### Performance & Rewards

It is a positive achievement cycle; it serves as a powerful motivational force for future growth. Success compensation refers to a salary component, various fringe benefits, performance-linked bonuses, stock options, etc. Compensation package emphasizes on performance, linked compensation, sharp increase in perks and allowances, recognition of special skills and abilities of individuals, increase in senior management remuneration, and salary increases for junior managers.

## HRM in 2020

*Now, we identify and discuss about five issues which are expected to affect the organizational HR in the future: (i) The corporations of tomorrow,(ii) Information age, (iii) Virtual corporation, (iv) Diversity, and (v) Social responsibility.*

## Corporation of Tomorrow

In future, there is a two-fold effect on Indian Industries, i.e.,(i) Generation of employment, and (ii) Industrial restructuring. We assume that in the future workplace, which may come true by 2020:-

- A majority of people worldwide will be connected through the IT infrastructure.
- Connectivity is the new frontier on the information highway to connect with one another.
- There are various factors on which the growth and expansion of connective technology will depend.
- The basic organizing unit in the workplace will be one individual engaging in business through connective technology.
- A learning culture will be festered by the technologies that will serve, entertain, and help people do their work. It will be basic workplace skill.
- Power in the organization of 2020 will be in flat structure.
- Culture and language will still move between the poles of traditionalism and modernism.

## Information Age

Information age has heralded a new way of doing business. IT has the power to change the most well-entrenched business paradigms. It has the power to link and connect people, and enable the exchange of products, services and capital, in an entirely different manner than in the past. IT has increased the efficiency of the human resource functions and reduced the burden of administrative work in the HR department, at the same time, helping to increase productivity.

## Virtual Corporations

A virtual company is usually a highly networked organization that extensively contracts out activities that were once performed in-house, allowing both speed and flexibility. The key to success in a virtual corporation is connectivity, i.e., the ability to network with a large number of independent companies.

## Social Responsibility

Change in technology results in a change in the structure, design and environment of an organization. It has four stages: (i) Acquisition of technology, (ii) adaptation of technology, (iii) utilization of technology, and (iv) improvement and development of technology.

Organizations of the future will operate in a workspace, which is likely to be much more broadly defined, than it is today. Connectivity within and outside the organizations, will create a world virtual reality organization.

Environmental problems fall into two broad categories, i.e., (i) Problems that arise out of poverty and inadequate development, and (ii) Problems that arise out of the process of development (threat of earthquake, deforestation, pollution of ground water).

# Bibliography


Aronson, E., Wilson: *Social Psychology.* New Jersey: Pearson, 2005.

Banks, S. : *Ethics and Values in Social Work: Practical Social Work Series,* London: Macmillan Press Ltd. 1995.

Bedi, M.S. : *Social Development and Social Work* , Himanshu, Delhi, 1994.

Charlton, G.: *Human Habits of Effective Organizations.* Pretoria: Van Schaik, 2000.

Chaturvedi, Pratima : *Social Work : Theories and Practices,* Book Enclave, Delhi, 2005.

Das, D.K. Lal : *Practice of Social Research : Social Work* Perspective, Rawat, 2000.

Dawson, T.: *Principles and Practice of Modern Management.* Kent:Hodder & Stoughton, 1993.

Devi, Ranjna K. : *Social Work, Philosophy, Concepts and Dimensions*, Omega, Delhi, 2009.

Drucker, P. F.: *Management: Tasks, Responsibilities, Practices.* New York: Harper & Row, 1974.

Fayol, H.: *General and Industrial Management,* London: Pitman, 1949.

Fink, A. E.: *The Field of Social Work,* New York, Henry Holt and Co., 1945.

Hicks, G.H., & Gullet, C.R.: *Organizations: Theory and Behaviour.* New York, NY: McGraw-Hill, 1975.

Iqbal, Shaikh Azhar : *Problems of Social Welfare and Social Work*, Sublime, Delhi, 2005.

Katz, D., & Kahn, R.: *The Social Psychology of Organizations.* New York, NY: John Wiley, 1978.

Kreitner, R. & Kinicki, A.: *Organizational Behaviour.* Boston:McGraw-Hill, 2007.

Linstead, S., Boje: *Passion, of organizing.* Copenhagen: Copenhagen Business. 2003.

Mayo, E.: *The Human Problems of Industrial Civilization.* New York: Macmillan, 1933.

Meyer, M. W.: *Theory of Organizational Structure.* Indianapolis: Bobbs-Merrill, 1977.

Nagpaul, Hana: *Social Work in Urban India*, Rawat, Delhi, 1996.

Pascusal Gisbert, S.J.: *Fundamentals of Sociology*, Orient Longman Limited, 1973.

Passer, M.W. & Smith, R.E.: *Psychology: the Science of Mind and Behaviour.* Boston:McGraw-Hill, 2004.

Rizwi, A K : *Social Policy and Social Work*, Mohit Pub, Delhi, 2008.

Schein, E. H.: *Organizational Psychology.* New Jersey: Prentice-Hall, 1980.

Scott, W. R.: *Organizations: Rational, Natural, and Open Systems.* Englewood Cliffs, NJ: Prentice-Hall, 1981.

Simon, H. A.: *Administrative Behaviour.* New York: Free Press, 1945.

Taylor, F. W.: *The Principles of Scientific Management.* New York: Harper, 1917.

Weber, M.: *The Theory of Social and Economic Organization.* New York, NY: Free Press, 1947.

# Index

## N



## O



## P



## R

❑❑❑